T0298742

Aid from International NGOs

International NGOs are increasingly important players within the new aid architecture but their geographic choices remain uncharted territory. This book focuses on patterns of development assistance, mapping, while analysing and assessing the country choices of the largest international NGOs. Koch's approach is interdisciplinary and uses qualitative, quantitative and experimental methods to provide a clear insight in the determinants of country choices of international NGOs.

The book aims to discover the country choices of international NGOs, how they are determined and how they could be improved. This work, which uses datasets created specifically for the research, comes to the conclusion that international NGOs do not target the poorest and most difficult countries. They are shown to be focusing mostly on those countries where their back donors are active. Additionally, it was discovered that they tend to cluster their activities; for example, international NGOs also have their donor darlings and their donor orphans. Their clustering is explained by adapting theories that explain concentration in for-profit actors to the non-profit context.

The book is the first on the geographic choices of international NGOs, and is therefore of considerable academic interest, especially for those focusing on development aid and third-sector research. Furthermore, the book provides specific policy suggestions for more thought-out geographic decisions of international NGOs and their back donors.

Dirk-Jan Koch has been working for the Netherlands Ministry of Foreign Affairs since 2004. He spent three years at their Civil Society Unit and is currently based in the Democratic Republic of the Congo, where he deals with humanitarian and development aid. He obtained his Masters Degree from the London School of Economics in Development Management. This current book serves as his PhD thesis for the Centre for International Development Issues Nijmegen of the Radboud University.

Routledge Studies in Development Economics

Aid from International NGOs

Blind spots on the aid allocation map

Dirk-Jan Koch

Routledge
Taylor & Francis Group

LONDON AND NEW YORK

First published 2009
by Routledge
2 Park Square, Milton Park, Abingdon, Oxon, OX14 4RN

Simultaneously published in the USA and Canada
by Routledge
270 Madison Avenue, New York, NY 10016

Routledge is an imprint of the Taylor & Francis Group

© 2009 Dirk-Jan Koch

Typeset in Times New Roman
by Taylor & Francis Books
Printed and bound in Great Britain by
CPI Antony Rowe, Chippenham, Wiltshire

British Library Cataloguing in Publication Data
A catalogue record for this book is available from the British Library

Library of Congress Cataloging in Publication Data
Koch, Dirk-Jan.
    Aid from international NGOS : blind spots on the aid allocation map /
Dirk-Jan Koch.
        p. cm. – (Routledge studies in development economics ; 70)
    Includes bibliographical references.
    1. Economic assistance–Developing countries. 2. Economic
development–Developing countries. 3. Non-governmental organizations. I.
Title.
    HC60.K567 2009
    338.9109172′4–dc22
                                    2008034973

978-0-415-48647-7 (hbk)
978-0-203-88217-7 (ebk)

Contents

PART III
Analysing the implications of the geographic choices of
international NGOs   125

List of Illustrations

Preface

The annual budget of World Vision International exceeds the official foreign-aid budget of Italy. Plan International outspends Greece on development projects. The budget of Save the Children Alliance exceeds that of Finland. According to Gatignon (2007), who provides the most complete estimate, the annual budget of international NGOs reached US$ 26.9 billion in 2005 and continues to rise.

As a policy advisor with the Civil Society Unit of the Netherlands Ministry of Foreign Affairs (2004–7) I followed these fascinating developments closely. Before joining the Ministry, I was a researcher at the Institute of Social Studies in The Hague, where I worked on one of many studies to determine what drives the country choices of official donors. When I came to the Civil Society Unit, I soon realised that the data I had been working with were incomplete: they excluded the aid provided to and through international NGOs, as well as the funds that international NGOs collected from the public. Since international NGOs had become major players on the aid scene, I felt that this 'blind spot' on the aid map needed to be filled.

The Ministry of Foreign Affairs was willing to support my efforts as long as my research would be relevant to its policies. I gladly accepted this condition and set as my objective to conduct an academic study of the country choices of international NGOs that would enable them, and their back donors, to improve these choices. This objective permeates all aspects of this research, from the research questions, to the design, to the focus on policy implications. It is the glue that holds the various parts of this research together. Having this research embedded within the research alliance between the Ministry of Foreign Affairs and the Centre for International Development Issues in Nijmegen, the IS Academy on Civil Society, which also explicitly aims to generate policy-relevant research, has undoubtedly strengthened its potential practical significance.

Intellectually, I owe a great debt to my promoter Ruerd Ruben. He commented constructively and swiftly various times on every single-draft paper that forms the basis of this book. I owe gratitude to Boriana Yontcheva and Axel Dreher who invited me as a Visiting Scholar to the International Monetary Fund Institute and the Swiss Economic Institute respectively to work together with them on the most advanced statistical parts of the research. Furthermore, 23 anonymous referees provided sharp comments on draft papers, which undoubtedly strengthened the research. I would also like to thank my 'informal reading group', consisting of Dieneke de Groot, Henk Molenaar, Joost Sneller and Jan Willem Nibbering who commented on nearly all chapters in great detail. I received additional useful comments from Kees Biekart, Koen Frenken, Don Kalb, Thomas de Hoop, Celina del Felice, Jelmer Kamstra, Willem Elbers and Wies Steur. Lara Yocarini and Jorim Schraven, taking their role as *paranimfs* seriously, grilled me repeatedly on my underlying assumption, and during this process I became increasingly confident that if I were to faint during my public defence, they could easily take over.

The research would not have been possible without very practical support from five very dedicated research assistants: Dik van de Koolwijk, Janno van der Laan, Judith Westeneng, Bart Loman and Geert Gompelman. They worked successfully for months on difficult research assignments, ranging from organizing interviews in remote parts of the Central African Republic, to composing historical datasets on the geographic choices of NGOs. My editors Karin Weber and Toby Adams repaired my sloppiness to the best of their abilities, and even though this same sloppiness prevents me from checking whether they actually did a good job, I am confident that they did.

This research was made financially possible by the Netherlands Ministry of Foreign Affairs. It granted me the much needed one-year research leave that enabled me to tie all loose ends together. Rob Visser is solely responsible for creating these research leave arrangements, which is a considerable achievement within an institution, whose natural tendency is to think that scientists, and not civil servants, should bridge the gap dividing academics and policy. Two colleagues and friends, Melle Leenstra and Ingeborg Denissen, who also chose to balance on this bridge, provided both moral and intellectual support.

The Centre for International Development Issues in Nijmegen of the Radboud University and the Institute of Social Studies in The Hague provided an enabling study environment, by providing facilities and sparring partners. The Institute of Social Studies (ISS), where I would start working at night when everybody else had left, supported me in the early phases of the project, when it was still viewed as either academically or politically irrelevant, or both. Special thanks goes to Wil Hout of the ISS, who – always behind the scenes – supported me when I most needed it.

More than 125 NGOs were interviewed for this research, more than 100 organizations cooperated by means of sharing data and responding to surveys, 40 organizations participated in gaming simulations and 40 organizations in focus group discussions. Their cooperation has simply been phenomenal. I hope that this manuscript will support them in their work, just as much as their cooperation helped this effort.

'Renowned publishers don't accept work from first-time authors, especially not a PhD thesis' was the answer I received from two top-level publishers. I am glad that Routledge decided to go against this tide and give this first-timer a chance. If my greenness still surfaces occasionally throughout the text, this is most certainly not due to the commissioning editor of the Routledge Studies in Development Economics list, Tom Sutton, who advised me aptly on this manuscript.

One can have all financial, intellectual and practical support in the world, but without an 'enabling environment' at home, this research would never have materialized. My family in the village 'Achterveld' provided the much-needed stable basis. My adorable daughter Olivia, who enlightened our home with her joyful presence, and my wife Annelies, who supported me throughout, are the strong women behind the scenes who made this all possible.

Brussels
July 2008

1   Introduction

Background

Many scholars focus on the country allocations of bilateral and multilateral donors (Feeny and McGillivray 2008; Collier and Dollar 2002; Hansen and Tarp 2000; Lensink and White 2000; Burnside and Dollar 1997). Many also research the geographic choices of NGOs at the sub-national level (e.g. Barr and Fafchamps 2005; Fruttero and Gauri 2005; Bebbington 2004; Zeller *et al.* 2001). However, hardly any research has been done on the country choices of international NGOs, the recent work by Nancy and Yontcheva (2006) being a notable exception, or on the determinants of these choices. This is surprising since these international NGOs have by now a combined budget of some US$26.9 billion.

Besides the increased size of international NGOs, there are also other recent development whose relationship with geographic choices are not evident, such as the sharp increase in the number of international NGOs, their intensified competition for funding, and their heightened financial dependence on official aid agencies.

The number of international NGOs runs into the thousands. Umbrella organizations of international NGOs in the OECD countries had more than 2,500 members in 2008. Coordination among organizations is known to be difficult, especially when large groups are involved (Brett 1993). It is not clear to what extent international NGOs are ensuring an even distribution of their activities, or rather, are displaying herding behaviour. An obvious research question is thus whether the multiplication of the number of international NGOs hampers geographic coordination among them.

Heightened competition for funds among international NGOs is another factor that influences the behaviour of international NGOs (Schulpen and Hoebink 2001). Back donors (official aid agencies) increasingly work through competitive tender systems, in which NGOs vie for contracts. Various scholars and international NGOs have claimed that this process of 'marketization' erodes their capacity to take risks and engage in the poorest areas (e.g. ECDPM 2004a). However, claims that international NGOs made more audacious geographic choices in the past, and have abandoned those because of competitive pressures, have yet to be verified and could be the subject of new research.

Over the past decades, official aid agencies have worked increasingly with and through international NGOs (Wang 2006; Edwards and Hulme 1998). Many donors, including the United States, Norway and the Netherlands, provide more than 20 per cent of their aid through international NGOs. Back donors argue that they channel aid through international NGOs because they are able to reach people who are beyond the reach of official donors because they live in countries characterized by endemic state corruption (UN Millennium Project 2005). Yet, the underlying assumption that international NGOs complement the efforts of official aid agencies and that they are effective in those types of countries has never been tested, and thus poses another research question.

Since back donors increasingly choose to work with and through international NGOs, the majority of them now receive more than half their budget from official donors. Many authors have strongly criticized this situation, casting doubt upon whether international NGOs are worthy of the name 'non-governmental' (e.g. Smillie 1997; Wallace 2000). Because of the growing infusion of public funds into international NGOs it is unclear whether they have become the executing subcontracting agencies of Northern governments or whether they are still able to make autonomous policy and country choices. This is yet another area for research.

There are various angles from which to analyse the ramifications of the increase in size and number of international NGOs, the heightened competition among them and their growing financial dependence on official donors. The operating procedures of international NGOs could be analysed, for instance, to ascertain whether their working practices are starting to resemble those of government agencies, as Fowler (1995) and Feldman (2003) suggest. Alternatively, it could be analysed how such increasingly large organizations create knowledge, as Porter (2003) and Tvedt (2002) have done, or whether they coordinate their efforts. This could be researched by determining to what extent international NGOs work on complementary themes, which Gauri and Galef (2005) did for Bangladesh.

This research takes yet another angle. It seeks to explore the implications of the trends discussed on the country choices of international NGOs, which has so far been uncharted territory.

Research outline

Independent evaluations of the long-term impact of international NGOs are still relatively rare. However, there are indications that international NGOs can have a substantial and lasting effect on poverty in the countries in which they work. Using panel regressions for 58 countries, Masud and Yontcheva (2005) demonstrate that aid from international NGOs contributed to a reduction in infant mortality rates during the 1990s. Bradshaw and Schafer (2000) find that growing involvement of international NGOs in a country leads to stronger economic development, more widespread provision of clean water and other facets of human development. Roberts (2005) corroborates these findings. He shows that the level of human development increased more in countries with strong ties to international NGOs in the early 1980s, than those with weaker ties, when controlling for other factors, in the subsequent two decades. The important contribution of international NGOs to pushing debt cancellation to the top of the G8 agenda has been widely documented, as well as the effects of these debts reductions on poverty in a number of developing countries (e.g. Hertz 2004; Hinchliffe 2004).[1]

This research thus refrains from questioning the 'raison d'çtre' of international NGOs (Hearn 2007; Petras 1997). It takes their existence and the potential benefits of their work as a given, and analyses critically one aspect of international NGOs: their country choices. In a sense, this research thus falls within the type of research of Mosse (2005), who shows that a critical research approach towards international aid actors can produce interesting insights in how aid policies and practices (co)-develop.

The following three questions guide the research:

1. What are potential determinants of the geographic choices of international NGOs?
2. What explains the geographic concentration of international NGOs?
3. What are the academic and policy implications of the research findings?

The research is divided into three parts, which each focus on one research question.

Part I: Mapping and testing potential determinants of the geographic choices of international NGOs

The first part of the research asks: what are determinants of the geographic choices of international NGOs? The following potential determinants are mapped and tested in Chapters 2 and 3:

1. poverty levels in recipient countries;
2. governance situation in recipient countries;
3. preferences of back donors;
4. processes of concentration (the preferences of other NGOs);[2]
5. NGO specific missions.

Part II: Explaining the geographic concentration of international NGOs

The second part asks: What can explain the process of geographic concentration of international NGOs?

1. Can an evolutionary economic geography approach help explain the geographic concentration of international NGOs (Chapter 4)?

2. Can poor country images explain why international NGOs exclude certain countries (Chapter 5)?
3. Can differences in the funding situation of international NGOs, for example due to competition among international NGOs and their level of financial dependence on back donors, explain differences in concentration of international NGOs (Chapter 6)?

Part III: Analysing the implications of the geographic choices of international NGOs

The last part of the research asks: What are the academic and policy implications of the research findings?

1. How does the concentration of international NGOs affect cooperation between them (Chapter 7)?
2. What are the academic and policy implications of the findings on the five determinants (poverty and governance levels in recipient countries, the importance of the preferences of back donors, geographic concentration, NGO-specific mission?) (Chapter 8).

Figure 1.1 illustrates how the different parts and chapters are linked. Part I (Chapters 2 and 3) focuses on mapping and testing five determinants of the geographic choices of international NGOs. This shows that the concentration of international NGOs is a prime determinant of their geographic choices. Part II (Chapters 4 to 6) subsequently analyses why this geographic concentration of international NGOs emerges. Each chapter focuses on a different level of the aid chain: Chapter 4 looks at recipient countries; Chapter 5 at international NGOs; and Chapter 6 at back donors. Part III (Chapters 7 and 8) builds on the two previous parts and assesses the findings of the research. Chapter 7 focuses specifically on the consequences of the concentration of international NGOs on cooperation among them in a recipient country. Chapter 8 discusses the academic and policy implications of the findings regarding the five determinants of the geographic choices of international NGOs that were mapped and tested in Part I.

Research approach

The five determinants that are the focus of this research (poverty levels, governance situation, preferences of back donors, concentration, NGO specific mission) by no means represent all potential determinants of the geographic choices of international NGOs. They are sometimes not even the pervasive drivers of such choices. However, they are cited frequently in the literature on the geographic choices of international NGOs. Furthermore, initial empirical research conducted for this study shows that this set of determinants provides a wealth of new and occasionally contradicting findings.

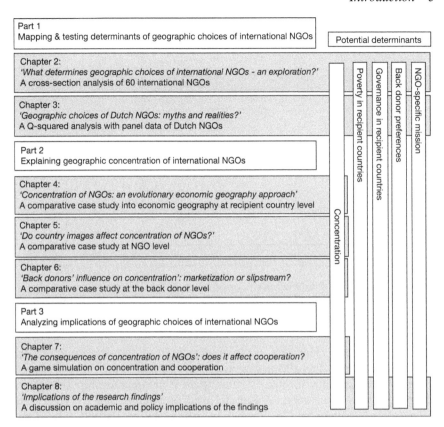

Figure 1.1 Analytic map of the research

'Poverty in recipient countries' is often considered the prime determinant of the geographic choices of international NGOs. Their decisions are therefore often analysed from this perspective (e.g. Nunnenkamp 2008; Dreher *et al.* 2007; Nancy and Yontcheva 2006). International NGOs are thought to be unsusceptible to geo-political pressures and therefore in a position to target the poorest parts of the world. An exploratory analyses of the data compiled for this research points in a different direction, however.

Figure 1.2 seems to suggest that international NGOs do not target the poorest countries and that they allocate more aid per poor person in Middle-Income Countries than in the poorest countries.[3] This relationship will be explored further in Chapters 2 and 3.

The second potential determinant included in this research is 'the governance situation in a recipient country'. As discussed in Chapter 2, the academic and policy literature suggests that international NGOs are effective in countries where other governmental actors are not, notably in countries with poor governance (UN Millennium Project 2005; Edwards and Hulme 1998;

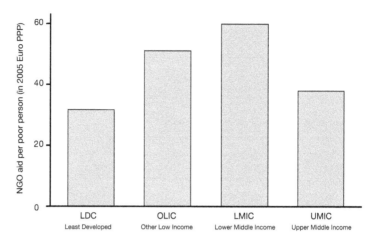

Figure 1.2 Figure 1.2 NGO aid per poor person over DAC classification
Source: World Development Indicators (2006), OECD (2007) and Koch, own data.

World Bank 1998). However, a preliminary scan of the data compiled for this research shows that this assumption may not hold true.

Figure 1.3 appears to suggest that there is no relationship between a country's level of democracy and its ratio of international NGO aid to bilateral aid. A country like Zimbabwe, which sits on the left side of the graph, receives the same ratio of international NGO aid to bilateral aid as a country like Ghana, which sits on the right side of the graph. This figure highlights a potential disconnect between the claims made in the literature and the actual geographic choices of international NGOs that deserves to be analysed.

The 'preference of back donors' is the third angle from which to analyse the geographic choices of international NGOs. It is heavily contested whether international NGOs can be considered truly non-governmental or not (e.g. Ferguson 2006; Kalb 2005; Biekart 1999; Fisher 1997). Some argue that international NGOs are mere implementers of the policies of their back donors. Others argue that international NGOs operate autonomously even though a large share of their budget is covered by back donors (Nancy and Yontcheva 2006). This research aims to contribute to this debate through a systematic analysis of the influence of back donors on the geographic choices of international NGOs.

The fourth determinant covered in this research is the concentration of international NGOs. The academic literature includes relatively little on the clustering of non-profit actors, Bielefeld and Murdoch (2004) being the exception. However, the data gathered for this research reveal that the geographic

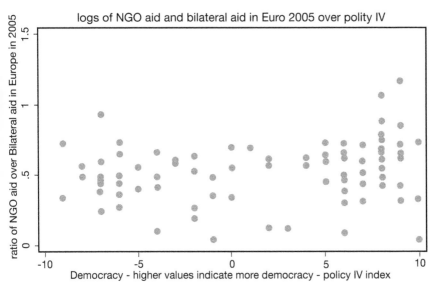

Figure 1.3 Ratio international NGO aid to Official Development Assistance over Democracy

Source: Koch, own data.

Note: The OECD/DAC data on bilateral data also include, in some instances, aid to and through NGOs. It appears that the DAC includes decentralized funding to NGOs in the country-wise breakdown of bilateral aid through NGOs. This could potentially lead to a bias in this graph, as arguably embassies and decentralized aid agencies in poorly governed countries provide relatively more aid to NGOs than to governments. However, an in-depth analysis of one of the major bilateral donors, the Netherlands, showed that there was no relationship between decentralized NGO funding and governance levels. Furthermore, the funding available for NGOs through decentralized funding is much smaller than the funding available for NGOs at the headquarters level.

choices of international NGOs are characterized by strong patterns of concentration.

Figure 1.4 illustrates how the activities of 61 of the world's largest international NGOs are concentrated.[4] The map shows per capita NGO expenditure (in Euros) in developing countries, with countries with a darker shade receiving more NGO aid per capita.

In 2005, the combined budget of the 61 international NGOs included in the sample was €6.9 billion and their average allocation per recipient country was €30.4 million. However, there are large differences between countries. For example, Zimbabwe, Sri Lanka, Bangladesh, Kenya, Sudan and Uganda receive amounts in excess of €100 million annually, while Guinea, Côte d'Ivoire and Yemen receive less than €10 million per year. The top recipients receive more than 20 times more on a per capita basis than the so-called donor orphans. Of the sample of 61 organizations, more than 40 are active

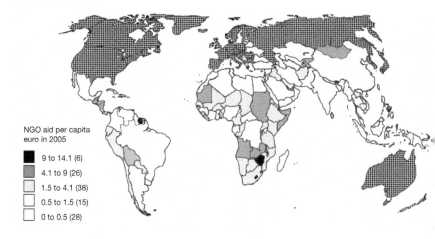

Figure 1.4 Distribution of NGO aid in 2005 (Euro per capita)
Source: Koch, own data (countries in cross-hatching are non-DAC countries and not covered by the dataset).

in countries like Sri Lanka, Uganda and Guatemala, while only a handful are active in countries like Yemen, Côte d'Ivoire and the Central African Republic. Concentration of aid also occurs within countries, as the example of Tanzania in Chapter 4 will illustrate.

An international NGO's mission is the fifth and last potential determinant addressed in this research. In his breakthrough theoretical work on non-profit organizations, Hansman (in Rose-Ackerman 1986) argues that their emergence is the result of the limits of governments. Non-profit agencies exist to provide services that government agencies cannot provide because the demands of users are too heterogeneous to allow for their universal provision. To clarify, Catholics in developed countries may prefer to support fellow-Catholics in developing countries to a larger extent than non-Catholics in developed countries are willing to support Catholics in developing countries. Catholics in developed countries may therefore decide to erect organizations that support fellow Catholics in developing countries. These organizations supplement official aid to developing countries. In sum, since it is expected that the mission of international NGOs and other organization-specific characteristics influence their geographic choices, this determinant is as much as possible included in the analysis.

Of the five potential determinants, most attention is paid in this research to the 'concentration effect' (discussed in Chapters 4 to 7). This is the least researched of the determinants, both empirically and theoretically. The literature on the relationship between the choices of international NGOs and the preferences of their back donors (e.g. Fowler 2005; Edwards and Hulme 1998; Fisher 1997) and between their choices and levels of poverty (e.g. Nunnenkamp *et al.* 2008; Nancy and Yontcheva 2006; Dreher *et al.* 2007) is extensive. Much less attention has been paid, however, to the link between the geographic choices of international NGOs and their concentration. This is remarkable since part one of this research finds that the clustering of international NGOs is one of the strongest determinants of their geographic choices. Chapters 4 to 7 therefore focus exclusively at this determinant.

This research recognizes that there can be other potential determinants of the geographic choices of international NGOs, such as the strength of the civil society in recipient countries and their security situation. Chapter 2 explores such factors and explains that they are not analysed further in this research because of meagre academic relevance and data constraints, among other things.

In public debates on this research some international NGOs said 'We do not work for countries, we work for people' (Ploumen 2007, p. 1). They claimed that it did not make sense to look at geographic choices between countries since this would obscure the fact that within countries, international NGOs reach the most marginalized segments of society. Geographic choices of international NGOs within countries are indeed relevant, but they do not make the choice between countries irrelevant. This research shows that the expenditures of international NGOs between countries differ strongly and, as the case studies of Tanzania and the Central African Republic highlight, that the geographic choices of international NGOs within countries do not necessarily lead to a stronger focus on the poor or a more even spread. Chapter 8 shows that there are in fact striking similarities in the geographic choices of international NGOs between and within countries.

This research uses a mix of quantitative, qualitative and experimental methods or a 'mixed-methods' approach, to answer the questions at hand.[5] Mixing methods and models has two clear advantages: it enables the triangulation of research findings and it promotes complementary research that leads to more comprehensive research findings (Creswell 2002). Typically, triangulation is proposed to overcome the validity weakness in quantitative methods and in the reliability and representative weaknesses of qualitative methods (Sumner and Tribe 2004).

Chapter 7 provides an example of triangulation. It shows how an experimental game simulation and a quantitative survey method can be used to analyse the same topic: cooperation among NGOs. Since participants in the game and respondents to the survey are the same, it is possible to detect and address potential biases in each research method. Chapter 3 contains another example of this approach. It discusses how findings of 20 in-depth interviews with international NGOs can be juxtaposed to the results of panel regression analyses.

Using a mixed methods approach also makes it possible to generate and link complementary research findings (Tashakkori and Teddlie 2003). Whereas quantitative methods can be used to test hypotheses at a general level, qualitative case-study methods can provide insights into informal processes and underlying motives. Chapter 3 provides an example of the use of complementary methods. In this example, a Q-squared research method, in which panel regressions are used to analyse the determinants of the geographic choices of Dutch NGOs at an aggregate level, is complemented by a case study of one Dutch NGO, which analyses why certain factors drive geographic choices within one organization and others do not. Chapter 4 presents another example of the use of mixed-method to obtain complementary findings: the so-called Q-questionnaire. Using a visual ranking method, respondents can sort statements on their importance for a certain decision-making process, in this case geographic choices. Respondents can write additional statements on the cards and include them in their ranking. This allows them to provide additional arguments for their choice. Researchers can translate the ranking of the cards into numerical results and consequently test them rigorously. This shows how a mixed-methods tool can combine, in this case, the breadth of a qualitative method and the depth of a quantitative method.

However, quantitative methods dominate this mixed methods research for two reasons. First, this research aims to complement existing quantitative research on the aid allocations of official donors, which overlooks allocations to and by international NGOs (e.g. Hout 2007; Neumayer 2003). Second, qualitative research and descriptive analyses of the geographic choices of international NGOs are abundant, as well as studies that provide normative statements on where international NGOs should be active (Steering Committee for the Evaluation of the TMF-programme 2006; Bebbington 2005; Chambers 2005; Fowler 2005). These qualitative findings and expectations have however never been tested statistically.

The quantitative methods used in this research range from simple t-tests to advanced statistical techniques such as Heckman regressions with clustered standard errors and two-step Generalized Methods of Moments regressions. The reasons for making use of a particular statistical method will be explained in the relevant chapters.

Relevance of this research

This research aims to present various empirical, theoretical and methodological contributions to the broader academic debate on development aid and in particular on decision-making processes within NGOs.

It contributes to filling an empirical vacuum in the aid allocation literature with two datasets that were developed especially for this research. The first contains data on the recent expenditure of 61 of the largest international NGOs by recipient country. The second contains data on the expenditure of the four largest Dutch NGOs over the last two decades.[6] Both datasets will be incorporated by the Centre for International Development Issues in Nijmegen (CIDIN) into a larger database that will be updated annually and will make this data available for future research. More information on these, and the other new datasets that this research have generated, can be found in Annex 1.

The research attempts to be innovative in theoretical terms in that it moves beyond the simple supply and demand paradigm that is usually used by non-profit location theories. Instead of focusing only on supply (the availability of funds) and demand (the needs of a population), it develops an evolutionary economic geography approach to non-profit location choices. This evolutionary economic geography approach provides a framework to explain why concentration of NGOs is occurring and integrates factors such as increasing returns to scale, labour mobility and path dependence into non-profit location theory. The research also borrows insights from other academic disciplines, such as business administration, to deepen the understanding of non-profit actors.

The potential methodological contribution of the research lies in its use of an experimental research method, a game simulation. The NGO GAME that was developed for this research, and which is described in greater length in the journal *Simulation and Gaming,* can be used to overcome certain shortcomings associated with more traditional forms of research in highly aid-dependent environments.

For those with an interest in choice processes within international NGOs, this research could provide more insight into the relationship between the five abovementioned potential determinants and choice processes within international NGOs.

However, an important objective of this research is to provide the material that enables better geographic choices of international NGOs. To enhance its policy relevance, efforts were made to involve stakeholders at each step of the process. This made it a very interactive process in which practitioners, policy makers and researchers all participated actively. The research also benefited from being part of the International Cooperation Academy on Civil Society, a research alliance between the Netherlands Ministry of Foreign Affairs and the Centre for International Development Issues in Nijmegen (CIDIN). This alliance provided numerous occasions for presentations and discussions on the topic of this research, which resulted in more public awareness on this research.[7]

Outline of the chapters

Part I: Mapping and testing potential determinants of the geographic choices of international NGOs

Chapter 2 provides a preliminary sketch of potential determinants of the geographic choices of international NGOs. Using a new representative dataset of 61 of the largest international NGOs from various OECD countries, it analyses the targeting of international NGO aid across a large number of recipient countries by considering potential determinants of international NGO aid in a multivariate regression framework. The findings of this analysis show that NGOs are active in the neediest countries, but they do not support the hypothesis that international NGOs complement official aid by engaging in so-called 'difficult' institutional environments. Rather, international NGOs tend to replicate the location choices of their back donors. Moreover, they follow the choices of other international NGOs so that aid becomes geographically concentrated. Finally, international NGOs tend to select recipient countries with the same religion or with which they are connected through a shared colonial past. Taken together, the findings suggest that international NGOs prefer to play it safe rather than distinguish themselves from their back donors and work under riskier conditions. Papers on which Chapter 2 is based are forthcoming in Palgrave MacMillan's *Development Aid: A Fresh Look* (Mavrotas and McGillivray 2009, forthcoming) and were published as a working paper of the KOF Swiss Economic Institute and are forthcoming in *World Development*. Axel Dreher, Peter Nunnenkamp and Rainer Thiele were co-authors to the KOF working paper and the World Development article.

Chapter 3 offers an in-depth analysis of the geographic choices of Dutch NGOs. There are various reasons for selecting Dutch NGOs for a case study; the size of their budgets (> €600 million annually) and their long history (1965 or older) both played a role. Also, the Netherlands' Government is one of the few that has, for decades, kept meticulous accounts of the distribution of NGO aid by country. This enables a dynamic statistical analysis to test a similar set of hypotheses as in Chapter 2. The chapter has a sandwich set-up. The first section discusses the outcomes of interviews with major stakeholders, such as former Directors General of the Ministry of Development Cooperation and former directors of the largest Dutch NGOs. In the next section, the assumptions coming out of these interviews are tested quantitatively. The last part analyses the case of Oxfam Novib, the largest Dutch NGO, to understand the organizational dynamics of geographic decision-making processes. The article that forms the basis of this chapter is available in Koch and Loman (2008).

Part II: Explaining the geographic concentration of international NGOs

Chapter 4 develops an evolutionary economic geography approach to explain the concentration of international NGOs from the point of view of recipient countries. This approach builds on recent literature in the field of economic geography and focuses on differences in returns to scale, labour mobility and path dependence. Field research in one 'donor orphan', the Central African Republic (CAR), and one 'donor darling', Tanzania, provides original empirical data. Statistical methods are used to contrast the diverging experiences of these two countries. The chapter concludes that the increased interest of international NGOs in Tanzania and their continued lack of interest in the CAR are self-reinforcing processes that go some way to explaining the concentration of international NGOs. Such concentration may lead to increased efficiency, but reduces the even distribution of NGO aid. The paper that forms the basis of this chapter, co-authored by Ruerd Ruben, is under review by *Economic Geography* and published as a working paper in the 'Papers in Evolutionary Economic Geography' of the Utrecht University (Koch and Ruben 2008).

Chapter 5 focuses on another level of the aid chain: the international NGOs themselves. This chapter asks whether country images affect the geographic choices of international NGOs. It shows that international NGO personnel are not neutral agents who make decisions on the basis of objective indicators. Instead, it shows that NGO personnel use simplified country images to inform their geographic choices. Their personal preferences interfere with an objective assessment of opportunities in potential recipient countries. The chapter shows that the lack of an emotional connection between NGO personnel and the CAR appears to lead to a negative bias in the country image. This negative country image leads to lower levels of involvement in the CAR, which in turn hampers the development of an emotional connection between NGO staff and the CAR, reinforcing its exclusion still further. The paper on which this chapter is based, co-authored by Dik van de Koolwijk, was presented at the International Society Third Sector Research conference in Barcelona in 2008 and is forthcoming in the conference proceedings.

Chapter 6 moves one step further up the aid chain and focuses on the back donors of international NGOs. The chapter explores whether back donors contribute to the concentration of international NGOs. Many international NGOs state that they are willing to invest more in 'difficult' countries, but are unable to do so because they are under pressure to show quick results to their back donor. Data on aid allocations of international NGOs and their competitive environment were collected from 15 international NGOs in Germany, Norway and the United States to test this. The German NGOs, which operate in the most protected environment, focus the least on difficult countries. This suggests that critics of the 'marketization of aid' overestimate its negative effects on country allocations. The chapter concludes that back donors do not influence geographic choices through the level of competition, but through the level of financial dependence they generate. NGOs that are more financially dependent on their back donors mimic the choices of their back donors to a greater extent. Since back donors also have their own orphans and donor darlings, replicating their country choices leads to a further concentration of NGO aid. The paper on which this chapter is loosely based was published in the *European Journal of Development Research* in 2007 (co-authored by Judith Westeneng and Ruerd Ruben).

Part III: Analysing the implications of the geographic choices of international NGOs.

Chapter 7 looks at the consequences of concentration among international NGOs. An experimental gaming approach was used in Tanzania to gain more insight into this issue. The results of the NGO GAME demonstrate that the willingness of local NGOs to cooperate with each other decreases the more NGOs operate in the same area. To check the validity of the game simulation results, they were compared to the results of a survey among the same local NGOs. Both point in the same direction: NGOs in highly concentrated areas operate more as competitors than as colleagues. Advantages of the game approach are that it permits one to control to some degree for socially desirable behaviour and that it has positive side-effects for participants, such as learning effects. Disadvantages are that the results of the game simulation depend heavily on the behaviour of the game leader and that it seems impossible to replicate real-life incentive structures precisely. Consequently, a combination of various research methods is likely to provide more robust results. The paper by Mayer and Mastik on which this chapter is based was published in the Conference Proceedings of the ISAGA 2007 conference (Koch 2007b) and in the journal *Simulation & Gaming*.

Chapter 8 again deals with the potential determinants of the geographic choices of international NGOs: poverty and levels of governance in recipient countries, back-donor preferences, concentration and NGO-specific mission. It outlines the findings for each potential determinant and their policy and academic implications. Chapter 8 also discusses to what extent these findings can explain geographic choices of international NGOs at other levels, e.g. within countries. The chapter concludes that the findings of this research merit some critical introspection on the side of international NGOs and their back donors. Their herding behaviour and their lack of focus on the poorest countries do not make sense given internationally agreed poverty reduction targets. International NGOs should increase their efforts to ensure more systematic needs and opportunity-based geographic decision-making processes and to better coordinate their efforts. Back donors are advised to be flexible and to provide NGOs with stimuli to do this. Parts of this conclusion have been published in a chapter in *Financing Development 2008* from the OECD Development Centre (Koch 2008b).

### Part I

Mapping and testing potential determinants of geographic choices of international NGOs

2 What determines geographic choices of NGOs?*

An exploration

Introduction

Donor governments hold the view that international NGOs have an important role to play within the international aid architecture. The share of bilateral official development assistance (ODA) channelled to or through NGOs exceeded 10 per cent in 2005–6 for various OECD countries, notably the Netherlands (19.5 per cent), Switzerland (17.2), and Spain (15.9).[1] Overall, the combined budget of international NGOs based in the member countries of the OECD's Development Assistance Committee (DAC) amounted to almost US$27 billion in 2005 (Gatignon 2007).

Notwithstanding the quantitative importance of NGO aid, little is known about where NGO aid is spent and how well targeted it actually is. If at all, NGO aid is analysed in country-specific studies.[2] The literature making use of cross-country regressions is largely confined to ODA, mainly because data constraints typically prevented performing cross-country regressions for NGO aid. For instance OECD/DAC data are seriously deficient with respect to NGO aid at the level of individual recipient countries (Nunnenkamp *et al.* 2008). This chapter aims to close this empirical gap by compiling and analysing a new dataset on aid allocation, collected for 61 NGOs based in 13 donor countries, and thus rather unique in its coverage. Data were collected from the annual reports of the international NGOs or provided by them on request.

The chapter is structured as follows. It commences with a review of literature, and comes with five propositions as to what determines the cross country choices of NGOs. It continues by describing the data and the multivariate regression methodology. The following section displays the results. Three sets of regression analyses are executed: (1) eligibility stage regressions for the total sample (what determines *if* NGOs become active somewhere?); (2) level stage regressions for the total sample (what determines *how* active NGOs become somewhere?); (3) eligibility stage regressions with reduced samples (on the basis of nationality of the NGOs). This chapter comes to a close by a discussion of the findings and a conclusion.

Literature review

The literature on the determinants of foreign aid is largely confined to ODA granted by OECD governments. Several earlier studies argued that targeting of ODA to needy recipient countries with reasonably good local conditions (in terms of basic institutions and economic policies) is far from perfect (Collier and Dollar 2002; Burnside and Dollar 2000).[3] Furthermore, economic and political self-interest of donors appears to have had an important influence on the allocation of bilateral ODA across recipient countries (e.g. Berthélemy and Tichit 2004; Alesina and Dollar 2000).[4] The effectiveness of ODA in promoting economic and social development in the recipient countries may be compromised in these ways. NGOs may provide more effective aid than official donors. Earlier analytical reasoning and empirical findings suggest five major determinants which will be subsequently discussed. Especially the first three determinants reflect the widely held view that NGO aid may be superior to ODA (e.g. Nancy and Yontcheva 2006). Otherwise, the recent literature also suggests various qualifications, or even counter-hypotheses, so that expected signs of the determinants of NGO aid often remain ambiguous a priori.

There are likely other factors that influence the geographic choices of (some of the) international NGOs. One can expect that security considerations for instance play a role for international NGOs, as they do not want their staff to run any risks. This is however not a very interesting potential determinant to explore in depth, since it is theoretically, empirically and practically not contested. Additionally, one can expect that the strength of local partners is a relevant deliberation one the side of international NGOs when making geographic choices (e.g. Borren 2007). Interestingly, this absorption capacity argument has an ambiguous impact on geographic choices: on one side NGOs need strong local partners to be able to work effectively, at the other hand a core mission of many of the international NGOs is to actually strengthen local civil society actors. This constitutes thus, in theory, an interesting research problem: do NGOs focus on the countries with already strong civil societies, or do they focus on those with weak ones? However, serious data prevent a meaningful analysis of this question. There are some efforts under way to create a 'civil society index', however its coverage is too thin to be of use for the cross-sectional analysis of this chapter (Heinrich 2005). Chapter 4 deals with local capacity at length. Thus, there are probably some other potential factors influencing geographic choices of international NGOs, but those are either not very relevant or nearly impossible to study in depth. The five potential determinants as listed in Figure 2.1 provide thus an appropriate analytical grid through which the country choices can – and consequently will – be analysed.[5]

Poverty in recipient countries

The popularity of NGO aid is at least partly a corollary of the widely perceived 'failure of official aid programs to reach down and assist the poor'

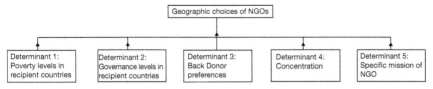

Figure 2.1 Analytic map of potential determinants of geographic choices of NGOs
Source: Koch, own data.

(Riddell and Robinson 1995, p. 2). NGOs can often circumvent governments in the recipient country and deal directly with target groups organized by local NGOs (Riddell *et al.* 1995, p. 25). It is claimed that they can reach the poor and the vulnerable, such as poor female heads of households and the landless, more directly than governments through their smaller scale of operation that offers better access to communities and grassroots organizations (Fowler and Biekart 1996). International donors finance NGOs for their role in reaching the poor (e.g. DFID 2006a).

This is why NGO aid would be expected to be strongly related to needs indicators such as the per-capita income of recipient countries or their economic and social development as measured by the Human Development Index. It could also be expected that NGOs would spend more of their resources in countries with an unequal income distribution, as indicated by the Gini coefficient, since many NGOs have their roots in the social justice movement, which focuses more on relative than on absolute poverty (Schulpen 1997).[6]

However, the view that NGOs have a clear focus on the poor has also been challenged. Research has shown that the claims of reaching the poorest of the poor have been exaggerated. Many case studies have shown that even if NGO interventions reach the poor, they usually do not reach the poorest of the poor (Steering Group 2002). For example, Sharma and Zeller show that NGOs services in Bangladesh 'are located more in poor pockets of relatively well-developed areas than in remoter, less-developed regions' (Sharma and Zeller 1999, p. 1).

NGOs may however also be reluctant to work in the poorest countries as they have to secure financial survival. According to the principal–agent model of Fruttero and Gauri (2005), the dependence of NGOs (the agents) on external funding (from official back donors as principals) tends to drive a wedge between organizational imperatives related to future funding and charitable objectives when making geographic choices. Principals have incomplete information on NGO projects, while future funding of agents depends on perceived success or failure of current projects. To demonstrate success, NGOs are as a consequence inclined to minimize risk, which weakens their incentive to operate in the poorest environments where failure may jeopardize future funding.

In a similar vein, the so-called marketization of aid is supposed to have unfavourable side-effects which bias the allocation of NGO aid towards recipient countries offering 'easier' environment (Cooley and Ron 2002; Fowler 2000; Lewis and Wallace 2000). The notion of marketization includes that NGOs increasingly have to compete for government and private funding. With the renewal of funding becoming less secure, however, NGOs may turn more risk averse and allocate aid strategically, by targeting recipients where success is easier to achieve.[7] The poverty orientation of NGO aid may thus be undermined by increasing pressure from co-financing governments to demonstrate project-related poverty impacts. This may appear counter-intuitive at first sight, but there is casual evidence to this effect. According to Bebbington (2004), increased intervention of the Dutch government into co-financed NGO projects in the Andes raised concerns with the NGOs that they might lose funding unless being able to demonstrate immediate project-related poverty impacts. Visible results are easier to achieve when projects address transitory forms of poverty, which may induce NGOs to shift attention away from the neediest recipients.

Alternatively, a lacklustre poverty focus might very well be related to a lack of absorption capacity in certain recipient countries. Most international NGOs rely on local partners for the actual execution of projects. Paradoxically, these organizations are often considered absent in the most needy environments, as Glasius points out: 'the poor and the marginalized are often too atomized and overwhelmed by a sense of powerlessness to have the confidence to set up vibrant associations. They also often lack the necessary skills and resources' (Glasius *et al.* 2004, p. 5).

There are four studies that use cross country regression on the expenditures of international NGOs (Nunnenkamp 2008; Dreher *et al.* 2007; Koch 2006; Nancy and Yontcheva 2006). The studies come to opposing results with respect to the poverty orientation of NGO aid. Nancy and Yontcheva (2006) present panel regression results on aid allocation by European NGOs (co-financed by the EU) in the 1990s. Poverty in recipient countries appears to be the major determinant of NGO allocations. Koch (2006) reports bivariate correlations between aid from Dutch NGOs and various indicators of need. NGO decisions of whether or not to engage in a particular country correlate to some poverty measures, such as the $1-a-day poverty head count, though not with other indicators of need such as per capita income, literacy, mortality and school enrolment. Conversely, levels of NGO funding are in general not correlated to needs indicators. Thus, the allocation of Dutch NGO aid seems at best partially based on human needs in the recipient countries. In a regression analysis of aid given by Swedish NGOs, Dreher *et al.* (2007) corroborate Koch's finding concerning the second stage of the aid allocation process. They also find that the amount of money that Swedish NGOs spend does not depend on levels of poverty in the recipient countries. In an analysis of the poor country targeting of Swiss NGOs, Nunnenkamp *et al.* (2008), find that NGO aid is generally not more poverty oriented than the aid from the Swiss government. According to this study, it rather depends on the measurement of recipient need whether NGOs out-performed the government. In sum, the academic debate on the poor country focus of international NGOs is far from concluded, and this chapter aims to contribute to it by analysing this relationship in depth for a large sample of international NGOs.

Governance in recipient countries

The second potential determinant of geographic choices is the quality of governance in recipient countries. This research employs a broad definition of governance; it encompasses both technical aspects, such as efficiency, and political aspects, such as democracy. Various scholars and institutes have concluded that NGO aid has a comparative advantage in countries with low levels of governance (Steering Committee 2002; Helmich *et al.* 1998; Edwards and Hulme 1998; Fowler and Biekart 1996), and that more NGO aid should consequently go to those countries. The World Bank publication 'Assessing Aid' was one of the first to propagate the notion that government-to-government aid should only go to countries that already had good governance. As the World Bank puts it:

> [i]n highly distorted environments the government is failing to provide supportive policies and effective services. That is why government-to-government financial transfers produce poor results. Effective aid in such an environment often involves supporting civil society to pressure the government to change or to take service provision directly into its own hands (or to do both).
>
> World Bank (1998, p. 104)

The United Nations Millennium Project share this opinion; in their report *Investing in Development: A Practical Plan to Achieve the MDGs* (2005), they state that there are

> countries that rank consistently low on civil liberties, political freedoms and human rights, while rating high on corruption, with little demonstrable will to achieve broad-based poverty reduction. In these cases, the international community can play a role in humanitarian assistance and deliver aid through NGOs.
>
> (p. 113)

The UK's Department for International Development states in categorical terms: 'NGOs will need to play a more active role in providing public services in fragile states where governments are weak and direct support to governments is not yet possible'(DFID, 2006b, p. 53). A report on Dutch government funding of co financing agencies (Steering Committee 2006, p. 15) argues along similar lines that NGOs should intervene in countries that are not eligible for bilateral aid because of governance deficiencies. 'These "bad governance cases" often demand politically more sensitive interventions, for which NGOs are thought to be better, and more appropriate agencies.'

Many academics subscribe to the view that bilateral aid to governments without reasonable policies does not help the poor and can even worsen their plight. Their argumentation is that such aid actually serves to prop up regimes that lack popular support (Bauer and Yamey 1982; Bauer 1971). It provides governments with the wrong incentives, since they are rewarded for bad policies (Easterly 2002). Many scholars suggest that if bilateral aid is not working, supporting non-governmental organizations is a good alternative (e.g. Easterly 2006).

However, NGOs may be unwilling to accept the role assigned to them by official donors, arguing against a scenario in which NGOs were to focus on the 'left-over' countries of bilateral aid (Borren 2007), or in which 'NGOs are seen as subcontractors who can be hired at will to clean up the institutional mess, after which Big Aid can move in and achieve nice results under conditions of good governance' (Monteiro 2007, p. 2). In addition, in cases where extreme adverse governance conditions prevail and where dictators forbid NGOs, interventions of international NGOs, if any, are likely to be limited in scale.

Empirical evidence is scant with respect to the relationship between the level of governance in recipient countries and the expenditures of NGOs. Of the four abovementioned cross-country regression studies, three address this relationship. Counter-intuitively, Koch (2006), Dreher *et al.* (2007) and Nunnenkamp (2008) find respectively that international NGOs from the Netherlands, Sweden and Switzerland do not focus more on countries with a poor governance situation. There thus appears to be a contradiction between what academics and policy makers expect, and what is actually happening. Since the abovementioned studies only cover NGOs from specific countries, this chapter analyses whether this paradox also surfaces when analysed with an internationally representative sample of NGOs.

Back-donor preferences

Targeting of ODA is likely to be affected by donor interests. Previous research has shown that many official donors tend to use aid to promote exports to recipient countries (e.g. Canavire *et al.* 2006; Berthélemy and Tichit 2004), while others 'buy' political support by granting ODA (e.g. Dreher *et al.* 2006a; Kuziemko and Werker 2006). Still others favour former colonies, which is at least partly because of maintaining political alliances, rather than a comparative advantage of working there. By contrast, the mission of NGOs engaged in international development cooperation is widely perceived to be independent of commercial and political interests of governments. Consequently, the allocation of NGO aid should be less or not affected by trade-related variables, such as bilateral exports, as well as political patronage variables, such as the voting behaviour of recipient countries in the UN General Assembly.

Nevertheless, the allocation of NGO aid is likely to be shaped by the geographical choices of official donors in the country in which the NGO is based. Recent literature increasingly questions the autonomy of NGOs, especially for those NGOs that strongly depend on government financing. Critics argue that NGOs are in fact subcontractors of the state (Kalb 2005) and see them as:

> organisations that political liberals cherish, and have for all practical purposes been reduced to serving as its [the state's] fire department, its expert toolbox, and its public relations group. These arenas may be necessary for the maintenance of hegemony but they hardly affect the core financial operations that are the undemocratic prerogative of the treasuries of their key sponsors.
>
> (Kalb 2005, p. 196)

Other critics of the supposed autonomy of NGOs are more moderate in their views and claim that:

> While the moniker 'non-government organisation' suggests autonomy from government organizations, NGOs are often intimately connected with their home governments in relationships that are both ambivalent as dynamic, sometimes cooperative, sometimes contentious, sometimes both simultaneously.
>
> (Fisher 1998, p. 451)

Edwards and Hulme (1996), for example, characterize the dependence of development NGOs on official donors as potentially 'too close for comfort'. As a consequence, NGOs might rather be expected to follow their back donors than to decide autonomously on where to locate their activities. Various critics suspect that government funding may have as a result that NGOs become 'the implementer of the policy agendas' of governments' (Edwards and Hulme 1996, p. 970).[8]

The limited empirical evidence available on the linkages between bilateral and NGO aid is inconclusive. Chapter 6 finds NGO and official aid to be correlated for Germany and Norway, but not for the United States. Since US-based organizations depend considerably less on their government than their German and Norwegian counterparts do, this result is consistent with the view that officially funded NGOs tend to follow the country-wise distribution of their back donors. Nunnenkamp (2008, p. 2) concludes that there is a high correlation between the expenditure distribution of Swiss aid and Swiss NGO aid, concluding that 'NGO aid is not so different after all'. Conversely, Nancy and Yontcheva (2006) register that projects from European NGOs and that are co-financed by the European Union do not follow the same geographic pattern of their back donor. This indicates that those NGOs have some degree of autonomy and do not merely implement EU aid policies.

Concentration

The existence of 'donor darlings' among bilateral and multilateral donors is a well documented phenomenon. Countries such as Uganda, Mozambique and Ghana were the flavour of the last decade (de Renzio and Hanlon 2007; Drechsler and Zimmerman 2007; Adam and Gunning 2002). In spite of this, the existence of NGO donor darlings countries has not been mapped statistically. There is some anecdotic evidence that there is a significant amount of NGO concentration in certain countries, such as Sri Lanka (Harris 2005) and in countries in the Balkans (Karajkov 2007).

Recently scholars have applied insights from the economic geography to the field of non-profit location theory, thereby shifting the focus to processes of concentration (Bielefeld and Murdoch 2004). These insights build on the work on for-profit firms by Krugman (1998). He focuses on economies of scale, labour mobility and path dependence to explain the concentration of economic actors. For example, when one international NGO has invested time and money in the strengthening of skills of local partners, it is attractive for other international NGOs to also work with these partners, instead of going to another country where partners still need to be trained. According to this theory, there are thus spatial positive externalities, contributing to a natural tendency of NGOs to cluster in the same countries. This theoretical argument will be explained in much more detail in Chapter 4, in which an evolutionary economic geography approach to explaining the geographic concentration of NGOs is elaborated upon. One key element of this economic geography approach is path dependence. This refers to the process whereby past choices narrow current and future room for manoeuvre. In the case of NGOs, path dependence occurs because of stakeholders who have an interest in maintaining the status quo (Cameron 2000). Research on the location decisions of NGOs by Bebbington (2004) – at a sub-national level – suggests that this is due to networks and institutions that both underlie and precede the existence of the agencies. He claims that the personal contacts of officers are important and notes that these 'are not accidental, and have a great deal to do with institutions, social networks, histories and political economic contexts within which they are embedded' (Bebbington 2004, p. 736). In short, informal and social networks are believed to shape the decisions of NGOs, and those networks tend to reinforce themselves.

Besides the economic geography arguments, the aforementioned principal–agent model of Fruttero and Gauri (2005) also suggests that NGOs face an incentive to locate close to where other NGOs are engaged as well. Conformity of location choices is supposed to render it more difficult for principals to assess the performance of individual agents, and may thus help preventing individual monitoring. Easterly (2002) calls this the blame-sharing effect, which is particularly relevant for NGOs with an established reputation. They have a lot to lose from failure, whereas less established NGOs have more incentives to distinguish themselves by engaging in countries where back donors can identify their specific contribution more easily. The NGOs in the sample are all more likely to belong to those with an established reputation, with annual budgets exceeding US$10 million, being active in on average 44 countries and having existed for decades.

The clustering of NGOs has not been tested systematically at the cross country level. This research is, to the best of knowledge, the first to engage in this effort. By contrast, the concentration of NGO activity has been widely researched at the sub national level. Fruttero and Gauri (2005) have found clustering of NGOs, especially micro-credit NGOs, within Bangladesh. According to Barr and Fafchamps (2005), NGOs are clustered in Uganda as well.

NGO-specific mission

NGOs have their specific mission, which enables them to raise funds from their constituents and donors. Their emergence can be explained by the heterogeneity of demands within a society, to which a government can impossibly respond adequately. The demands are so diverse, and there might be so little of a common denominator between them, that a government cannot fulfil all these requests (Hansman in Rose-Ackerman 1986). This stimulates the creation of common interest groups that will deliver the specific services desired by these groups.

NGOs have thus more discretion than state agencies to allocate aid according to specific group characteristics. As argued by Lipsky and Smith (1990), service delivery by state agencies requires not only unambiguous eligibility criteria, but also unambiguous indicators showing whether and to what extent beneficiaries meet those criteria. As a result, the selection of official aid recipients is, at least seemingly, rules-based; favouring one group of countries over another requires 'elaborate rationales' (*ibid.*, p. 631). By contrast, NGOs can afford to be more selective in their choice of aid recipients. To choose particular recipients according to religion, language, location or similar factors may violate the universalistic criteria underlying public development cooperation, but NGOs may well allocate their aid according to such factors without being criticized for doing so. Indeed, the focussed missions, are widely considered the 'raison d'être' of NGOs (e.g. Williams 1990).

What are these specific interests to which international NGOs are a response? Many of the international NGOs arose as a desire to support the evangelical and missionary work of Christians abroad (Lissner 1977). Their mission statements reflect their religious inspiration, which is also likely to permeate in their geographic choices. Furthermore, other common traits that might also foster additional solidarity are a shared language and a shared colonial heritage. It is worthwhile to investigate the importance of these special interests, as there might be a trade-off between this and equity concerns (Schmid 2003).

In summary, this chapter attempts to gain deeper insights into the targeting of NGO aid across recipient countries by jointly considering the major potential determinants of NGO aid allocation identified above in a multivariate regression framework. Some potential determinants, notably the clustering of NGOs in specific recipient countries, have received scant attention in previous empirical work, while the evidence on other potential determinants has remained inconclusive and limited to specific donor countries. The present analysis makes use of a unique dataset covering aid allocations of 61 international NGOs from a number of OECD countries, allowing us to investigate the determinants of NGO aid in a cross-section of countries. Hence, the econometric estimations are more likely to be representative than the previous studies on this topic. At the same time, it is possible to compare the allocation behaviour of NGOs based in different donor countries. The dataset and the method of estimation will be described in some detail in the next section.

Material and method

Data

The data situation on NGO aid is extremely poor with respect to its distribution across recipient countries. Information on aid allocation published by NGOs in Annual Reports is often confined to regions or major recipient countries. In order to assess the allocation behaviour appropriately, however, it is equally important to know which countries received minor amounts of aid, or none at all. Therefore, 98 NGOs that met two criteria have been contacted: (i) the annual aid budget exceeded €10 million in 2005 (about US $12.5 million at the average annual exchange rate in 2005); and (ii) they were not mainly humanitarian organizations.[9] Humanitarian NGOs, such as the Red Cross and Médecins Sans Frontières, were not contacted as their aid allocations are highly dependent on exogenous shocks and emergencies, such as a tsunami. A cross-sectional analysis of their country-wise expenditures is likely to be driven by a few outlying observations. Foundations such as the Ford Foundation are included in the sample. Even though they do not receive public funding, they do fulfil the criteria. They are non-governmental, non-profit, and are not primarily humanitarian organizations.

The figures that were provided by the international NGOs provide insight an overview of a large part of international NGO aid. It does however not cover all aid that individuals and official donors give to NGOs. Direct funding by decentralized aid agencies to independent local subsidiaries of international NGOs do not surface in the data provided by the international NGOs for this research. This needs to be considered when interpreting the results.

The response rate to the data request was high: 62 per cent. The sample of NGOs included in the subsequent analysis represents about two thirds of the total budget of all NGOs contacted (see Annex 3 for the sample of NGOs). In most cases, aid data refer to the year 2005.[10] Taken together, the sample of NGOs granted aid in the order of € 4.6 billion (US$5.7 billion) to recipient countries. This amounts to almost 40 per cent of overall grants by all NGOs as reported by the OECD for 2005 (US$14.7 billion).

The NGO sample also appears to be sufficiently representative with respect to donor country coverage. Apart from some minor DAC countries with a combined ODA share of about 8 per cent, it is only for Japan that there is a lack of information on NGO aid. However, the case of Japan is unlikely to generate a serious sample selection bias; aggregated OECD data suggest that NGO aid plays a marginal role for this otherwise important donor. Three-quarters of NGO aid in the sample is from NGOs based in the United States, the United Kingdom, Germany and the Netherlands. This share almost exactly resembles the combined share of these four countries in NGO aid as presented by the OECD. Finally, the sample clearly reflects that the US share in NGO aid is considerably higher than its ODA share. The non-response of NGOs from Italy, Denmark and Spain does not lead to biases; according to the OECD DAC data none of these countries contribute to more than 1 per cent of the total NGO aid.

All countries that were on the list of DAC aid recipients in 2005 have been included in the regressions. Small island states are excluded (e.g. Tonga and St Lucia).[11] The final sample consists of 114 countries. Annex 1 gives the top recipients of NGO aid. As can be seen, the more populous countries dominate the list of prime recipients when absolute amounts are considered. Conversely, small countries dominate when focusing on per capita expenditures. The list of absolute top recipients consists of ten Anglophone countries, whereas this pattern is more diverse considering the NGO aid per capita list. Approximately half of the top recipients are considered to be Least Developed Countries by the OECD/DAC (indicated with *).

To assess the role of poverty in NGO allocations (determinant one), three indicators are employed in the regressions.[12] In line with most previous studies, (log) GDP per capita has been chosen as the standard needs indicator. Alternatively, the Human Development Index is used, which provides a broader measure of need by including life expectancy at birth, literacy rates, and school enrolment rates, next to GDP per capita (United Nations Development Programme 2006). To capture whether NGOs are driven by relative rather than absolute levels of poverty, the Gini coefficient is included (Gilles *et al.* 1996).[13]

What 'good governance' actually means and how it can be measured are contested (Hout 2007; Arndt and Oman 2006). Criticisms relate to the fact that most of them are perception based, and that the criteria often reflect political preferences of the designers of the indicators. The same could be said of the indicators, that are used in this research. Nevertheless, the indicators that will be employed are standard ones that are used in virtually all aid allocation regressions (e.g. Neumayer 2003). To assess the relevance of the governance situation in recipient countries (determinant 2), the Polity IV index of democracy is used (Marshall and Jaggers 2004). The index ranges from -10 to 10, with higher values representing more democracy. Alternatively, the first principal component of the six 'Governance Matters' indicators from the World Bank is used (Kaufmann et al. 2005). Finally, the sum of the Freedom House (2006) indicators of Political Rights and Civil Liberties is also used, ranging from 2–14, with higher values indicating less democratic governance.[14]

The preference of back donors (determinant 3) is proxied by (log) bilateral aid that a country received (in 2004) from the home country of the NGO as reported in the Creditor Report System of the OECD/DAC (net official aid flows).[15] To check whether donor interests also shape the choices of NGOs, the share of the recipient country in total exports of the donor country is included. In addition, a variable that represents the political interests of the donor country is incorporated: conformity of voting of the recipient country with the home country of the NGOs in the United Nations General Assembly. These variables are standard in the aid allocation literature (e.g. Canavire et al. 2006; Alesina and Dollar 2000).

To test for the effect of the presence of other NGOs – the so-called concentration effect, determinant 4, this research uses (i) the number of other NGOs from the sample which are present in the same recipient country and (ii) the total amount of aid that all other NGOs in the sample spend in the same country. Ideally, a lagged variable of the number of other NGOs would be used, as this would have enabled to better capture whether NGOs operate in the slipstream of other NGOs. Unfortunately, for the time being the data on international NGO aid are cross-sectional in nature. In the next chapter, regarding Dutch NGOs, panel data exist and we can test lag the concentration data.

To test whether the country choices of NGOs reflect the NGO-specific mission (determinant 5), dummies are included for countries that share certain key characteristics with the NGO (dummies for shared religious beliefs and former colonial status). The first dummy is one if the NGO has Christian foundations and the recipient country is predominantly Christian, and zero otherwise.[16] The second dummy is one when a recipient country was a former colony from the home country of the donor NGO. Finally, in accordance with standard aid allocation regressions, a country's (log) population size is included.

The dependent variable in the regression analysis relates to the efforts of international aid NGOs, as assessed by their expenditures in the countries in the sample. The (logged) absolute amounts of aid have been taken rather than aid per capita as the dependent variable. This is to account for the fact that donors are more likely to allocate a fixed overall amount of money on a country basis than on a per capita basis (Neumayer 2003). The log value is used, as the data were not normally distributed.

Arguably, some of the explanatory variables may not be exogenous to the NGOs' decisions. For instance, effective aid may be supportive for raising per capita income in recipient countries. Aid may also be helpful stabilizing (un-)democratic governments. For several reasons, however, reverse causation is unlikely to distort the empirical results. Various aid items are unlikely to have *short-term* effects on economic outcomes (Clemens *et al.* 2004). Concerning the impact on democratic institutions, in particular, short-term effects are not likely to be expected. According to Burnside and Dollar (2004, p. 4), 'researchers coming from the left, the right, and the centre have all concluded that aid as traditionally practiced has not had systematic, beneficial effects on institutions and policies'. Nevertheless, all the explanatory variables are lagged by one year (i.e. refer to the year 2004), as is recommended by Gujarati (2002, p. 662)

Common cause interdependence is a cause of concern for this chapter, as there is a likelihood that there is a relationship between potential unobserved effects and one of our independent variables, the geographic choices of other NGOs. After all, it is probable that factors that influence the geographic choices of the NGOs in the dependent variable, but are not in the model, also affect the geographic choices of the other NGOs, in the independent variable. Consequently, this might lead to an upward bias in these estimation results, as the independent variable 'number of other NGOs' captures these unobserved effects.[17] On theoretical grounds it can be argued that this omitted variable bias is limited, but non-negligible. The five determinants cover the most often recurring elements in the literature review. In addition, adequate indicators were found to represent these elements. Nevertheless, certain unobserved characteristics of recipient countries, notably the absorption capacity of local organizations, were left out of the equation due to a lack of conceptual clarity and data constraints. These country characteristics could influence both the dependent and the independent variable and would ideally have been included in the model. However, empirical tests indicate that the bias is limited. A comparison of results of regressions with and without the 'number of other NGO' variable shows that excluding this variable reduces the explanatory power of the model, but not disproportionately so.[18] Other potential factors that influence both regressor and regressand have been analysed and were found not relevant. For instance, a dummy for disasters in the period 2002–4 was included to see whether this would influence the results, as disasters could influence both the numbers of other NGOs and the NGO in the regressand.[19] The effects of common cause interdependence, if any, were thus contained.

Method

There are basically two options for dealing with the bounded nature of the dependent variable: a Tobit approach and a two-stage Heckman approach. The Tobit approach assumes that the same set of variables determines both whether a country is selected as aid recipient and how much money is being allocated to that country. Under this assumption, Tobit is considered the preferred method. The Heckman approach assumes that NGO donors decide in a first stage whether to allocate aid to a country at all, while – in a second step – they decide on the amount of aid to be given once a country has been selected as a recipient. For the first stage of this model, Probit is the adequate technique of estimation.

Employing this Heckman selection model implies to impose restrictions on the allocation equation. As Neumayer (2003) argues, it is not obvious which variables should be excluded from the allocation stage and could be argued to be important for selection exclusively. He therefore suggests OLS as an alternative method of estimation, ignoring the bias. The bias associated with OLS might be reasonably small when the sample contains a limited number of zero observations. However, the number of countries where NGOs are not active at all is fairly large in the sample. Therefore, this research does not present OLS results but prefers to employ the Heckman estimator.

In this research shared religion is excluded from the allocation equation. There are several arguments to support this choice. Most importantly, NGOs that selected recipient countries on the basis of shared characteristics such as common language or historical ties have often done so several decades ago. Former decisions of this sort are rather unlikely to shape current decisions on the amount of aid to spend in these countries. It fits into this reasoning that the religious match becomes completely insignificant when running OLS regressions (reported in Koch *et al.* 2008) for the countries selected as recipients of NGO aid (while it is significant in the Probit selection equation reported below). There are thus both theoretical and statistical justifications for the assumption that the religious match affects selection rather than allocation, even though the OLS estimate has to be interpreted with caution as it may suffer from selection bias.

Throughout the analysis, the units of observation are the allocations made by individual NGOs. Consequently, individual location decisions are analysed, some of which may be lost when aggregating data on the country level (e.g. Cheng and Stough 2006). For all the estimations, standard errors are therefore clustered at the country level.

Three sets of results that are discussed in this chapter. First, the results of the Probit analysis on the selection of recipient countries of the entire sample are presented in Table 2.1. Second, the Heckman estimates for the entire sample, testing the determinants of levels of funding, are presented in Table 2.2. The last table in the chapter, Table 2.3, displays the Probit selection estimates for NGOs grouped by home country.

Results

The Probit model results regarding the entire sample, addressing the selection of recipient countries, are presented first. The dependent variable takes the value of one if a country has been chosen as recipient by a particular NGO, and zero otherwise. In testing the determinants outlined in the 'Literature review', one variable representing one of the five determinants enters the basic specification, including variables that figure prominently in the ODA allocation literature (Hout 2007; Dollar and Levin 2006; Alesina and Dollar 2000): (log) GDP per capita, the Polity IV index of democracy, and (log) population. The basic specification also includes the dummy for joint religion, (log) bilateral per capita aid, and the number of other NGOs present in the same recipient country.

Column 1 Table 2.1 shows the results of the base regression. The estimation correctly predicts 73.4 per cent of the observations. This means that the model can predict correctly in 73.4 of the cases whether an NGO is, or is not active, in a certain country. NGO appear more likely to select countries with lower per capita GDP, though only at the 10 per cent level of significance. NGOs are more likely to become active in countries with higher levels of democracy, at the 10 per cent significance level. At the 1 per cent level, NGOs are more likely to be active in countries (i) which receive higher levels of bilateral official aid from the donor country in which the NGO is based, (ii) where more other NGOs are engaged, (iii) which share the same religion, and (iv) which have larger populations. Contrary to hypothesis 2, however, NGO aid increases with rising levels of democracy. The first results seem to suggest that international NGOs favour countries that are more democratic, rather than working in difficult environments.

As concerns the size of the effects, a 1 per cent increase in GDP per capita reduces the probability of receiving NGO aid by 1.3 per cent (marginal effects coefficient). Improving democracy by one point on the polity index (ranging from −10 to +10) increases the probability of being selected by 0.2 per cent. A 1 per cent increase in bilateral aid and the presence of one more NGO from the sample in a recipient country increases the probability of being selected by 4.5 per cent and 1 per cent, respectively. The marginal effect for joint religion is 18.9 per cent, which points to a remarkably strong influence of the NGO specific mission on NGOs' geographic choices.

In the following columns of Table 2.1, one variable for each hypothesis is changed at a time to test the robustness of the findings.

Replacing GDP per capita by the Gini coefficient (column 2) or, respectively, the Human Development Index (column 3) shows that these two alternative indicators of need are not significant at conventional levels. This result runs counter to the claims that NGOs make use of relative poverty indicators or broader notions of human need when deciding whether to become active in a country. GDP per capita is only significant in two of the nine specifications, indicating that at the evidence that NGOs become active in poorer countries is flimsy. Later in this chapter, though, it will become clear that there is a relationship between the amount of aid NGOs give to countries and poverty levels in those countries where they are active.

Table 2.1 The selection of recipient countries by international NGOs Probit estimates for 2005

	(1) Base—standardized coefficients	(2) Poverty	(3) Poverty	(4) Governance	(5) Governance	(6)	(7) Back donor	(8) Concentration	(9) Common traits
GDP p.c. (log & lag)	−0133 (1.79)*			−0.024 (1.03)	−0.013 (0.62)	−0.032 (1.44)	−0.040 (1.74)*	0.010 (0.31)	−0.010 (0.69)
Polity (log & lag)	0.00284 (2.46)*	0.004 (1.11)	0.005 (1.53)			0.007 (2.09)**	0.007 (1.99)**	0.010 (2.05)**	0.011 (3.89)***
Bilateral aid (log & lag)	0.04563 (10.96)**	0.140 (10.65)**	0.134 (11.39)**	0.128 (11.46)***	0.127 (11.33)***	0.128 (10.40)***	0.155 (12.15)***	0.140 (11.05)***	0.118 (9.78)***
# of other NGOs	0.01035 (11.57)**	0.030 (11.72)**	0.031 (13.00)**	0.030 (12.22)***	0.031 (14.31)***	0.030 (11.32)***	0.028 (10.56)***		0.032 (14.04)***
Religion	0.18900 (9.57)**	0.494 (8.88)**	0.488 (9.54)**	0.518 (10.81)***	0.527 (10.82)***	0.50 (8.85)***	0.480 (8.79)***	0.505 (8.91)***	
Population (log)	0.01456 (2.74)**	0.031 (2.24)*	0.035 (2.31)*	0.042 (2.64)***	0.033 (2.46)**	0.054 (2.70)***	0.042 (2.63)***	0.051 (2.29)**	0.033 (2.47)**
Gini coefficient (log)		0.0003 (0.48)							
Human Development Index (lag)			0.026 (0.22)						
Freedom House (lag)				−0.011 (1.49)					
Governance (lag)					0.009 (0.45)				
Recipients' share in total exports (lag)						−4.902 (1.99)**			

(continued on next page)

Table 2.1 (continued)

	(1)	(2)	(3)	(4)	(5)	(6)	(7)	(8)	(9)
	Base–standardized coefficients	Poverty		Governance			Back donor	Concentration	Common traits
UNGA Voting (lag)							0.519 (4.57)***		
Expenditures other NGOs (log)								0.265 (8.81)***	
Colony, dummy									0.314 (3.80)***
Constant	-1831 (9.83)**	-1954 (8.44)**	-2016 (10.03)**	-1.826 (10.07)***	-1.870 (9.87)***	-2.060 (7.89)***	-2.126 (9.95)***	-6.147 (14.19)***	-1.834 (10.33)***
Observations	5409	4653	5531	5999	6059	5118	5349	5406	5409
# recipient countries	95	82	97	105	106	90	94	95	95
Pseudo R2	0.16	0.16	0.16	0.16	0.16	0.16	0.16	0.16	0.15
log likelihood	-2878.82	-2516.02	-2932.84	-3204.40	-3226.34	-2759.45	-2847.21	-2894.48	-2914.16

Notes:
Robust z statistics in parentheses
* significant at 10%; ** significant at 5%; *** significant at 1%.

Columns 4 and 5 substitute the index of democracy taken from Freedom House and, respectively, the World Bank's governance index for the Polity index of democracy. The two indicators are not significant at conventional levels. In five of the nine specifications, more democracy in recipient countries seems to stimulate international NGOs to select those for intervention, and does so significantly. This is in contrast to what was predicted on basis of the literature.

Bilateral exports in total donor country exports (column 6) are significant at the 5 per cent level when included in the regression, showing that increased trade reduces NGO aid. While the negative coefficient may be somewhat surprising, it can be concluded that, as hypothesized, NGO aid appears not affected by the economic interests of back donors.[20] Voting in the General Assembly (UNGA voting) is highly significant, with a positive coefficient (column 7), which could suggest that, in addition to simply following back donors, NGOs prefer to be engaged in countries with which their back donor has friendly ties.

Column 8 includes (log) expenditures of other NGOs instead of the number of other NGOs being present in a particular country. NGO aid is both rising with the amount of aid granted by other NGOs, and with the number of other NGOs active in the country, at virtually all times at the 1 per cent level of significance.

The dummy for former colonies is significant at the 1 per cent level (column 9). This strengthens the finding of the base regression that common traits are an important selection criterion.

Note that the coefficients of most variables are strikingly robust throughout the various specifications of the Probit model. Bilateral aid is significant at the 1 per cent level in all specifications. The same is true regarding the number of other NGOs and religion (at the 5 per cent level at least). The index of democracy and GDP per capita, however, become insignificant in many specifications. The Probit model thus provides evidence in favour of determinants 3 to 5, while there is weak evidence in favour of determinant 1 on poverty. Determinant 2, on the engagement of NGOs in comparatively difficult environments finds no support by the data. If there is any evidence on the importance of governance levels in recipient countries, it points in the other direction, as the base regression and some of the other regressions shows a positive relationship between democracy and NGO selection.

Whereas Table 2.1 focuses on the determinants of whether an NGO becomes active in a country, Table 2.2 displays the results on how active NGOs become (for the entire sample). It uses a Heckman estimator and omits the shared religion – and the colonial dummy – from the allocation equation. Throughout, the Inverse Mills Ratio is not significant at the 5 per cent level (as reported at the bottom of the table which indicates that Ordinary Least Squares results such as reported in the World Development article, can be assumed to be unbiased). The results reported for the levels of NGO aid largely mirror the findings for the eligibility stage, with one important distinction; poverty is a much more robust determinant for the level of NGO aid. Given that the determinants of selection are to some extent different from those determining the amount of aid, the above noted assumptions underlying a Tobit specification do not hold, indicating that a Heckman procedure is a preferred statistical approach.

Column 1 of Table 2.2 shows the results of the base regression with respect to the levels of expenditures of international NGOs. The base regression shows that international NGOs allocate more to countries with higher levels of poverty. The variable is significant at the 1 per cent level. Since the regression is mostly a log-log regression, the coefficient indicates changes in terms of percentage. Thus a 1 per cent increase in GDP per capita, reduces aid from NGOs by 0.14 per cent. The governance situation in a recipient country is not significant, which mirrors the earlier findings in the Probit regression. Determinant 3, the back donor preferences, exerts a considerable influence on the level of NGO financing. The variable is significant at the 1 per cent level and its coefficient indicates that a 1 per cent rise in bilateral aid leads to a 0.14 per cent increase in aid from NGOs to that country. The relevance of the fourth determinant, the concentration effect, becomes visible in the base regression of the Heckman regression. The presence of other NGOs has a stimulating effect on the expenditures of NGOs in that country at the 1 per cent significance level. The presence of one additional other NGO in the country is associated with 0.03 per cent higher expenditures.

In the following columns of Table 2.2, the robustness of the findings is checked by replacing for each determinant the base-variable by an alternative comparable variable.

While the Gini coefficient (column 2) does not appear to influence the allocation pattern of international NGOs, the Human Development Index (column 3) does. Higher levels of Human Development lead to lower levels of NGO allocations (at the 1 per cent level). Thus besides the fact that GDP per capita is a robust determinant of levels of NGO aid, also the Human Development Index, is significant. This strengthens the case that NGOs hardly consider levels of poverty when deciding to be active somewhere, but do include that in their considerations when deciding on *how* active to become in those countries in which they are active.

Other variables that represent levels of governance in the recipient countries are tested in columns 4 and 5. In line with earlier findings, there is no indication that there is a relationship between levels of governance in a country and the level of NGO allocations, as neither the Freedom House nor the governance indicator produce significant results.

Columns 6 and 7 report the relationship with other donor interest variables, such as the trade between donor and recipient country and the conformity of voting in the United Nations General Assembly. There is no relationship between the levels of trade and the levels of NGO aid. There appears to be however, a negative relationship between the conformity of UN-voting and NGO allocations. This contrasts with the findings for the

Table 2.2 The levels of expenditures per recipient countries by international NGOs Heckman estimates for 2005

	(1)	(2)	(3)	(4)	(5)	(6)	(7)	(8)
	Base	Poverty		Governance		Back donor		Concentration
GDP p.c. (log & lag)	-0.14493			-0.13994	-0.10946	-0.13880	-0.14222	-0.10774
	(4.32)***			(5.05)***	(3.78)***	(3.98)***	(3.77)***	(3.11)***
Polity (lag)	0.00614	0.00473	0.00308			0.00789	0.00775	0.00383
	(0.81)	(0.59)	(0.40)			(1.02)	(1.02)	(0.55)
Bilateral aid (log & lag)	0.14978	0.16317	0.15323	0.15606	0.15498	0.14781	0.08905	0.11955
	(6.14)***	(6.88)***	(6.15)***	(6.77)***	(6.71)***	(5.95)***	(3.31)***	(3.98)***
# of other NGOs	0.03104	0.03448	0.03209	0.03172	0.03255	0.02948	0.03020	
	(6.15)***	(6.14)***	(5.96)***	(6.66)***	(6.73)***	(5.64)***	(5.25)***	
Population (log & lag)	0.06103	0.04026	0.06802	0.05234	0.04359	0.10512	0.05679	0.05469
	(1.64)	(1.06)	(1.75)*	(1.54)	(1.25)	(2.48)**	(1.51)	(1.55)
Gini coefficient (lag)		-0.00356						
		(1.07)						
Human Development Index (lag)			-0.74594					
			(3.40)***					
Freedom House (lag)				-0.01470				
				(1.17)				
Governance (lag)					-0.03396			
					(0.85)			
Recipients' share in total exports (lag)						-9.10483		
						(1.40)		
UNGA Voting (lag)							-1.27777	
							(5.23)***	
Expenditures other NGOs (log)								0.20690
								(3.33)***
Constant	11.88935	11.27454	11.24944	12.06832	11.88589	11.20073	12.97476	9.48470
	(19.26)***	(18.25)***	(17.63)***	(20.44)***	(19.29)***	(15.65)***	(19.72)***	(6.28)***
Observations	5407	5191	5395	5997	6057	5360	5401	5406
Inv. Mills (Prob>chi2)	0.18	0.13	0.22	0.06	0.08	0.36	0.90	0.24
# of recipient countries	95	80	94	105	106	90	94	95

Notes:
Robust z statistics in parentheses
* significant at 10%; ** significant at 5%; *** significant at 1%.

eligibility stage, where conformity of UN voting exercised a positive influence on being selected as a recipient country. Thus, while bilateral aid influences NGO allocations in both the Probit and Heckman regression, the findings with respect to donor interest variables is ambiguous at best.

Column 8 tests another measure of the concentration effect. It considers the level of expenditures of other NGOs (instead of the number of other NGOs). This variable is again significant at the 1 per cent level and the coefficient is sizeable. It indicates that a 1 per cent increase in expenditures of other NGOs in the recipient country contributes to a rise of 0.2 per cent of expenditures of the NGOs.

Table 2.3 moves on to an analysis at a more specific level. The sample of NGOs is broken down along donor country lines. Only results are presented from countries with three or more NGOs in the sample (Australia, Austria and France are hence excluded). The Probit results are presented since samples sizes would become rather small when presenting the Heckman estimates.[21]

The results confirm most of the earlier findings when the sample is split along national lines. There is some variation across donor countries. The variable that is most versatile is the GDP per capita variable. Whereas in some donor countries there is no relationship between GDP per capita in the recipient countries and location choices (e.g. Belgium and Canada), there is a positive linkage in one country (Germany) and a negative relationship in other countries (Ireland and the United Kingdom). The results with respect to the reverse poverty targeting of German organizations might seem odd at first sight, but is clearly substantiated in a case study on German organization in Chapter 6 of this research.

The governance variable is generally not significant, and if its coefficients are positive. This indicates that more democratic countries have a higher chance of being selected by NGOs from some countries, notably Germany. This corroborates the earlier findings that there is no evidence for the second determinant, and if it is present, it points in the other direction (better governance situations leading to more NGO aid).

Back-donor preferences are positive and significant for all regression. There is some variation on the coefficient across countries. American organizations are least influenced by their back donor preferences and Belgium organizations most. Chapter 6, which also presents a case study on the American organizations, confirms that American organizations are indeed more independent from their back donor than organizations from other countries.[22]

With respect to the fourth determinant, the concentration effect, this is found present in nine of the ten countries. Only Swiss organizations are not influenced by the preferences of other organizations, which appears related to the focus of Swiss organizations on Asia.

Lastly, in the overwhelming majority of the cases (eight out of ten) a positive and significant relationship exists between a shared religion and the chance that NGOs select a country.[23]

Table 2.3 The selection of recipient countries by international NGOs, per donor country Probit estimates 2005

	(1) Belgium	(2) Canada	(3) Germany	(4) Ireland	(5) NL	(6) Norway	(7) Sweden	(8) Switzerland	(9) UK	(10) USA
GDP capita (log & lag)	0.169 (1.40)	-0.035 (0.39)	0.148 (3.00)***	-0.544 (2.86)***	-0.128 (2.01)**	0.065 (0.84)	-0.014 (0.15)	-0.098 (1.61)	-0.092 (1.72)*	0.027 (0.68)
Polity (lag)	0.001 (0.03)	0.024 (1.71)*	0.030 (3.07)***	-0.017 (0.61)	0.015 (1.48)	-0.030 (2.16)**	0.019 (1.08)	0.016 (1.70)*	0.013 (1.30)	0.010 (1.40)
Bilateral aid p.c. (log & lag)	0.565 (5.43)***	0.178 (2.66)***	0.126 (2.71)***	0.166 (1.95)*	0.143 (3.21)***	0.338 (5.33)***	0.113 (1.89)*	0.187 (5.95)***	0.099 (3.11)***	0.076 (2.97)***
# of other NGOs	0.040 (3.90)***	0.035 (4.58)***	0.033 (5.10)***	0.088 (6.43)***	0.032 (4.67)***	0.033 (2.91)***	0.04 (3.69)***	0.003 (0.61)	0.051 (8.20)***	0.026 (5.63)***
Religion	0.764 (2.75)***	0.011 (0.06)	0.641 (4.36)***	1.718 (5.01)***	0.597 (3.84)***	1.004 (4.73)***	-0.321 (1.77)*	0.698 (4.91)***	-0.780 (2.97)***	0.262 (1.70)*
Population (log & lag)	-0.299 (2.37)**	-0.077 (1.30)	0.183 (3.52)***	0.112 (1.09)	-0.009 (0.17)	-0.226 (3.84)***	0.133 (1.89)*	0.102 (2.41)**	0.028 (0.53)	0.030 (0.90)
Constant	1.128 (0.64)	-0.113 (0.13)	-5.059 (6.50)***	-1.347 (0.73)	-0.702 (0.84)	1.525 (1.82)*	-4.015 (3.67)***	-1.771 (2.67)***	-1.442 (1.91)*	-1.981 (3.69)***
Observations	258	282	595	285	644	380	285	570	623	1032
# of countries	86	94	85	95	92	95	95	95	89	86
log likelihood	-77.34	-145.95	-325.67	-77.21	-310.01	-169.24	-110.11	-333.74	-296.56	-587.89
(Pseudo) R2	0.37	0.16	0.21	0.52	0.19	0.24	0.26	0.09	0.28	0.10

Notes:
Robust z statistics in parentheses
* significant at 10%; ** significant at 5%; *** significant at 1%.

Overall, the Probit regressions (both for the entire sample and for the sample divided along donor country lines) and Heckman regressions provide strong support for determinants 3 and 4. The preferences of back donors and the country choices of other NGOs matter a great deal for NGOs when they make their geographic choices, both when they decide on *if* and *how* active they become somewhere. Interestingly, while poverty levels in the potential recipient countries are not of importance when NGOs decide on *if* they become active in a country (as the Probit results show), they clearly are of importance when they make decisions on *how* active they become in those countries (as the Heckman regressions indicate). There is thus only limited evidence that poverty affects the NGO's choice to be active in a country, whereas poverty is shown to have an impact on the amount of aid that is spent. Concerning NGO-specific missions, it is found that these characteristics matter for the selection of recipients rather than the allocation of aid amounts. The second determinant, regarding the impact of governance levels in recipient countries on NGO choices, was found of little use when attempting to explain the geographic choices of NGOs.

Discussion and conclusion

This chapter provides one of the first, if not the first, comprehensive cross-country analysis of the driving forces of NGO aid, based on new data from a representative group of 61 of the largest NGOs from various OECD countries.

The widely held view that NGOs provide well-targeted aid is supported in two respects. First of all, poverty levels in recipient countries affect the levels of expenditures of NGOs in those countries positively. Second, commercial interests such as the promotion of exports, often supposed to shape the allocation of official aid, have not systematically affected the allocation of NGO aid.

On the other hand, this chapter indicates that NGOs do not complement official aid through engaging in so-called difficult institutional environments. Rather, NGOs tend to replicate the location choices of official 'back donors' from whom NGOs get part of their funding. This casts doubt on the notion of autonomous NGO behaviour. Moreover, NGOs appear to follow other NGOs so that aid becomes clustered, further adding to the divide between so-called donor darlings and donor orphans. Donor darlings of international NGOs such as Tanzania, Kenya, Malawi and Sri Lanka, Zambia and Uganda received more than US$100 million annually, whereas countries such as Côte d'Ivoire, Congo-Brazzaville, Guinea, Yemen and the Central African Republic received significantly less than US$10 million annually. Finally, NGOs prefer recipient countries with common traits related to religion or colonial history, which appears to demonstrate the importance of NGO-specific missions in geographic choice processes.

This chapter has presented a comprehensive cross-country analysis of the driving forces of NGO aid. The following chapter will test whether the same five determinants can also contribute to an explanation of the historical geographic choices made by NGOs from one specific OECD country: the Netherlands.

3 Geographic decisions of Dutch NGOs
Myths and realities*

Introduction

As stated in Chapter 2 little is known about where NGO aid is spent and what its determinants are. This chapter contributes to this discussion by identifying and analysing the determinants of the country choices of Dutch NGOs. There are two major reasons for selecting the Dutch NGOs to study determinants of NGO-aid allocation. First, no previous research on this subject has ever been performed in the Netherlands. Second, the Dutch civil society programme is one of the largest (> US$700 million annually) and oldest (since 1965) in the world. Oxfam Novib, the largest Dutch NGO, will be analysed in more depth because of its size and its reportedly unique geographic allocation system (Borren 2007).

This chapter is structured as follows. In the first section, key features of the Dutch co-financing system for NGOs are described, including their geographic characteristics. In the second section, the five potential determinants of Chapter 2 are contextualized in the Dutch case by means in-depth interviews. In the third section a quantitative analysis is used to rigorously test these determinants. In the last session, a case study is provided of one of the NGOs, with the aim of identifying major mediating factors, which actually influence those potential determinants.

Methodology

For this research, a Q-squared approach is applied to single out a social phenomenon. This method was primarily developed for poverty research, but its interesting mix of qualitative and quantitative aspects has inspired this research (Kanbur 2001).

After an analysis of the Dutch setting in the first part of this research, the second part is qualitative and enables the research to discover the probable determinants of country aid allocation by Dutch NGOs. One central element of this qualitative research is the use of open-ended questions within unstructured surveys of non-random samples. Chambers (2001) argues that one of the advantages of qualitative methods is that they enable researchers to generate testable hypotheses. The elements touched upon during the interviews were compiled based on a review of relevant literature. This research makes use of 16 interviews with the relevant decision-makers within the main Dutch development NGOs. Those decision-makers were involved in the NGOs' geographic choices between 1965 and 2005. Interviewees include managers and ex-managers within all four large development NGOs, former heads of the Civil Society Unit, as well as former top-level civil servants from the Netherlands Ministry of Foreign Affairs. In addition, external stakeholders were interviewed that were involved as researchers or consultants to those organizations on this topic. For a full overview of interviewees, see Annex 5.

The third part is quantitative and makes it possible to test the drivers that emerged during the second part with a structured quantitative analysis. Kanbur (2001) states that quantitative analysis enables an assessment of causal relationships and changes over time. This research makes use of advanced statistical techniques developed by Nancy and Yontcheva (2006) at the International Monetary Fund, which allows this research to test the causality of relations. A longitudinal dataset has been compiled of aid allocation of the largest Dutch NGOs to all recipient countries between 1989 and 2005. The source of these data were the annual financial reports of the NGOs to the Netherlands Ministry of Foreign Affairs. The sole legally binding constraint on NGOs in their (public) aid allocation decisions was that they should spend it in DAC countries. For this reason, only countries that were present on the DAC list at any time during the research period are included in the sample (N = 121). For an overview of the summary statistics of the variables used in this section, see Annex 6.

The final part of this research is a largely qualitative and descriptive case study. This research uses interviews and supporting materials to examine which mediating factors can explain why in certain instances the potential determinants were found to have a substantial impact on the geographic choices and in some instances, they were not. In line with Ravallion (2001), a case study is deemed superior in comparing the results of quantitative methods to experiences 'on the ground'. By using this approach, the research attempts to exploit fully the comparative advantages of the various research methods. This research draws heavily on the experience of the Q-squared approach. As a case study, Oxfam Novib has been selected for various reasons.[1] First, Oxfam Novib was the first Dutch organization to develop a formalized selection system for their 'core' countries. Second, Oxfam Novib is the largest Dutch development NGO in terms of adherents and budget. Lastly, the director of Oxfam Novib claimed during presentations of the preliminary quantitative findings that they did not apply to her organization. This case study combines an analysis of relevant internal documents from the organization and in-depth interviews with stakeholders. Findings regarding Oxfam Novib are thus not necessarily representative for the average Dutch geographic decisions, and deviations from the general pattern will be highlighted.

The Dutch setting

Background of the Dutch co-financing system

The Dutch co-financing system has displayed a high degree of continuity in terms of the NGOs receiving subsidies. The government started funding three NGOs in 1965. These organizations reflected the divisions within Dutch society: Cebemo was a catholic organization; ICCO was its protestant equivalent; Oxfam Novib (called Novib at that time) was secular and social democratic. Very occasionally, the Dutch government added another organization such as the humanistic HIVOS in 1977 and child-centred *Plan Nederland* in 1999.

The main objective of the system in the early years was 'social justice and self reliance' (Netherlands Ministry of Foreign Affairs 1976). Since 1992, the main objective of the system and the co-financing agencies was changed to the structural alleviation of poverty.

The size of the co-financing system has increased continuously during its 40-year existence. For the entire period covered by this research (1989–2005) a legally fixed percentage of Dutch aid has been allocated to the co-financing organizations. This rose steadily from 4 per cent in the 1970s to 11 per cent at the beginning of the twenty-first century. Since 1995 the level of Dutch aid was pegged to the Dutch GDP, which also grew continuously during this period. Therefore, the total growth in the Dutch co-financing programme was phenomenal. It increased from 2.4 million Euros (nominal prices) in 1965 (Schulpen 1997) to 418 million Euros in 2005. Government funding accounted for around 85 per cent of the total income of the organizations. Interestingly, the government did not decide on the division of the funding between the organizations. Instead, until 2002 the organizations themselves could decide on the distribution key. From 2002 onwards, an external advisory committee judges the quality of the proposals and the amounts of funding organizations receive. Besides the formal co-financing system, the Ministry of Foreign Affairs formalized many other relationships with smaller thematic Dutch NGOs in 2003. Allocations to these NGOs had been low, but have risen steadily in recent years in this sample to about 80 million Euros annually.

In the 1980s and 1990s, the Dutch government moved gradually from project to programme funding, and from programme funding to institutional funding. This heralded the emergence of the 'Dutch model of co-financing'. This model was considered internationally unique because of long-term financing based on a general agreement, ex-post accountability, supervision from a distance and autonomous decision-making (Boesen, in Steering Group 2002). Dutch organizations thus have a long history of full legal autonomy in their country aid allocation decisions and have, in their own opinion, maintained a high degree of autonomy in their activities (German and Randel 1999, p. 169).

The allocation of Dutch NGO aid in the dataset

The quantitative research on Dutch NGOs covers the period from 1989 to 2005. In this period, these NGOs spent US$3,838 million (real prices – 2000 levels) received from the Dutch government on development assistance in developing countries. On top of that, the Dutch government spent US$20.69 billion (real prices – 2000) in developing countries during the same period. For both of these aid distribution channels, the budgets rose during these years.

Figure 3.1 indicates the distribution of NGO aid across five regions over three periods (early 1990s, late 1990s, early 2000s). This regional partitioning of aid shows some changes over the period. The NGOs in the dataset decreased their spending in Latin America. This relates to the high share that Dutch NGOs spent in Latin America in the late 1980s and the criticism that was voiced against this (Steering Committee for the Impact Study on the Co-financing Programme 1991). Shares to other regions, notably Africa, increased. Whereas most aid in the beginning of the 1990s went to Latin America, this shifted to Africa and Asia in the beginning of the third millennium. However, the most aid per country over the entire period went to Latin America (on average more than US$50 million per country).

Table 3.1 provides an overview of the top recipients of Dutch NGO aid from 1989 to 2005. The NGO aid per capita list contains a high number of small Latin American countries, such as Belize, Nicaragua, Bolivia and El

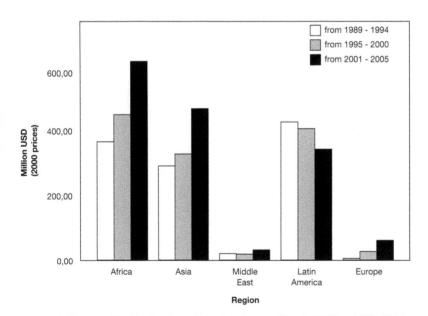

Figure 3.1 Geographic distribution of the four largest Dutch NGOs, 1989–2005
Source: Koch, own data.

Table 3.1 Overview of top recipients of total Dutch NGO aid (constant US dollars), 1989–2005

NGO aid per capita		Total NGO aid (million)	
Country	Dollars	Country	Dollars
Suriname	23.9	India	372.7
Belize	22.5	Brazil	235.5
Nicaragua	16.7	Peru	199.1
Bolivia	15.7	South Africa	166.2
West Bank and Gaza	12.6	Philippines	152.3
Botswana	11.3	Bolivia	131.7
Guinea-Bissau	10.2	Bangladesh	125.9
Albania	9.6	Tanzania	101.3
El Salvador	8.9	Indonesia	95.6
Peru	7.8	Uganda	94.5

Source: Koch, own data.

Salvador. Former Dutch colony Suriname tops the list with the average person 'receiving' on average US$23.90 from Dutch NGOs during the period of research. There is one country from the Middle East (West Bank and Gaza), one from Europe (Albania) and two from Africa (Guinea-Bissau and Botswana). Only one country, Guinea-Bissau, is qualified by the Development Assistance Committee as a Least Developed Country (in the first published DAC list in 1996 as well as in 2005). The list of countries that receive most in absolute terms looks different. Populous countries, such as India and Brazil, top the list. This list also shows a more equitable spread of countries across regions; four Asian countries (India, the Philippines, Bangladesh and Bolivia), three Latin American countries (Brazil, Peru and Bolivia) and three African countries (South Africa, Tanzania and Uganda). No more than three of these recipients are a Least Developed Country (Bangladesh, Tanzania and Uganda). Annex 8 shows a breakdown of the top recipients for three different periods (including Least Developed Country status).

A qualitative scan of determinants

The literature on NGOs provides a plethora of factors, which could or should influence NGOs' decisions on which countries to provide aid to. Chapter 2 provided an overview of the literature, thus this section restricts itself to the results of the interviews on the five potential determinants: (1) poverty levels in recipient countries; (2) governance levels in recipient countries; (3) the preferences of the back donors; (4) concentration; and (5) NGO-specific mission.

These factors were consistently brought up during the interviews, despite the use of open-ended questions to allow other factors to surface. Even though interviewees from time to time used different wordings to describe these factors, they often referred to one of the five factors outline above. While these five factors appear to represent a large number of the considerations of NGOs, they do not cover all of them. For instance, some NGOs referred to the 'quality of the local partner portfolio'. The previous chapter has already explained that the data situation regarding this element is insufficient to permit a thorough analysis of it.

Poverty levels

As shown in Chapter 2, it is widely assumed that NGOs gear their efforts towards the poor (Tendler 1982). While many bilateral donors are inclined to allocate their resources according to strategic preferences (Alesina and Dollar 2000), NGOs are assumed to target poor and vulnerable countries.

During the interviews, Dutch NGOs indicated that 'needs' have always been one of the primary criteria in country-selection processes. NGOs had various ways of putting this into practice. One organization mentioned to focus on poor target groups in countries regardless of the countries' income level in the 1970s and 1980s, and started to work with income indicators only later, beginning with Gross Domestic Product per Capita and later shifting to Social Watch's Capabilities Index. Others claim to use the Human Development Index or the percentage of people living below the poverty line. Another organization claimed to use relative, instead of absolute, measures of poverty. Substantial differences came to light in the way organizations applied these indicators. One NGO periodically organized formal screenings of its country portfolio, systematically using these indicators. Other organizations had informal bargaining systems for country allocations in which those indicators only played a minor role, for instance when desk officers decided to make use of them to substantiate their budget claims. However, one organization categorically refused to use national-level poverty statistics as a selection criterion for a country, as 'our background and expertise are neither to work directly with the poorest segments in a society, nor with the poorest societies'.

Governance in recipient countries

Chapter 2 has illustrated that both academics and funding agencies are of the opinion that NGOs ought to engage relatively more in countries with a poor governance situation. Dutch policy documents argue along similar lines: '[i]n cases of bad governance bilateral aid relationships are often underdeveloped; co-operation from civil society to civil society is the only way' (Netherlands Ministry of Foreign Affairs 2001, p. 5).

The interviews produced a mixed message on the involvement of NGOs in countries with bad governance and it appears that NGOs themselves, especially these days, are less inclined to stress their unique capabilities in countries with poor governance. In the early years of the co-financing programme, organizations needed to have a 'letter of consent' from the governments of countries where projects were to take place (Netherlands Ministry of Foreign Affairs 1966). This restricted the possibility to disburse aid in authoritarian, notably socialist, countries. This requirement was eased in 1976 (Netherlands Ministry of Foreign Affairs 1976). NGOs claimed unequivocally that they started working in certain countries in Latin America, South Africa and the Philippines because of the exploitative governance situation. They worked with small grass roots, sometimes underground, organizations to stimulate democratic change (cf. Biekart 1999). They also acknowledged that certain Ministers of Development Cooperation encouraged them to do this because 'we could work in those countries where the Netherlands government could not'. They also added that they considered these kinds of requests simply as logical or even as part of a natural division of labour. Since some Ministers also provided extra funds for projects in those countries, NGOs were willing to increase their involvement.[2] Some NGOs claimed that they reduced their involvement in those countries when the situation had become more democratic.

At the same time, NGOs also argued against the basic assumption that they were the best-placed to focus on 'the "left-over" countries of bilateral aid'. One former director general of the Ministry of Foreign Affairs concurred: 'Some of the social-democrat ministers might have wanted the NGOs to be more active in those countries with bad governance, but Christian democratic thinking stipulates that civil societies in all types of countries merit support'. In addition, in some of the badly governed countries the NGO legislation is so strict that organizations cannot become active there.

The preferences of back donors

An evaluation of Dutch development aid in 1969 noted that 'It is striking that 140 of the 190 co-financing projects of NGOs are in priority countries of the Dutch government' (Werkgroep Evaluatie Nederlandse Ontwikkelingshulp 1969). The interviewees stated however that the bilateral donor never had any formal say over the location and allocation of their co-financing aid through NGOs.[3] They mentioned that managers of the civil society unit of the Ministry of Foreign Affairs had on occasion suggested that activities in certain politically sensitive countries (e.g. Cuba or Fiji) needed to be reduced. However, in practice this reduction never occurred.

There were actually two mechanisms by which the Ministry could still influence the aid allocation of the NGOs: financial incentives and general policy messages. There was a wide array of financial incentives that could be used to tempt organizations into certain countries. One method was conditioning future allocations through the co-financing programme to specific countries. This happened in the case of the former Yugoslavia in the mid–1990's. It was made clear to the organizations that their budget would be increased if they were to invest more in the former Yugoslavia, which they agreed to. Furthermore, the NGOs were also provided with extra finances when bilateral aid could no longer be channelled through regular channels, as was the case in Central America in the late 1980s. In addition, various thematic and regional departments of the Ministry financed NGOs separately, and they restricted this supplementary co-financing to particular countries. One former director pointed out that some of the Ministry's country units would turn to his organization, especially towards the end of the year, to find out whether his organization could help them to exhaust their budget.

Besides financial stimuli, general policy statements also appear to have had an impact. During the 1990s, one of the implicit messages emanating from the Ministry, based on the impact evaluation of 1991, was that NGOs should increase their focus on Africa at the expense of Latin America, and organizations appear to have internalized that message (e.g. Netherlands Ministry of Foreign Affairs 1995). The financial dependence of organizations on the Ministry furthered the acceptation and adoption of these general policy messages. Thus, although NGOs claim that the government has no direct impact on their country allocations, financial and informal stimuli may infringe this autonomy.[4]

In general, the Netherlands Ministry of Foreign Affairs stimulated NGOs to become active in the same countries as where they were active. This was assumed to strengthen possibilities to work in 'complementarity' (e.g. Ardenne 2004). There was one exception to this rule, who was Eveline Herfkens. During speeches in the beginning of her mandate as Minister she suggested that NGOs should become only active in those countries that were not selected for bilateral aid (Netherlands Ministry of Foreign Affairs 2000). However, this call never materialized in the following official policy documents.

Concentration

Chapter 2 has shown that international NGOs are concentrating in the same countries. This was theoretically explained by the fact that NGOs tend to remain in those countries where they are already active (path dependence), and that new NGOs tend to become active in those countries in which other NGOs are already operational (and prepared the ground).

Bebbington researched the geographic choices of Dutch NGOs and concluded that they were highly path-dependent (a more in depth explication on path dependence is given in Chapter 4). He suggested that path dependence is due to networks and institutions that both underlie and precede the existence of the agencies. He claims that the personal contacts of officers are important and notes that these 'are not accidental, and have a great deal to do with institutions, social networks, histories and political economic contexts within which they are embedded' (Bebbington 2004, p. 736). In short, informal and social networks are believed to shape the decisions of NGOs, and those networks tend to reinforce themselves.

Interviews confirmed this path-dependent process. One former director did even not agree with the term 'geographic choice', 'as it implies some kind of reasoning from macro to micro with clear indicators. We prefer to let our practice grow organically, based on our personal networks, and this is how it should be'. Furthermore, a number of interviewees questioned their own organization's flexibility. They compared their organizations to an 'oil tanker', as it worked with multi-annual plans and multi-year commitments. In addition, they argued that 'employees really disliked to see the budget for *their* country and *their* partner organizations diminished, which resulted in internal lobby campaigns for their country'. This was not necessarily through fear of losing their job, but through a very strong sense of loyalty, sometimes dubbed 'exaggerated commitment' to partner organizations. Having to cease a partner relationship was by many seen as an 'abortion'. This contributed to a certain form of organizational inertia. Changes in geographic choices were made possible by increases in funding; old networks were maintained, and additional finance was used to venture into new countries.

The role that solidarity movements played in the geographic choices of NGOs highlights the importance of the personnel of NGOs in these choices and the networks in which they operate. The solidarity movements, related to for instance Chile and Nicaragua, lobbied the personnel of the NGOs successfully to become active in those countries. Furthermore, the NGOs ended up hiring people who were active in the social movements as they had experience working in those countries. Those newly hired staff had close ties with those countries and ensured that the NGOs remained active there.

Yet path-dependent processes do not lead automatically to concentration. If all NGOs remain where they are and they are not active in the same countries no concentration is occurring. Two NGOs even claimed in the interviews that when they had to make geographic choices, their organization preferred to become active in those countries where the other Dutch organization were not yet present. The quantitative analysis try to find whether there is empirical evidence that supports this claim.

NGO-specific missions

The largest Dutch NGOs were founded based on four main 'pillars' of Dutch society, which reflected the segregation in religion and ideologies. There was one Catholic organization, one Protestant organization, one secular organization, and later also a humanistic organization. Their background provided a stable network for the NGOs in developing countries; they could allocate their funds to like-minded local counterparts. For instance, the Catholic organization funded projects in countries where Dutch missionaries lived.

The interviews confirmed the importance of the NGO-specific mission, and how it influences geographic choices. One of the founding directors of one of the agencies almost declined to accept an interview on the geographic policy of his organization between the 1960s and 1980s as 'there was no such policy'. During the interview, he pointed out that 'it is out of the question that there would have been any kind of conscious country selection policy during the 17 years that I was director.' They were intermediary financing agencies, whose main task was to channel subsidy requests from their missionaries in the South to the Dutch Netherlands Ministry of Foreign Affairs. Still, even though there was not a geographic policy, the choice to work with missionaries did have geographic implications.

In sum, the interviews showed a clear-cut picture of the factor of poverty. All organizations, except for one, claimed that high levels of poverty encouraged them to become more active in those countries. With respect to the governance situation, the relationship appears more ambiguous. Whereas there are clear examples of Dutch NGOs venturing into countries that were suffering from autocratic regimes, some of the representatives of Dutch NGOs claimed that this had never been a selection criterion. However, it is assumed that Dutch NGOs could consider poor governance as a potential factor for aid allocation. Regarding autonomy, the Dutch government did not directly influence Dutch NGOs. However, the Dutch government did influence Dutch NGOs by means of financial incentives and general policy messages. Furthermore, the interviews showed that Dutch NGOs often decided to fund projects based on previous relationships and therefore tended to be rather path-dependent. Yet, this was claimed to not lead to clustering as NGOs would chose to become active in countries where other Dutch NGOs were not active. Lastly, the interviews showed that the NGO-specific mission influenced the geographic choices of NGOs. In sum, not all potential determinants turn out to influence geographic choices. The case study on Oxfam Novib (see 'A case-study approach' section below) aims to explain why certain potential determinants rise to predominance and others do not. In the next section, the five abovementioned potential drivers are analysed more thoroughly using a quantitative analysis.

A quantitative analysis

Statistical method: General Methods of Moment

The research now turns to testing the factors presented in Chapter 2, which were discussed in relation to the Dutch case in the previous section. To test the potential determinants, this research uses the methodology developed by Nancy and Yontcheva (2006). In their efforts to discover the determinants of the country choices made by NGOs that received aid from the European Commission, they employed a General Methods of Moment (GMM) estimation, which is a dynamic panel estimation. This research makes use of a GMM system estimator, that not only use the equation in first differences, but also instruments the equation in levels. The most important reason for selecting this method is that it can effectively solve unacceptable levels of serial correlation in ordinary least squares panel estimations (Arellano and Bover 1995). This section presents the result of the two-step GMM as it is considered the most efficient estimator (Roodman 2006).

In this research, the dependent variable in the regressions is the amount of NGO aid that countries received per year from one of the four NGOs in our sample. This variable is measured in real terms in Euros (2005). The source of the data is the Netherlands Ministry of Foreign Affairs, to whom organization had to report their country wise expenditures annually. In all regression, the dependent variable is thus NGO aid per country per Dutch NGO (four Dutch NGOs in sample). The amounts of aid were selected as an indicator for geographic choice as they provide a more precise indication of how committed organizations are to various countries than for instance the number of projects in a country or whether or not an organization is active in a country. The dependent variable is thus similar for the dependent variable in Chapter 2, with the main difference that currently only Dutch NGOs are in the sample and the sample covers 17 years.

The independent variables represent the five potential determinants. There is one base regression, regression 1, in which all potential determinants are tested simultaneously. The remaining regressions, numbers 2 to 5, are robustness checks in which the independent variables are swapped. To test the first potential determinant, poverty, the 'GDP per capita' is included in the base regression. This indicator is selected since it was present for nearly all developing countries and years in the sample. In the robustness checks for this determinant, regression 2 and 3, respectively the life expectancy at birth and the Gini coefficient from the World Development Indicators are included.

To gauge the relationship between NGO aid and the level of governance, the Freedom House data on Civil Liberties and Political Rights is included. While acknowledging the limitations, these indicators are selected, since they are the only ones that were available for the entire research period for nearly all countries. To test the robustness of the finding with respect to governance as a potential determinant, the Bureaucratic Quality indicator from International Country Risk Guide is included in regression 4.

To approximate the influence of back-donor preferences, the research uses bilateral allocations (net of NGO allocations) to developing countries, just as in the previous chapter. These data were lagged by two years as it is assumed that NGOs need some time to adjust to changes in bilateral preferences.

To test for the concentration effect two indicators are included. First, the number of other NGOs Dutch NGOs (ranging from 0 to 3) in the year prior was included in the regression to discover whether NGOs responded to the geographic choices of their Dutch peers. Second, to assess the path dependence of Dutch NGOs, the allocation of the NGO five years prior are included in the regressions simultaneously. The decision to include a five-year lag was made since most development programmes by NGOs are longer than one year. As a robustness check on the path dependence of NGO, the NGO data with a lag of ten years in regression is included.[5]

Please note that in this model the geographic impact of the NGO-specific mission, determinant 5, is not included. This was a deliberate choice, since the static dummies that capture these effects, a dummy for religion and former colony (see Chapter 2), are of no use in a dynamic panel analysis.

Endogeneity and serial correlation

The number of other NGOs active in a country is expected to be endogenous to the model, as it could be affected by the dependent variable (the expenditures of an NGO in a country), even though it is lagged. The standard method to deal with endogeneity is to work with instrumental variables. This presents us with difficulties, since it is hard to discover variables that relate to the number of other NGOs present in a country, but not to the NGO that is the unit of analysis. One of the merits of GMM model estimation is that it allows instrumentation by means of including lagged variables of the endogenous variables. This is considered as an appropriate method, as it is assumed that past levels of numbers of other NGOs only affect NGO allocations through numbers of other NGOs in t-1 (and not directly) (Gujarati 2002).[6] The Hansen test of over-identifying restrictions shows whether the instruments were indeed appropriate for dealing with the endogeneity problem (the Hansen test should preferably produce a test score close to 100). All other independent variables were considered exogenous, since e.g. no evidence has been found that aid from Dutch NGOs had influenced the economic growth and life expectancy at national levels.[7]

An advantage of the GMM model is that it differences the data, which normally reduces serial correlation. The results of the Arellano Bond first differences tests verify that serial correlation has indeed effectively been dealt with (AR(1) should be significant, AR(2) not). The results are presented in such a way that it can be ascertained that all regular problems associated with panel regressions have been addressed, such as serial correlation and invalid instruments.

Scatter-plots

Four scatter-plots provide a first, tentative, visual insight in the relationship between the levels of Dutch NGO aid and indicators reflecting the potential determinants described above.

The two-dimensional scatter-plot in Figure 3.2(a), suggests that there is no clear relationship between for instance life expectancy and NGO per capita aid. If there is a relationship, it is a negative one, as countries with lower levels of poverty receive more aid. This could be explained by the high average life expectancy in Latin America (69.9 years during the period) and high allocations per capita. Actually, a breaking point appears in countries where life expectancy is between 65 and 75 years.

Looking at the governance situation in a country, Figure 3.2(b), there appears to be no clear relationship between the level of governance as assessed by the Freedom House indicators and the level of NGO involvement. The

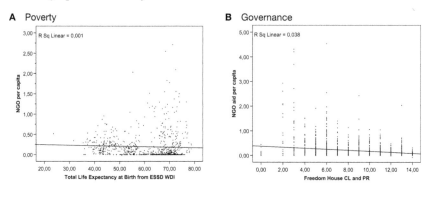

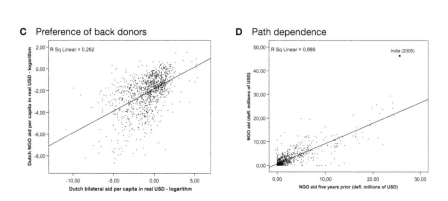

Figure 3.2 Scatter-plots of potential drivers of allocation

graph shows less involvement in countries with low or high levels of governance, and more in countries with medium levels of governance.

One of the potential indicators that could reflect whether the NGOs are influenced by the preferences of their back donor is to assess the relationship between expenditures of the Netherlands Ministry of Foreign Affairs and NGOs. The subsequent panel analysis provides insight into a causal relationship between bilateral and non-governmental geographic decisions, Figure 3.2(c), shows that there is a positive relationship between NGO aid allocation and the bilateral aid allocation; countries that receive more from the Netherlands Ministry of Foreign Affairs, also receive more aid from the Dutch NGOs which are funded by them. The correlation is 0.59 (significant at 1 per cent level).

A standard way of measuring path dependence, which could contribute to concentration, is to look at the relationship between previous and current allocations, as was done in Figure 3.2(d). This graph provides a scatter-plot of the NGO aid (x-axis) and NGO aid five years prior to it (y-axis, the L indicates lag). There is a clear relationship between the two indicators (the correlation is 0.86 per cent). External shocks cause the two aberrations from the clear pattern. One outlier represents India in 2005. This sudden rise of NGO flows to India could be explained by aid in the aftermath of the tsunami.

Results

Table 3.2 presents the base specification estimated over the entire sample, which is an unbalanced panel of 118 countries, for four NGOs, from 1990 to 2005, totalling 2,437 observations. For each regression, the research reports the Hansen J test of over-identifying restrictions. It does not reject the joint null hypothesis that the instrument, lags of bilateral aid, is valid (i.e., uncorrelated with the error term). In addition, it shows that the excluded instruments are correctly excluded from the estimated equation. Examining the p-values of the AR(1) and AR(2) tests of autocorrelation, it can be seen that, as expected, the null of no first order serial correlation in residuals is rejected. Hence, no evidence is found for second-order serial correlation at 10 per cent significance. It is therefore concluded that the regression specifications are correct. This table reveals some important and apparently rather robust results. The results for each independent variable will be discussed.

The base regression indicates the following with respect to the potential determinants: neither the poverty determinant, nor the governance determinant, was found to determine the geographic choices of NGOs. The third potential determinant, the preference of back donors, appeared to be a driver of geographical aid allocation. An increase in bilateral allocations led to an increase in NGO allocations two years later. Also, the fourth potential determinant, the concentration of NGOs, appears relevant, as the number of other NGOs active in a country influences the geographic choices of NGOs one year later. Furthermore, path dependence appeared important as expenditures with a lag of five years still impacted positively on current expenditures.

The robustness checks confirm the results of the base regression. Regardless of how poverty is assessed, be it by means of a social indicator (life expectancy, regression 2) or by a relative poverty indicator (Gini, regression 3) there is no causal link with NGO aid allocations. Thus, these results from the panel regressions corroborate the absence of a positive relationship with poverty, which was already suggested by the cross-sectional scatter-plots on poverty. Furthermore, also the governance indicator from the ICRG does not turn out to be influencing the geographic choices of NGOs (regression 4). In addition, in all regressions the geographic choices of the bilateral donor are influencing the choices of NGOs two years down the line.[8] With respect to the concentration, the positive results appear robust as well. The number of other NGOs is influencing the level of expenditures of NGOs in all regressions. The path-dependence effect is significant in all regression, but not when the lag is increased until ten years (regression 5).[9]

Table 3.2 GMM estimation of Dutch NGO allocations, 1989–2005

Dependent variable: NGO aid (log)	1	2	3	4	5
	Base	Robustness checks			
		Poverty		Governance	Concentration
Determinant 1: Poverty *GDP per capita (log & lagged)*	-0.193 [0.6353]			-0.196 [0.7192]	-0.126 [0.8754]
Determinant 1: Poverty *Life Expectancy at Birth (log & lagged)*					0.091 [0.8638]
Determinant 1: Poverty *Gini coefficient (lagged)*			0.036 [0.3867]		
Determinant 2: Governance *Freedom House (lagged)*	-0.257 [0.2279]		-0.186 [0.4931]		0.875 [0.0857]
Determinant 2: Governance *Bureaucratic Quality ICRG (lagged)*				0.387 [0.6868]	0.112 [0.8617]
Determinant 3: Bilateral aid *Bilateral aid (log & double lagged)*	0.786 [0.0179]**	0.784 [0.0189]**	0.927 [0.0073]***	0.243 [0.0570]*	0.875 [0.0857]*
Determinant 4: Concentration *Number of other NGOs (lag)*	0.690 [0.0497]**	0.639 [0.0585]*	0.905 [0.0144]**	1,242 [0.0025]***	0.806 [0.0585]*
Determinant 4: Concentration *NGO aid 5 years ago*	0.290 [0.0106]**	0.286 [0.0086]***	0.249 [0.0697]*	0.511 [0.0878]*	
Determinant 4: Concentration *NGO aid 10 years ago*					0.227 [0.3652]

(continued on next page)

Table 3.2 (continued)

Dependent variable: NGO aid (log)	1	2	3	4	5
	Base	Robustness checks			
		Poverty		Governance	Concentration
Country in Europe	−2,504 [0.0041]***	−2,676 [0.0021]***	−1,645 [0.1027]	−2,311 [0.0107]**	−3,164 [0.0564]*
Constant	7,363 [0.0532]	5,615 [0.5473]	2,264 [0.4221]	2,845 [0.4199]	4,214 [0.6020]
Observations	2358	2434	2129	1950	1735
Number of countries	114	118	102	92	114
AR 1	0.002	0.001	0.003	0.008	0.000
AR 2	0.206	0.191	0.331	0.485	0.265
Hansen test	46.39	50.33	47.8	51.76	36.57

Source: Koch and Loman (2008)
Notes: (1) p values in brackets; (2) * significant at 5% level; ** significant at 1% level; (3) GMM results are reported with robust standard errors (Windmeier adjusted); (4) a full set of year and regional dummies is included in all specifications – only those that are significant are included; (5) the instrument includes lags of the number of other NGOs in a country (t−2 and earlier) as instruments in level and system equations; (6) GDP per capita, population and population squared are considered exogenous

In sum, Dutch NGOs do not appear to focus as much on poor countries as the interviews suggested. As for the governance of countries, the results are in line with those of Chapter one, as they seem to contradict the internationally held assumption that NGOs focus on countries with poor governance. In addition, the scatter-plots showed a strong relationship between Dutch bilateral and NGO aid, which was confirmed by the regression results and strengthens the findings of Chapter 2. The interviews already provided insight into the way in which the Dutch government has influenced the aid allocation of NGOs. Lastly, the regression results show that Dutch NGOs also tend to concentrate as they tend to become more active in countries where other Dutch NGOs are already present, despite the fact that the interviews pointed in a different direction. In general there is thus a large similarity in the statistical findings of Chapter 2 and the present chapter.

A case-study approach

The purpose of this case study is to identify mediating factors that influence the determinants of geographic choices within an NGO. The second section of this chapter has explained why Oxfam Novib was selected as a case study. The set-up of this case study is as follows. After providing a general overview of the geographic decision-making process at Oxfam Novib, this section reviews the five potential determinants of aid allocations. For the set of potential determinants, it is first established whether Oxfam Novib deviates from the general pattern as described in the previous sections of this chapter, and second attempted to explain which mediating factors can contribute to an explanation as to why certain potential factors became to determine geographic choices and others not. The findings of this section are tentative only, as they are based on the case study of Oxfam Novib only.

Historical geographic developments

In 1956, Oxfam Novib started their work in two countries, Greece and Sudan. The number of countries had expanded to 74 by 1996, after which it declined to 63 in 2006. Until 1996, the geographic policy of Oxfam Novib was geared towards selecting new countries for intervention. Personal networks played a dominant role in the early stages of (Oxfam) Novib's development. The most striking reason why Oxfam Novib was active in certain countries, especially until the late 1980s was: 'we were active where we were active, because we had always been active there'. Oxfam Novib's support became more oriented towards political empowerment during the 1970s, and this was also reflected in its geographic choices. It resulted in a focus on democratization projects, for example, especially in dictatorial Latin American regimes. Its focus on Latin American countries was so strong in the early 1980s that the board of Oxfam Novib decided to hire a new programme director without any links with Latin America. The aim of this was to facilitate a gradual shift towards other geographic regions, notably Africa. Many identification missions to African countries followed. However, nearly a decade later Latin America was still receiving most funding, while allocations to Asia had increased more rapidly than those to the African continent. An impact study in 1991 reiterated the importance of shifting geographic priorities towards Africa. As the organization's budget was constantly increasing, it was possible to reduce the percentage of funding that went to Latin America, while still increasing absolute funding considerably there. The same impact study also indicated that the organizations were spreading their resources too thinly and that a concentration of activities was desirable. Oxfam Novib paid no heed to this advice, however, and the number of countries of operation continued to grow. These rather natural geographic 'choices' came to a rather abrupt end in 1998 with the advent of the Guidelines for Resource Allocation Priorities.

The Guidelines for Resource Allocation Priorities (GRAP)

In 1998, the director of Oxfam Novib wrote in a memo to its staff:

Novib's investment practices have known an organic development over the last four decades, through contacts, networks and opportunities as they manifested themselves. Policy developments evolved with our practice, but prior to 1996 there was no attempt to provide a transparent substantiation to answer the question how much money Novib was spending in one continent or in one country in comparison with others and why.

(Novib 1998, p. 1)

A report by the GRAP project group claimed that: 'The lack of a resource allocation policy and criteria can be seen as an amateurish hang-over from a previous era, quite inappropriate for a professional and transparent development cooperation agency in the present context.' (Meeting of Project Group, Tuesday 21 February 1996, in Teune and Dietz 2003, p. 24). The Guidelines for Resource Allocation Priorities (GRAP) established an obligatory rating system that desk officers had to use to assess all developing countries. The GRAP exercise was executed in 1996, 1998 and 2000, and was meant to be executed every two years. In the GRAP, desk officers were asked to rate countries in their region based on 'needs', 'capacities of others' and 'Novib's comparative advantage' which resulted in a priority ranking. Based on these ratings, the project group proposed a list of eligible countries to the management team including whether current efforts required modification. Normally, a two-day workshop for key-staff at Oxfam Novib concluded the GRAP during which the proposals of the project team were discussed and a final decision was proposed. The final proposal contained an optimal continental allocation scenario for four years later. The GRAP was instrumental in making concrete recommendations about the continental and national division of Oxfam Novib's aid disbursement, but it was also useful for regional desks to subdivide their budget.

The GRAP 1996 report stipulated (again) that investment in Africa needed to be increased (to 35 per cent), at the expense of Latin America. The second GRAP report in 1998 showed similarities to the first GRAP. For instance, once again, one of the conclusions was that more resources needed to be allocated to Africa. This was partly a result of insufficient follow-up on the recommendations of GRAP-1 (Teune and Dietz 2003). In 2000, the organization executed a similar exercise including other Oxfam organizations. This joint 'GRAP' exercise was actually considered less successful and was not repeated because the costs (e.g. preparation and negotiation) were deemed to outweigh the benefits. Many other Oxfam organizations could not meet the expectations of more coordination, because of low levels of unrestricted funding. The GRAP exercises led to some changes and contributed, for instance, to the phasing out of aid to certain Latin American countries. However, its effect on country allocations was not as great as the 'focus discussion'.

The focus discussion and beyond

Various external evaluations, notably the Impact Evaluation of 1991 and 2001, and various external actors, such as the Project Pool Commission, strongly advised Oxfam Novib and other organizations to reduce the number of countries in which they were operating. In 2002, the 'Commission Box' decided on the subsidy application of Oxfam Novib. This commission concluded that Oxfam Novib was not focusing sufficiently on specific themes and countries, and therefore cut its funding (Commissie MFP-breed 2002). Consequently, the management team decided to reduce the number of countries in operation to 18, and started another rating exercise to this effect. Novelties this time included that Oxfam Novib consulted external agencies, such as its Southern partners, Dutch NGOs and other Oxfam members. In addition, other departments within Oxfam Novib, such as those dealing with fundraising and campaigning, contributed to the focus discussion process from the outset (this process became known as GRAP-4). Countries were ranked based on needs, the activities of other actors, and the potential added value of Oxfam Novib (this time assessed through a risk and opportunity method). The project team proposed 22 'core' countries. Then followed a decision-making workshop and finally, Oxfam Novib narrowed the list of core countries down to 18. Simultaneously the concept of 'regional and thematic programmes' was conceived. These thematic and regional programmes allowed for spending in non-core countries, and amounted to nearly half of the budget from 2003 onwards.

As a preparation for the new subsidy application in 2006, some minor changes were made to the existing list of countries. In a discussion on this topic, the director of Novib argued that the work of Oxfam Novib is akin to 'acupuncture' in which strategic pressure is exercised to strengthen the power of certain actors in a process of continued social change. She argued that three main questions play in its four-yearly in-depth consideration of its country choices:

How poor is a country? What civil society actors can we find to work with, and can they achieve concrete results for people living in poverty (with our help)? How good are the partners at connecting their local work with national and global social movements and campaigns?

(Borren 2007, p. 2)

She claimed that 'The hard thing is to weigh these different criteria and come up with country and regional choices which achieves as much as possible for men, women and children living in poverty, while also changing the structural causes of poverty'.

The next step in this case study is to assess how the experiences of Oxfam Novib relate to the determinants of particular areas of interest to this research: poverty, levels of governance, preferences of the back donors, concentration and NGO-specific mission, and why certain of those potential determinants have risen to prominence and others have not.

Poverty levels in recipient countries

Even though Oxfam Novib spent only 34 per cent of its budget in the Least Developed Countries in 2000, this was substantially more than other large Dutch organizations. Hivos, for example, spent only 11 per cent of its resources in those countries (Steering Group 2002).[10] Oxfam Novib was not satisfied with the low correlation between its expenditure and the Human Development Index (Novib 2003), and to address this it developed stricter poverty criteria for its core countries. Countries needed to be listed as a 'Least Developed Country' or 'Other Low Income Country' on the 2001 DAC list. Oxfam's strict application of these criteria ensured that the organization further strengthened its position as being the most poor-country oriented of the Dutch NGOs.[11] For instance, six out of the top ten core countries receiving most aid from Oxfam Novib in 2005 were listed as 'Least Developed Countries'.[12] For the other large Dutch organizations, this averages only three out of ten. In the period 2003 to 2005 Novib spent 48 per cent of its resources in the Least Developed Countries, whereas this was only 31 per cent for the other organizations.

Which mechanisms ensured that Oxfam Novib focused more on the poorest countries than the other Dutch organizations? What appears to be an important factor is the commitment of the management of Oxfam Novib to increase the poverty targeting of its operations. Their endorsement of a formalized rationalization process, in which needs indicators played a decisive role and their active follow-up on the results of those exercises, reflect this.

Governance levels in recipient countries

Oxfam Novib had a tradition of engaging in countries in which the democratization process had yet to take place, such as Chile, South Africa and Philippines. The use of needs indicators in GRAP-1 and GRAP-2 reflected this commitment to people in countries that suffered from autocratic regimes, since they included indicators that related to the political situation. Oxfam Novib dropped this governance criterion during the focus discussion, and the DAC poverty status became the sole needs indicator. Nevertheless, Oxfam Novib continued to focus more on countries with severe democratic deficits than its Dutch counterparts did. In 2005, on its list of top ten core countries, five were considered as 'not free' by Freedom House, while for other Dutch organizations this is the case for only one or two countries. Having said this, there is still no significant correlation between governance levels and allocations from Oxfam.

The governance situation was a determinant neither for Oxfam Novib, nor for any other organization. In the transmission mechanism from poverty indicators to increased poverty targeting, the commitment of senior management and a systematic transfer of this into geographic allocation decisions played a substantive role. In the case of governance as a potential determinant, both commitment and follow-up were absent. Senior management did not consider an extra focus on countries with poor governance to be relevant. Consequently, this criterion was removed from the selection criteria during the last, and most important, selection round. Oxfam Novib's strong focus on poorly governed countries appears to be a by-product of its focus on the poorest countries, more than a consequence of deliberate policy.

Preferences of the back donors

Interviews with Oxfam Novib staff indicated that they considered themselves 'totally free' in deciding which countries they were active in, even though they accepted the principle of restricted funding for specific parts of the organization. Despite this perceived autonomy, there was a strong relationship between the distribution of aid through Oxfam Novib and the Ministry of Foreign Affairs. The correlation coefficient hovered at around 0.5, which is roughly comparable to that of the other organizations.

What explains this apparent substantial discrepancy between the perceptions of Oxfam Novib personnel on one hand and the high correlation between Oxfam Novib spending and the Netherlands as a bilateral donor on the other? Part of the explanation is that the high correlation between the expenditure of Dutch organizations and the bilateral expenditure has existed for decades. Furthermore, as discussions on complementarity between Dutch NGOs and the Ministry failed to come to consistent conclusions over recent decades this basic pattern was not altered (Borren 2007).[13] Senior management of Oxfam Novib was also unclear on this issue. It has promoted certain countries, such as Niger and Nigeria, to 'core country' status, although they were not on the Dutch government's list of priority countries; at the same time, they included 'complementarity with Dutch bilateral aid' as one of the additional criteria in the same focus discussion. It appears that the ingredients that fostered change, such as the commitment of senior management and systematic translation into policy, were absent in this case. This, in combination with pockets of restricted funding, for instance, has contributed to the continuation of past policies, and as a result, the strong geographic correlation between Dutch bilateral aid and Oxfam Novib's aid has been maintained.

Concentration

Since 2000, a joint mapping exercise has been put into practice, showing which Oxfam organizations are operating in which countries. These maps show, for instance, that a large majority of Oxfams (nine out of 13) are active in Guatemala and Mozambique, while none at all is present in Guinea or the Central African Republic. However, the joint mapping exercise was not followed by systematic joint planning, even though Oxfam Novib has made efforts to this effect. Thus despite Oxfam's recognition that they are clustering their efforts, they do not appear to succeed in curbing this trend.

Despite the GRAPs and the focus discussion, there was a significant correlation (at the 1 per cent level) of above 0.5 between Novib's national funding allocations in both 1991 and 2004. In fact, this applies to all Dutch agencies, confirming their path dependence. A clear example of this with respect to Novib are the 'regional programmes'. The regional programmes were a new type of programme that emerged from the focus discussion. Regional programmes were neither aimed exclusively at solving regional cross-border problems, nor implied exclusive partnering with regionally active organizations. An analysis of the regional programmes shows that in quite a number of them, the bulk of activities deal with national problems and with national organizations (e.g. Oxfam Novib 2007). In fact, regional programmes were never defined at the beginning. When asked about the role of these regional programmes, the interviewees stated that the definition of a regional programme was rather vague and that in some instances regional departments used their discretion to continue old practices. Also, there was also no ceiling in terms of the funds that could be spent on regional programmes. This led to the surprising situation that some countries, which are not core countries, are still among the top ten recipient countries, such as Peru, Bolivia and Brazil.[14] Interviewees claimed that the regional programmes evolved over time, and they have now become more 'regional' than in the beginning. They also stated that the regional programmes were also, but not exclusively, meant as a buy-in for those parts of the organization that would otherwise be faced with too much radical change.

Which mechanism can explain for Oxfam Novib this mix of continuities, with sudden discontinuities? It appears that the senior management of Oxfam

Novib set most of the nominal changes in motion, such as the GRAP-1 and GRAP-2, and also the focus discussion. Often these adjustments were made in reaction to external inputs, such as evaluations. Nevertheless, senior management only forced the organization to significantly move its course after the negative assessment of their major grant request, which resulted in a 25 per cent reduction in the subsidy requested by Oxfam Novib. All the relevant interviewees argued that this exogenous shock triggered the discussion on geographic concentration. The unexpected decision of the 'commission Box' led to a sense of urgency among personnel, which the management team was able to use to convince them that changes were called for.

NGO-specific mission

Oxfam Novib has an explicit aim in its mission: the creation of a 'just' world. This is more than just a world free of economic poverty. In the vision of Oxfam Novib also the poor have a right to be heard. Consequently, lobby and advocacy by and on behalf of the poorest groups in the world is a key activity. This specific mission of Oxfam Novib influences their geographic choices. The ability of local organizations to contribute to international lobby objectives was one of the criteria on which countries were rated and did influence the choice of countries of being selected as a core country (Borren 2007).

The aim of this case study was to find intra-organizational mediating factors, which contribute to an explanation as to why potential determinants become actually driving forces of country choices. It became clear this occurred when (a) there is an exogenous shock and (b) there is commitment of senior management to stimulate organizational change.

Discussion and conclusion

Generality of findings

The NGOs in the sample received an overwhelming part of the funding that the Netherlands Ministry of Foreign Affairs has directed to NGOs. Nevertheless, the Ministry has also funded many smaller organizations in the Netherlands (Steering Committee for the Evaluation of the TMF-programme 2006). The geographic choices of NGOs financed through 'thematic co-financing', as it is known, are broadly similar to those made by the larger NGOs. For example, back donors have no direct influence on their geographic choices either. The Steering Committee's evaluation of the thematic programme added that there was a considerable overlap between the geographic choices of both types of organizations. They concluded that the thematic organizations were targeting neither the poorest countries, nor the countries with worst governance.[15] For this reason the results appear, at least for the Dutch case, fairly representative.

Conclusion

How have the geographic choices of the Dutch NGOs evolved over the four decades of their existence? In the first decades of the co-financing agencies, geographic choices were not deliberate and the result of pre-existing and self-reinforcing networks, often based on the religious and ideological background of the NGOs. Organizations became more active and stayed in those countries where they knew people and organizations. By the late 1980s, expanding budgets and political preferences had led to a situation where Dutch NGOs had spread their resources over many countries with a strong focus on Latin America. During the 1990s, there was a process of rationalization in which some organizations sought to develop a more systematic geographic decision-making process, of which Oxfam Novib was a clear exponent. During the 1990s, the long-awaited shift towards Africa materialized at the same time as a small reduction in the number of recipient countries.

This chapter has sought to understand the determinants of geographic decisions of Dutch NGOs. The statistical findings demonstrate interesting parallels between the determinants of the geographic choices of Dutch NGOs and their international peers. Just as in Chapter 2, Chapter 3 shows that poverty and governance levels in recipient countries were not main determinants of geographic choices. The preference of back donors, the NGO-specific mission and concentration were better able to explain them. The panel data also made it possible to analyse path dependence of organizations, which was found to be high.

The interviews and the case study of Oxfam Novib provided a more in depth insight into why certain factors became key determinants of country choices. The case study revealed for instance that exogenous shocks, such as significant grant reductions, appeared to be one of the main mediating factors inducing changes in geographic choices. Besides these exogenous shocks, a strong commitment of senior management to geographical change was found essential to overcome organizational inertia.

Now that determinants of geographic decisions of NGOs have been mapped and tested in Part I of this research, the next part of this research (Chapters 4 to 6) will attempt to provide a more profound understanding of one of the identified key-determinants, concentration. Part II is divided into three parts that all seek to explain the underlying reasons of NGO concentration, albeit at different levels. Chapter 4 focuses on factors that induce concentration at the recipient country level, Chapter 5 on factors within international NGOs, and Chapter 6 on factors at the back donor level.

Part II

Explaining the geographic concentration of international NGOs

4 The concentration of NGOs

An evolutionary economic geography approach*

Introduction

The Central African Republic (CAR) is an extremely poor, landlocked country, where 75 per cent of the population of 4 million live below the poverty line. Tanzania, meanwhile, is a coastal country with a population of about 38 million, of whom 11 million live below the poverty line. Accordingly, one would expect Tanzania to receive greater support from international development NGOs – in equivalent terms, about three times as much. The real difference, however, is much greater. 61 Of the world's largest non-governmental development organizations spend only around €1 million a year in the Central African Republic, compared with around €70 million a year in Tanzania. The Central African Republic is an example of a 'donor orphan', and this is all the more striking when one considers that the CAR ranked 172nd out of 177 countries on the Human Development Index (HDI) (UNDP 2006a). More alarming still is the drop in social indicators during the last ten years. Life expectancy has fallen dramatically from 49 years in 1988 to 42.7 in 2003 (UNDP 2006a), and the situation in the education and health-care sector is bleak (World Bank 2007) (UNDP 2006b). For Tanzania, meanwhile, the figures tell a different story: the Human Development Index rose from 0.45 in 1985 to 0.52 in 2005. Tanzania is now 159th on the list.

Current non-profit location theories cannot provide an adequate explanation for this seemingly disproportionate distribution of aid. These theories either consider non-profit organizations as altruistic organizations that address the needs of the population, or as entities that make geographic choices based on budget-maximization, or as a combination of both. These theories virtually all rely on a neo-classical supply (funding) and demand (need) framework (Zeller *et al.* 2001; Smith and Wiest 2005; Fruttero and Gauri 2005; Nancy and Yontcheva 2006), and fail to provide an adequate explanation of the real levels of aid concentration observed. They do not take the insights from evolutionary economic geography into consideration.

This chapter proposes a non-profit agency location theory: an evolutionary economic geography approach to non-profit organizations. The approach is better able to clarify the existing patterns of geographic concentration among non-profit organizations, particularly development NGOs. The research uses core concepts from evolutionary economic geography. It focuses on increasing returns, labour mobility and path dependence, while paying due attention to contextual factors (Boschma and Frenken 2003; Arthur 1994). This chapter suggests that many of these economic geography elements, which are normally used to explain concentration of for-profit companies, can also be set to work to understand concentration among non-profit organizations. Please note that this chapter focuses on the factors at the recipient country level that can contribute to the clustering of NGOs, while the following chapters (5 and 6) focus on factors within international NGOs and at the back-donor level respectively.

The remainder of this chapter is structured as follows. First, the chapter commences by outlining the contours of the proposed evolutionary economic geography approach to non-profit organizations, drawing extensively on the evolutionary economic geography approach. This approach is then applied to two case studies that represent two contrasting outcomes in terms of NGO concentration: Tanzania and the CAR. Tanzania, and in particular the Arusha region – which is the focus of this research – is characterized by a large-scale expansion in the foreign-funded NGO sector. No such expansion has been observed in the CAR. These two contrasting cases will enable the research to analyse the determinants of clustering among NGOs in depth. Finally, the chapter discusses how the approach can be refined in light of the findings of the case studies.

An Evolutionary Economic Geography approach to non-profit organizations

In literature on the geography of voluntary and non-profit organizations, many have noted that one of the salient characteristics is its unequal spatial coverage (e.g. Bryson *et al.* 2002; Fyfe and Milligan 2003; Sakabe and Eloundou-Enyegue 2006; Milligan 2007). When non-profit location theories are applied in an attempt to explain such inequalities in aid distribution among non-profit organizations, a supply and demand analysis is mostly used (Wolch and Geiger 1983; Weisbrod 1988; Wolch 1999; Gronbjerg and Paarlberg 2001; Barr and Fafchamps 2005). Supply factors often include financial and human resources that are available to non-profit organizations in certain locations, while demand is reflected in the level of poverty among the local population (e.g. Bielefeld 2000; Beckfield 2003; Taylor 2004; Dreher *et al.* 2007). With some exceptions (e.g. Bielefeld and Murdoch 2004), these analyses are static and cross-sectional in nature and do not pay attention to dynamic processes at work in non-profit clustering. Most studies, for instance, correlate indicators of needs with indicators of NGO presence and simply conclude that NGOs succeed (or not) in reaching the poorest segments. These studies refrain from explaining current patterns of inequality.

The economic geography discipline basically deals with the distribution of economic activity across space (Clark *et al.* 2000). Since the uneven distribution of one set of economic actors, non-profit agencies, is the phenomenon that this chapter seeks to explain it is a logical step to rely on economic geography literature. However, a severe *methodenstreit* has been raging within economic geography over the last decades (Hudson 2003; Lagendijk 2003; Markusen 2003a; Markusen 2003b; Peck 2003; Martin 1999). Extending insights from 'economic geography' to the non-profit domain involves much more than just 'copy-pasting' an unequivocal and coherent body of economic geography theory. A theoretically well-founded economic geography approach to non-profit actors requires explicit choices with respect to underlying assumptions, the importance of contextual factors and the conceptualization of time (e.g. whether it is mainly a static or dynamic analysis). Moreover, such an approach needs to provide guidance into which methodologies can be used to demonstrate the validity of the theoretical concepts. Boschma and Frenken (2006) identify three approaches to economic geography: a neo-classical; an institutional and an evolutionary approach. This chapter develops an evolutionary economic geography approach, while benefiting in some aspects from the strengths of the institutional approach to compensate for certain relative weaknesses of a strict evolutionary approach.

The evolutionary economic geography approach which has been developed by Boschma and Frenken provides the theoretical tools for a dynamic analysis of concentration. The evolutionary economic geography approach is consistent with evolutionary thinking in other disciplines, as it explains a current state of affairs from its history. The authors state that:

> The current state of affairs cannot be derived from current conditions only, since the current state of affairs has emerged from and has been constrained by previous states of affairs. Evolutionary theory deals with path dependent processes, in which previous events affect the probability of future events to occur. In this view, small events can have large and long-lasting effects due to self-reinforcing processes.
>
> (Boschma and Frenken 2006, p. 280)

There are various reasons why the concentration of NGOs might be a research topic that is amenable to an evolutionary economic geography analysis. Foremost, Chapter 3 has shown that past geographic choices of international NGOs were a clear determinant of current choices of international NGOs. However, how this path dependence exactly works does not become clear from those panel analyses. An evolutionary economic geography might thus provide interesting insights in how historical developments have an impact on current concentration tendencies. Second, an evolutionary approach can also move beyond descriptive case studies as it proposes more formalised ways of theory testing. Since there are already various ethnographic and qualitative case studies available on the geographic choices of NGOs, which provide anecdotic evidence of the importance of path dependence (e.g. Bebbington 2004), the evolutionary approach can stimulate a more systematic way of analysing the assumed self-reinforcing patterns.

Due to the relative novelty of this evolutionary economic geography approach, an articulated critique on it has not yet surfaced (Martin and Sunley 2006). Nevertheless, there are certain still relative underdeveloped aspects of the evolutionary economic geography sub discipline, which can be compensated by integrating some strong elements of an institutional economic geography approach. For instance, one of the preferred method of many evolutionary economic geography studies is formalized modelling. Since the concentration of non-profit actors has hardly been empirically researched at all, it appears more suitable to first gather more insight in potential drivers of this concentration, before turning to abstract models. That being said, also within evolutionary economic geography an increased use of surveys and questionnaires can be noted (e.g. Boschma and Weterings 2005; Wenting *et al.* 2008). Also the focus of the evolutionary approach on how *organizational routines* impact the competitiveness of firms (and how spin-offs copy those routines from mothers firms) does not tally very well with the focus of this research. The competitiveness of individual firms is not the prime focus of this research. Instead it focuses on the mechanisms that enable emergence of non-profit clusters as a whole, and analyses therefore complementarities between organizations within a cluster, support organizations and how contextual factors contribute to the emergence of clusters. Therefore, it appears advisable, especially from a methodological point of view, to also draw on some of the strengths of the institutional economic geography approach, notably the Italian industrial district approach.

The institutional economic geography approach, notably the Italian industrial district approach, can contribute to a profound analysis of the geographic choices of international NGOs. While the industrial district approach hardly produces testable hypothesis, studies in this tradition share some methodological common traits that can enrich the understanding of non-profit clusters.[1]

First, the industrial district approach is rooted in detailed empirical work on specific regions and stresses the social, cultural and political foundations of local sector growth and cluster formation. The approach pays due attention to cluster effects, such as tacit knowledge spill-overs and joint collective efficiencies (e.g. Schmitz 2000; Visser 1999). The industrial district approach is thus particular useful in analysing contextual factors that have assisted or hindered the development of certain regions and sectors. Recent literature on the growth of NGO sectors suggests that contextual factors are indeed of clear importance (Mitlin *et al.* 2007). Large-scale cross-country regression analysis has also been used to analyse geographic choices of international NGOs. This method was helpful in establishing that the international NGO sector can be characterized by strong concentration. It provided, however, less insight into the mechanisms provoking these concentration tendencies. The foci of studies within the industrial district tradition, with its clear contextual analysis, can make these mechanisms more explicit.

Second, the industrial district approach looks beyond firms (or in our case NGOs) when analysing concentration processes. It includes the role of other institutions, such as universities, professional associations, umbrella organizations and relations between them. Such a broad approach appears essential as earlier research on the clustering of NGOs has demonstrated that there are strong complementarities between NGOs and other economic and political actors (e.g. Laan 2007). By broadening the focus beyond the prime actors of interest of the research, it is prevented that all other actors become mere contingencies (cf. Markusen 1996).

There are several weaknesses of the institutional approach (to which the industrial district belongs), which explains why this research takes evolutionary economic geography as the main starting point. These criticisms come, among others, from the proponents of the other traditions, notably the new-geographical economics approach (Krugman 1998) and the evolutionary geography approach (Boschma and Frenken 2006), but also by less outspoken adherents of one particular approach (Markusen 1996; Grabher and Hassink 2003). Three main concerns are voiced against an institutional approach. First, it is argued that numerous case studies of the institutionalists have become so specific that too little attention has been paid to the potential generality of the findings, as well as to factors outside the specific case that may have impact on its results (Markusen 2003a). Second, another weakness that critics point out is that contributions in this realm are often not tested systematically (Krugman 1998). A third criticism relates to its still rather static ways of analysing concentrations. Conversely, in an evolutionary framework, the analysis focuses on the degree to which institutions are flexible and responsive to changes. Institutional differences between regions or nations are then part of that what needs to be explained, as institutions co-develop with processes of industrial dynamics and technological innovation.

There are also various arguments against using the new economic geography approach to explain the concentration of non-profit organizations. While this approach provides interesting insights into the clustering of economic actors, three reasons render it not fully suitable to explain concentration of non-profit actors. First, one of the underlying assumptions of this approach is the profit maximization of economic actors, which appears rather problematic when applying it to non-profit actors. Second, one of the main determinants of concentration in those models is transport costs, while these appear relatively unimportant for NGO location choices. Transports costs do not appear to play a major role in the decisions of international NGOs as they are mainly involved in financial and knowledge transfers. They transfer funds to local organizations, in exchange for which local organizations engage in development activities *sur place*. Lastly, new economic geography applies a classic market-oriented demand and supply framework, albeit with other assumptions regarding competition and returns to investment.

However, various studies regarding international aid point out that it can hardly be considered as a market, since supply considerations dominate and feedback mechanisms are largely absent (Easterly 2002; Rogerson 2004).

Therefore, to explain the drivers of concentration of international NGOs, an approach that draws most on evolutionary economic geography appears best suited. As explained, in this research also some of the strengths of the institutional economic geography approach will be taken into consideration, notably its focus on contextual factors and on other actors (than just the actors that are the prime focus of the research).

In the proposed evolutionary economic geography of non-profit organizations three main theoretical constructs can be identified: increasing returns, labour mobility and path dependence. These three elements surface virtually always as drivers of concentration in the relevant literature (e.g. Boschma and Frenken 2006; Sforzi 2002; Antonelli 1990 and 2000; Keeble *et al.* 1999; Amin and Thrift 1995). Interestingly, different terms are used by authors for virtually similar concepts. For example, whereas some authors use the term increasing returns to scale (Sforzi 2002) and others agglomeration economies (Bielefeld and Murdoch 2004) and pecuniary externalities (Antonelli 2000), they all imply that average production costs go down in case of geographic concentration. The three concepts that are used in this research, can be considered as a common analytical core that permits to understand the main drivers at the recipient country level for spatial concentration of international NGOs. Traditionally, an evolutionary economic geography approach might focus exclusively on increasing returns to scale and path dependence (Boschma and Frenken 2003; Arthur 1994). Yet, for reasons explained in detail below, in the case of NGOs, 'labour mobility' deserves special attention, as especially international staff are highly mobile and contributors to concentration. We will first discuss the relevance of each the concepts and then provide an empirical illustration.

Increasing returns to scale

Increasing returns to scale is one of the key factors which lead to concentration (Bellandi 2003). Increasing returns to scale emerge from two types of economies of scale: internal (within an organization) and external (between organizations). Internal economies of scale arise when an organization can achieve more of its aims when clustering its activities. In this respect, for NGOs that work with field offices, it becomes efficient to reduce the number of countries where they operate. The investment and overhead costs involved in setting up a new base in a new country can be reduced by hiring another program officer in a country where the organization is already present.[2]

External economies of scale arise when a group of organizations can achieve more of their aims when they combine their activities. Economic geographers show that a decrease in average costs, for instance because of cost sharing and cheaper inputs, stimulates organizations to locate close to each other (Bielefeld and Murdoch 2004).

Labour mobility

Labour mobility contributes in two ways to concentration of NGOs; (1) qualified labour tends to move towards incipient concentrations since salaries and living conditions are better and (2) labour tends to be more mobile between organizations within incipient concentrations. Both of these labour mobility effects have a positive impact on concentration tendencies in the long term.

The mobility of international NGO staff contributes to concentration of NGOs, notably of those working with field offices. Labour mobility depends on the flexibility of workers to move from one region to another. The factors driving people to migrate to another region are related to the expectation of receiving a higher real wage or a better living standard (Brakman and Garretsen 2003). If real wages (or quality of life) become higher in a region, some part of the labour force is likely to move. The movement of (inter) national NGO staff from one aid 'hotspot' to another, be it Kosovo, East-Timor or Sri Lanka, illustrates that they are highly mobile.[3] The movement of international labour is not without consequences. International staff can transfer skills that are considered indispensable for the NGO sector, such as writing log frame-proposals or negotiating funds with head offices. These skills increase the chance that local organizations will be able to attract more funding (Townsend *et al.* 2002; Wallace 2000). International NGO staff bring the network to reach the international donors. In summary, the presence of international staff can lead to further concentration of NGO activity. International aid staff prefers to work in more advanced cities where already many other expatriates are present, setting in motion a pattern of cumulative causation (Collier 2007).

A second reason why labour mobility can lead to further NGO concentration is based on the movement of personnel between organizations. Personnel bring the skills they have acquired in one organization to another organization. This movement creates knowledge spill-over, also called learning effects. The labour mobility among local organizations leads to a broadening and deepening of the skill-base of workers and facilitates the exchange of tacit knowledge (Saxenian 1994; Maskell and Malmberg 1995). This may enhance their organizational capacity, thereby triggering the interest of foreign donors and enhancing concentration.[4]

Path dependence

A path-dependent process or system is one whose outcome evolves because of the process' or system's own history (Martin and Sunley 2006). Different forms of path dependence can be distinguished: the dynamic increasing returns effect; the technological lock-in effect; and the institutional hysteresis effect (*ibid.*). Since the increasing returns effect has already been discussed above, and technological lock-in effect is somewhat less applicable for NGO sectors, this discussion focuses on institutional hysteresis.[5] Institutional hysteresis is 'the tendency for formal and informal institutions, social arrangements and cultural forms to be self-reproducing over time, in part through the very systems of socio-economic action they engender and serve to support and stabilize' (Martin and Sunley 2006, p. 400). There are various angles for analysing this institutional hysteresis type of path dependence. This chapter focuses on the effects of self-reinforcing networks of international NGO staff and the importance of professional capacity building organizations, as several other authors have shown the importance of these elements (see below).

Research regarding the location decisions of NGOs at the sub-national level by Bebbington (2004) suggests that networks and institutions both underlie and precede the existence of agency choice. It is claimed that personal contacts of relevant officers are of key importance and these personal contacts are not accidental, but have a great deal to do with the institutions, social networks and histories within which they are embedded. Informal and social networks shape the decisions of NGOs, and they tend to reinforce themselves easily, contributing to exclusion and marginalization.[6] This is in line with Granovetter's (1985) view on the effects of interpersonal networks on economic activity. In addition, an empirical analysis of Fafchamps and Owens (2006) finds that successes of local NGOs in attracting grants from international donors depend mostly on network effects.

It is not only networks, but also the effects of past investments on current levels of professionalism within organizations that enhance path dependence, and thus stimulate the process of concentration. International capacity-building organizations will target regions where a local NGO sector is already emerging and will prefer to set up local offices there. Such capacity-building organizations contribute to the 'institutional thickness' of Amin and Thrift (1995). They argue that supporting institutions, such as training institutes and professional associations, can make a substantial contribution to the economic development of a region. If capacity-building organizations are successful, local civil society can present itself as a stronger entity to international donors. International donors may consequently increase their funding to local organizations in this region, thereby contributing to further concentration.

Methodology

Selection of the case studies

Data on spending by 61 of the world's leading international NGOs has been collected. It appears that 37 of these organizations are present in Tanzania and that they spent €68 million there in 2005. Tanzania is not an extreme case; international NGOs spend in total about €5.05 per poor in this country. Tanzania falls in the middle category in terms of concentration (see Introduction). It is comparable to countries such as Nepal, Senegal and Ecuador. Yet, also within Tanzania there is actually a fairly high degree of concentration. Particular regions are overrepresented and commentators have criticized organizations for their neglect of the poorest and most remote parts of the country (The Express, in Mercer 2003). The Arusha region was selected for this research, since a large concentration of NGO activity has taken place there. Research by Zoete (2006) on the allocation of foreign aid to civil society organizations in Tanzania shows a significant concentration of organizations in the Arusha region. Almost 20 per cent of foreign-funded NGOs are active in this region, although only 4 per cent of the country's population lives there (Mercer 2003; May and Magongo 2005; Devdir 2007). Arusha has historically already played an important role for colonial authorities and missionaries which will be elaborated upon later in this chapter.

The Central African Republic does not attain the same level of popularity. Of the 61 NGOs in the sample, only four are active in the CAR, and they spent about €1.2 million in 2005, which equals €0.40 on a per poor basis. The CAR is not an extreme case in terms of neglect by NGOs either, though it does belong to the countries that receive least on a per capita basis.

Various practical reasons have led to the decision to compare specific elements of a country (Central African Republic) with a region (the Arusha region of Tanzania). The sheer number of NGOs in Tanzania, and the desire to map a region where a real take-off of the local NGO sector has taken place were paramount to this decision.[7]

Table 4.1 demonstrates the remarkably different growth paths over the 1997–2007 period. The information shown in Table 4.1 illustrates the sharp rise of the foreign-funded NGO sector in Arusha region of Tanzania and its virtual standstill in the CAR. Whereas the number of international donors with more than one grantee and the number of international organizations that are physically present in the CAR has remained stable over the last ten years, there has been a steep rise of those in the Arusha region. There is more international NGO activity in this single region of Tanzania than in the entire CAR, although the latter is three times as populous and substantially poorer (UNDP 2006a). For each local organization, the number of foreign donors reached 2.7 in Arusha, while this was only 1.3 in the CAR. Note that this figure already excludes all organizations without international funding. The threefold real-terms increase in the average budget of organizations working in Arusha region, in conjunction with increasing levels of dependence on foreign donors, exemplifies the sharp increase in the interests of international NGOs in the Arusha region. The total foreign budget available to NGOs in Arusha tripled six times over the last ten years. This is in marked contrast to the involvement of international actors in the CAR: though the share of international donors in the budget has fluctuated, NGOs in the CAR receive on average less currently than a decade ago.

Table 4.1 International NGO involvement in Central African Republic and the Arusha Region of Tanzania, 1997-2007

	Central African Republic**			Arusha region, Tanzania**		
	Inhabitants: 3.7 million			Inhabitants: 1.3 million		
	1997	2002	2007	1996	2011	2006
International NGOs with more than one local partner	5	5	7	1	6	9
International NGOs present*	7	7	6	4	10	14
Number of international NGO donors per local organization	0.7	0.8	1.3	1.3	1.7	2.7
Average percentage of budget that is foreign funded	74%	66%	76%	64%	65%	72%
Average budget of foreign funded organization (in 2005 Euros, nominal values)	117,054	86,213	118,921	29,063	75,448	149,416
Total NGO inflows (in millions Euro, real values)	2,412	1,961	3,075	887	2,546	4,935

Source: Koch, own data.
Notes: *The definition of international NGOs applied here is: (1) organization must have an annual budget larger than ten million Euro; (2) organization must spend

Methods

Two research methods were employed in this chapter: (1) a Q-questionnaire of 43 international NGOs at the level of their headquarters; (2) structured interviews with 92 local NGOs with offices in the Arusha region of Tanzania or in the CAR. The Q-questionnaire provided insight into the determinants of the funding decisions of international donors with respect to Tanzania and the CAR, and to what extent they rely on determinants that fall within the purview of the evolutionary economic geography approach. The structured interviews in the Arusha region and the CAR with development NGOs provided insight into the level of concentration among NGOs in each region, as well as the extent to which evolutionary economic geography factors are actually prevalent. This two-track approach was chosen to highlight the interaction between concentration effects in the field and the decisions of donors in the headquarters, which could be mutually reinforcing.

The Q-questionnaire of international development NGOs

The Q-questionnaire is a research method in which respondents are invited to address questions by means of relative visual ranking. In this case, they ranked reasons why they are (not) active in Tanzania and/or the CAR. The Q-methodology is a means of identifying subjective opinions. The aim of the Q-methodology is to collect and explore the variety of reasons that people construct. The instrumental basis of Q-methodology is the Q-sort technique that conventionally involves the rank ordering of a set of statements (from agree to disagree). It requires participants to sort a number of items along a continuum (Cross 2005). In this case, 12 cards displayed arguments that could affect decisions on involvement in Tanzania and the CAR. These arguments were derived from the evolutionary economic geography approach proposed here and from the literature on the geographic choices of NGOs. If participants had the impression that cards did not offer all relevant argumentation, they could fill in additional cards and rank those as well. The Q-methodology is an appropriate means of discovering the various thought processes involved in making geographic choices, as these are often based on complex decision processes without clear formal guidelines. The Q-methodology thus allows the diversity of actors and factors that influence the decision-making process to be taken into account. 45 per cent of the 100 largest international NGOs that were invited to participate did so.

Structured interviews with NGOs based in Tanzania and the Central African Republic

The researchers conducted interviews with managers of local NGOs based in both countries. The criteria for being interviewed were: (1) independence from the government and non-profit base; (2) foreign-funded; (3) executing development projects in the region/country; (4) having an office in the region/country. The organizations could be local, national or international in scope. Offices of international NGOs that were executing projects themselves thus count as local NGOs in this research. This resulted in a list of 72 potential organizations in the Arusha region, of which 47 were interviewed. Composing a list of organizations that matched the criterion 'foreign-funded' proved to be harder in the CAR, since more organizations did not have any foreign funding. Eventually, a list of 45 organizations was composed, which comprised all organizations that had at least a structural relationship with foreign donors.

This research relies on two methods applied in two cases, which does not suffice to confirm the circular causation hypothesis of evolutionary economic geography. To establish whether an increase in interest among foreign donors in one country has changed the local setting to such an extent that consequently more foreign donors are coming to that country, requires at least four measuring points: (a) the opinions of donors prior to increased involvement of donors; (b) the local situation with respect to NGOs prior to increased international involvement; (c) the local situation after this involvement; and (d) the opinions of donors with increased international involvement. This can illustrate whether a mutually reinforcing nexus of expanded interest of foreign donors, an improved aid 'investment' climate, and again increased interest of foreign donors exist. No systematic data on past attitudes of foreign donors exist and a full reconstruction would not be reliable. It was therefore opted to retrieve elements (a) and (b) from one pre-involvement case study and (c) and (d) from a post-involvement case study. This method is thus based on time-for-space substitution, which can be considered a classical research method in geography and appropriate for this kind of research (Paine 1985). Yet, it is important to note that not all differences with respect to NGOs in the Central African Republic and Tanzania can be automatically ascribed to the fact that one is a post-involvement case and the other a pre-involvement one. Other factors, which did not necessarily present themselves at the beginning of the research period (1996), could have contributed to these divergent experiences as well. In the following, we address differences that presented themselves before 1996, and in the discussion it will be indicated whether after 1996 other factors can contribute to the diverging paths.

Setting and recent developments regarding NGOs

The data analysis is based on the evolutionary economic geography of non-profit organizations developed in this research. As explained, this approach takes the social, political and historical factors that contribute to concentration into consideration.

There are important similarities between the two regions, such as the roughly similar level of economic development, their degree of ethnic homogeneity, and simultaneous backgrounds of colonization and decolonization. In the early 1990s, the number of NGOs was higher in the CAR than Tanzania (Fisher 1998), as 20 years ago, virtually no NGO existed in Tanzania at all (Igoe 2003; Shivji 2004). This was mainly related to the Tanzanian single-party political system that attempted to bring all organizations (such as youth and women's organizations) under the party umbrella, and even affiliating rural cooperatives to the party (Klinken 2003). Even though there was thus a substantial flow of aid to Tanzania, relatively little was channelled through NGOs (Hoebink 1988). The aid that international NGOs provided went mostly to local (para)-statal agencies (Black 1992). In the CAR, development NGOs existed earlier, many of them linked to Catholic dioceses (Cordaid 2006). These NGOs filled the vacuum of an almost non-existent state outside the capital city areas (Oosten and Badjeck 2006).

A preliminary analysis of the geographic expenditure of international NGOs suggests that there are two major historical determinants that can contribute to an explosion of foreign-funded NGOs in one country and the stagnation of this sector in another: (a) the colonial heritage; and (b) presidential legacy. These are not the only differences between the two countries, but come to the fore as two of the most relevant ones. The importance of colonial ties was discussed in Chapter 2, and the importance of country images – of which the image of its leaders forms a part – will be discussed in the following chapter.

Tanzania (during the colonial period known as 'Tanganyika') first was a German colony, and after the First World War a British trusteeship, under the League of Nations and later the United Nations, while the Central African Republic was for a long time a French overseas territory. The differences between the French and British methods of colonization were manifold, yet one important difference relates to the role that was assigned to the state during and after colonialism. Whereas France exported a state-led development model that dominated its colonies in the post-war period, the British Empire had long since been applying a more laissez-faire approach. Consequently, the British colonies maintained a far more vibrant (nationalist) civil society as they became independent when compared to their French counterparts (Ferguson 2004; Veen 2004). The aid modalities of the French and the English further reinforced the respective roles of the state. Whereas the United Kingdom has always – and especially during the last 20 years – supported (local) non-governmental organizations, the French government used to deal almost exclusively with the governments of their former colonies. It is clear that the 'associational revolution' (Salomon *et al.* 2003) manifests itself stronger in the Anglo-Saxon world and this clearly had its influence on the geographic location of international NGOs. It is illustrative that the ten largest international development NGOs all have their head offices in the Anglo-Saxon world, and eight of the ten largest recipients of aid from NGOs are former English colonies.[8]

A second historical difference that still influences the current unequal size of the foreign-funded NGO sector relates to the international appeal of the two of the most important presidents in the two countries. Bokassa, the president of the CAR from 1966 until 1979, was widely known for crowning himself Emperor in the exact same way as Napoleon did. Opponents ousted him in a coup in 1977, but for many people Bokassa is still the first thing that comes to their mind when the CAR is mentioned. In the Q-questionnaire, 21 per cent of the respondents still spontaneously associated the CAR with 'Bokassa' before anything else. Whereas Bokassa is seen as personifying all the vices of Africa, such as nepotism and authoritarianism, Nyerere represents all its virtues (Meredith 2005). He was president of Tanzania from 1964 to 1985 and was one of the first African leaders to step down voluntarily. Many international NGOs were attracted by his (party's) 'African socialism', considered a truly African alternative to the communist and capitalist model. For 21 per cent of the respondents, Nyerere was still the first idea that came to mind when thinking about Tanzania. Various NGOs claim that they started their first activities in Tanzania because of Nyerere's personality and development policies.

Results: unravelling non-profit concentration

The results of the Q-methodology represent the first step in applying the evolutionary economic geography to the case studies (see Table 4.2). NGO

Table 4.2 Arguments for (non)-involvement in the CAR and Tanzania

Score −2: major argument against involvement Score −1: minor argument against involvement Score 0 : argument both against and in favour Score +1: minor argument in favour of involvement Score +2: major argument in favour of involvement	*Central African Republic (N=30[1])*		*Tanzania (N=37[1])*		*Asymp. Sig. (2−tailed)*
	N	*Mean*	*N*	*Mean*	
Evolutionary economic geography arguments:					
Local organizational capacity*	**17**	**−0.18**	**30**	**0.9**	**0,008****
(Absence of) Local (in)formal network	**16**	**−1.44**	**9**	**−0.44**	**0,042***
General NGO climate	**15**	**0.07**	**22**	**1.32**	**0,001****
Overhead concerns and spending pressures	15	−1.67	15	−1.53	0.35
Possibility to achieve results	17	0.94	32	1.09	0.663
Other arguments:					
Interest of general public	**15**	**−0.93**	**13**	**0.38**	**0,007****
The interest of donors	**19**	**−0.95**	**26**	**0.15**	**0,009****
Security situation	**15**	**−0.6**	**18**	**0.5**	**0,002****
Image of country	14	0.36	20	1.1	0.053
Local corruption	16	−1	20	−0.9	0.539
Needs in the country	25	1.72	28	1.75	0.868
Possibilities for local fundraising	7	0.14	13	0.62	0.461

Source: Koch, own data.
Notes: [1]45 NGOs responded, but not all of them filled in all elements of the Q-questionnaires, which explains that N is below 45. There is no reason that the non-respondents could lead to a bias. Significant differences in bold. ** is significant at 1% level, * is significant at the 5% level.

managers were invited to select and rank key arguments underlying decisions concerning location. They could select five cards that were related to the evolutionary economic geography approach to non-profit organizations developed for this research: (a) the capacity of local partners; (b) the potential to achieve results; (c) the availability or absence of informal networks; (d) the local climate for NGO operations; and (e) overhead concerns and spending pressure. These arguments form part of the evolutionary economic geography theory as they involve a clear endogenous element: the evolutionary economic geography approach predicts that these become increasingly relevant arguments when more international NGOs are involved in a country. The other arguments are more exogenous and relate to general demand or supply-side issues. Decision makers within NGO headquarters located in OECD countries were invited to rank the motivation cards on a continuum between 'major argument against involvement' to 'major argument in favour of involvement'. If evolutionary economic geography elements are of importance, a significant difference should exist between the ranking regarding the CAR and Tanzania. For instance, arguments such as 'local organizational capacity' are expected to be rated more positively in Tanzania compared to the CAR. In line with research into the differences between clustered and non-clustered regions (Visser 1999), the Mann–Whitney U test was used to assess statistical differences between the two countries.[9]

The N column in this table represents the number of times that respondents selected the card. If organizations did not 'rank' the card, this means that this argument is not considered when deciding on their (non)-involvement in the country. For instance, 17 out of 30 respondents (57 per cent) rate 'local organizational capacity' in the CAR as a relevant argument, and 30 out of 37 rate this for Tanzania (81 per cent). Interestingly, the average score that the respondents gave to this argument was -0.18 for the CAR. Scores close to zero imply that the argument worked 'both against and in favour of involvement'. Thirty of the 37 respondents rated the same element for Tanzania, producing an average score of 0.9, which is closest to '1' and thus classified as 'a minor argument in favour of involvement'. Moreover, these scores proved to be significantly different for the two countries. Another example is the 'absence of a local (in)-formal network'; 16 of the 30 respondents used this reason to explain their (non)-involvement in the CAR. On average, they scored this argument with -1.44, which indicates something between a major or a minor argument against involvement. For respondents in the Tanzanian case, the absence of a local formal or informal network was not an important argument against involvement, as only nine respondents (of 37) ranked it. This table shows that international NGOs consistently ranked the five evolutionary economic geography arguments more positively in Tanzania than in the CAR, indicating that the economic geography approach developed for this research might contribute to a better understanding of the concentration of international NGO aid.

This table also clearly shows that there are also other relevant arguments for international NGOs to opt for Tanzania instead of the CAR. These include the lack of interest of back donors in the CAR and the favourable security situation in Tanzania. The large amounts of Official Development Assistance flows to Tanzania (approximately US$1 billion annually) in comparison to meagre flows towards the Central African Republic (about US$60 million) support this. The differential rating with respect to security appears to be comprehensible. In the Central African Republic an NGO aid worker was shot by rebels in 2007, while such incidents were not reported for Tanzania (Polgreen 2007). These arguments do appear to reflect different enabling environments for NGOs in Tanzania and the Central African Republic. Strikingly, NGOs do not rate the demand side argument, needs in the two countries, differently, but do so for supply-side arguments, such as donor preferences.

The above results provide a first impression that the location choices of international NGOs – just as those made by for-profit firms – could be considered as being partly driven by self-reinforcing endogenous motives such as past involvement that increases the organizational capacity of local organizations, thereby attracting more foreign donors. To enhance the robustness of the findings, the chapter now turns to findings derived from the structured interviews in the Arusha region and the CAR. These will enable us to analyse in more depth the drivers towards concentration elaborated upon earlier, namely (a) increasing returns to scale; (b) labour mobility and (c) path dependence.

Increasing returns to scale

One central factor contributing to concentration is related to the phenomenon known as increasing returns to scale. Due to cost-sharing opportunities and reduced prices of input purchase, economic actors that are operating in a concentration are thought to be more competitive than those that are not. (Porter 2000; Morosino 2004; Eifert *et al.* 2005). To analyse the presence of increasing returns to scale, local organizations were asked whether they shared costs with other organizations with respect to (a) cars and transport equipment, (b) staff hiring and (c) other (variable) inputs (see Table 4.3). These elements were selected because they often comprise a large share of the operational budgets of NGOs. The research analysed their statistical difference with the two-tailed Mann–Whitney U test (i.e. the non-parametric equivalent of the t-test). In all cases, NGOs in Tanzania realize significantly more benefits from cost sharing: Tanzanian NGOs more often share cars, staff and other inputs than their counterparts in the CAR.

In another procedure for testing whether increasing returns to scale are indeed relevant for NGOs, this research explored the differences in prices of inputs. Specialized agencies can provide cheaper and better inputs. The extent to which NGOs use specialized agencies to provide inputs is therefore likely to influence the buying price and delivery quality of inputs. Keeble *et al.* (1999) have shown that this contributes to clustering among for-profit firms in, for instance, the Cambridge region in the United Kingdom. For instance, if local NGOs can make use of research institutions rather than generating

Table 4.3 Differences in increasing returns to scale-cost

Are you engaged in sharing the following elements with other NGOs?' % refers to + answers	Central African Republic (N=45)	Arusha region (N=47)	Significance (a-asymptotic, 2-tail)
Transport equipment	4%	36%	0.000**
Staff	13%	42%	0.002**
Other inputs	2%	45%	0.013*

Source: Koch, own data.
Notes: Significant differences in bold. ** is significant at 1% level, * is significant at the 5% level.

research themselves, they can save money in that category. Table 4.4 provides an overview of the extent to which organizations in Tanzania and the CAR make use of external agencies for input provision.

It can be observed that Tanzanian organizations make statistically significant more use of every sort of external service providers than their Central African counterparts. In four of the eight cases, these differences are significant. Tanzanian NGOs make significantly more use of service providers for fundraising, research, personnel affairs and recruitment, and for advertisements.[10] Probably, such increasing returns to scale do not only exist between NGOs, but can also become an externality for attracting foreign direct investments. Internationally funded tourism companies in the Arusha region often make use of the same internet providers, taxi companies and security firms as NGOs. By sharing providers, NGOs stimulate the market for these services, eventually leading to a general decrease in prices for internet services and auditing costs (cf. Keeble *et al.* 1999). Because international NGOs can consequently mobilize many inputs locally, operating costs are driven down. This is in stark contrast to the situation in the CAR, where the notable absence of such a market for inputs leads to higher prices for inputs to NGOs.[11] The findings of the Q-questionnaire illustrate this: 37 per cent of the respondents saw overhead costs as a major argument against involvement in the CAR, whereas the figure was only 22 per cent for Tanzania.

Labour mobility

In the evolutionary economic geography approach put forward by this research, labour mobility is an important determinant of concentration processes. Labour mobility leads to an influx of qualified (international) labour towards concentrated areas, which bring with them access to more international

Table 4.4 Differences in increasing returns to scale-external inputs

'Do you make use of external suppliers for ...?' % refers to positive answers	Central African Republic (N=45)	Arusha region (N=47)	Significance (a-asymptotic, 2-tail)
Accountancy	44%	51%	0.529
Management consultant	40%	46%	0.588
Personnel and recruitment	**16%**	**36%**	**0.025***
Advertisement	**27%**	**49%**	**0.029***
Research	**32%**	**57%**	**0.012***
Fundraising	**9%**	**33%**	**0.007****
Computer services	60%	72%	0.213
Printing services	51%	64%	0.22

Source: Koch, own data.
Notes: Significant differences in bold. ** is significant at 1% level, * is significant at the 5% level.

funds. Similarly, labour mobility among firms and organizations in a concentrated area can strengthen the skills base of the labour force. The structured interviews addressed the question of whether NGOs benefited from
personnel that previously worked at another non-profit organization. In addition, to analyse the influx of foreign personnel, the chance that an international staff member represented the organization during the reporting events
of this research was used as a proxy (see Table 4.5).

These results show that there is indeed more movement of trained personnel among organizations working in Arusha region compared to those
operating in the CAR. With respect to international staff, this difference is
also significant. The influx of foreign personnel appears to be both a cause
and an effect of concentration. Arusha has always been an attractive place
for foreigners to reside. The already high number of foreigners provided a
network for donors during the early years of development assistance. The
1952 census of Tanzania showed that of the 8,000 inhabitants of Arusha,
fewer than 50 per cent were actually Africans (Finke 2006). This high
number of foreigners was probably due to geographic factors. Tanzania had
traditionally one of the lowest mortality rates of settlers in Africa (Acemoglu
et al. 2001). Arusha, at an altitude of 1,500 metres, has a temperate climate
and no malaria. It is, therefore, perhaps unsurprising that more than 90 per
cent of respondents from international NGOs expressed a desire to visit
Tanzania, whereas this was less than 60 per cent for the CAR. The high
number of expatriates has created a physical and social infrastructure, which
attract further foreigners and NGO activity.

Concentration can also lead to greater learning effects. It is illustrative to
note how geographical proximity is related to the training opportunities for

Table 4.5 Labour mobility between and to NGOs in CAR and Tanzania

	CAR	Tanzania	Significance (a-asymptotic, 2-tail)
Staff previously worked at other NGO	64% (N=45)	79% (N=47)	0.13
International staff	5.6% (N=71)[1]	21.1% (N=38) [1]	0.015*
Question to international NGO personnel			
Would you like to visit?	56% (N=40)	92% (N=39)	0.002**

Source: Koch, own data.
Notess: [1] The N refers here to the number of attendees to the reporting events after
  the two case studies in the two countries. Whereas 71 people visited these events in
  the Central African Republic, this was 38 in Tanzania. ** is significant at 1% level,
  * is significant at the 5% level.

local personnel in Arusha. Almost all interviewees (> 90 per cent) know of workshops in which NGOs exchange 'best practices'. More than 70 per cent of the interviewees in Arusha state that their organization has become 'more innovative' because of the presence of other NGOs. These learning effects can enhance the attractiveness of Tanzania for international NGOs.

Path dependence

Path dependence can contribute to a further explanation of concentration tendencies. The responses to the questionnaire among international NGOs enabled the respondents to fill in blank cards. Five NGOs stated that 'they had historically no relationship' with the CAR and were therefore not interested in it. Furthermore, various NGOs justified their continued presence in Tanzania by 'having a decades-long partnership with Tanzania'. The past choices of NGOs still have repercussions today (i.e. path dependence). For reasons explained in the theoretical section, two elements enhancing path dependence will be further explored: (a) the role of 'networks'; and (b) the importance of capacity building.

Many Northern organizations considered the absence of a formal or informal network as an impediment to becoming active in the CAR. To test whether there was indeed a significant difference between the informal networks that exist between the staff of international NGOs in the two countries, respondents were asked whether they had ever visited (not in their current capacity) the two countries, or whether they knew anybody from there (see Table 4.6).

Actually, only 3 per cent of the professional staff of International NGOs in this sample had ever been to the CAR, compared to two-thirds for Tanzania. The same holds true for personal informal networks. Whereas 88 per cent of the respondents knew a Tanzanian, this was only 16 per cent for the CAR. The difference between the answers on how often they hear something about the two countries is also significant.

Table 4.6 Networks of Northern NGO personnel

	Central African Republic (N=40)	Tanzania (N=39)	Significance (a-asymptotic, 2-tail)
'Have you ever been to... (not in your present capacity)'?	3%	67%	0.000***
'Do you know somebody from ...?'	16%	88%	0.000***
Do you hear at least regularly something about ...?	31%	68%	0.001***

Source: Koch, own data.
Notes: ** is significant at 1% level, * is significant at the 5% level.

International capacity building organizations, financed by international NGOs, might entrench path dependence. In the Central African Republic, no international organizations (for-profit and non-for-profit) that have local capacity building as their prime task are present. In the Arusha region of Tanzania, two international organizations (one of them is for-profit, and one non-for-profit) focus exclusively on the capacity building of local NGOs. Paradoxically, capacity-building organizations are present in those regions in Tanzania where already most local capacity is present. By focusing on the Arusha region, they are actually further strengthening the organizational capacity of organizations in a region that is already fairly well organized. This was strongly related to access to international funding of local NGOs; capacity building is mostly financed by international donors, and as they are more present in Arusha, this attracts capacity builders to the areas (Laan 2007). This contributes to a further professional gap between NGOs in the Arusha region and those in the CAR.

Discussion

This chapter has sought to develop and empirically test an evolutionary economic geography approach to explain the concentration of non-profit agencies. This discussion will highlight the constraints of this approach, by focusing on three aspects that surfaced during the case studies: (1) the importance of other contextual factors; (2) the restraint needed in applying this approach to concentration at different geographic scales; (3) the prudence required if extending this approach automatically to different geographic units of the same scale. It is important to be aware that NGO concentration remains the result of multiple factors. Interferences based on just two case studies, especially case studies that differ with respect to initial situation and contextual trends, can only be modest.

Not all differences for NGO clustering between the two countries ought to be attributed to concentration effects. There are also other contextual factors that might have influenced this process, which either were already present before the time-frame of this research or evolved later on. With respect to historical differences, the 'setting section' showed that both the different colonial heritages and presidential legacies mattered. Also, during the research time-frame changes emerged between the two countries that possibly explicate the divergent paths of the two NGO sectors, namely: (1) increasing Official Development Assistance to Tanzania and its stagnation with respect to the Central African Republic; (2) stronger patterns of urbanization in Tanzania; (3) superior economic growth in Tanzania; and (4) improving governance situation in Tanzania.

First, Chapters 2 and 3 have already demonstrated the importance of the choices of back donors on the NGO location decisions. During the period of research, official aid allocations rose with approximately 80 per cent for Tanzania (from US$600 million to US$1 billion) and remained stable in the Central African Republic (US$60 million) (OECD 2007). Hence, the increased interest of NGOs in Tanzania coincided, probably not incidentally, with increased interest from official donors. Second, urbanization, linked by Glasius *et al.* (2004) to the rise of a civil society, was much more pronounced in Tanzania than in the Central African Republic during the research. This arguably attracted international NGOs looking for strong local partners. Third, economic development, which is associated with a rise in local non-profit activity (Howard 2003), was negative in the Central African Republic during the research period and positive in Tanzania. This probably has had a reinforcing effect on the reliance of external agencies and for the costs of inputs. Fourth, during the research period Tanzania became slightly more democratic and the Central African Republic slightly less (Freedom House 2006). Since international NGOs tend to be more active in more democratic countries this can also have contributed to their increased focus on Tanzania. These four above-mentioned factors provided favourable conditions in Tanzania in which the local NGO sector could further develop. It is thus important to remind that the evolutionary economic geography factors identified in this research contributed to processes of concentration, but are by no means the sole driving forces.

A second limitation of the evolutionary economic geography approach developed in this research is that it cannot automatically be applied to concentration at all geographical scales (Martin 1999). Even though Annex 9 shows that clear patterns of NGO concentration also characterize the geographic choices of NGOs at the sub-national level, this cannot be automatically ascribed to evolutionary economic geography. Three broad categories of concentration-enhancing processes can be derived: (a) processes that contribute to intra- and inter-country inequality, (b) processes that solely explain inter-country inequality and (c) processes that solely clarify intra-country inequality. A key factor that affects both intra and inter-country concentrations is labour mobility. The fact that qualified staff prefer to work in regions with higher real wages or better standards of living holds just as much as at the sub-national as at the international level. An example of an argument that holds at the inter-country level but not the intra-country level is the colonial tradition. Colonial traditions differ between countries and can thus elucidate differences between countries. Lastly, there are also factors that contribute to a specific explanation of differences at the sub-national level (but that do not hold at the cross-country level). For instance, in regions of a country where political opposition is powerful, there is often a vibrant civil society (Clarke 1998), which could clarify why foreign donors flock to that region. Despite these differences, the core elements of the evolutionary economic geography that were elaborated in this chapter (i.e. increasing returns to scale, labour mobility and path dependence), appear relevant concentration-enhancing effects at different geographical levels. Yet, to arrive at a complete picture a multi-level and preferably interactive, approach would be required (e.g. Beugelsdijk 2007).

A third and last reservation relates to the restraint that is needed when extending this approach to different geographic units at the same level (countries), also known as horizontal generalizations. The economic geography approach developed here appears to play a role in illuminating the differences in NGO activity in the CAR as compared to Tanzania, but this does not necessarily mean that it can also be used to explain differences between Nicaragua and Yemen, or Zambia and Guinea. A clear case in point that merits attention is 'the place dependence of path dependence' (Markusen 1996; Martin and Sunley 2006). Different contexts shape the importance and characteristics of path dependence. The effects of religion can be used to illustrate this relationship. Many international NGOs and local NGOs maintain a relationship based on shared religious denominations. There are indications that religious international NGOs have more profound relationships with Southern NGOs with a similar religious denomination than with lay partners (see Chapter 2). This makes path dependence stronger in those places where religiously-inspired organizations with close links to like-minded organizations in the North are at the origin of the concentration. Another example of context-specificity within path-dependence refers to the kind of aid that NGOs provide. NGO aid with a short time horizon and which is distributed by outside actors, such as emergency aid (the so-called 'Come 'N' GO's'), usually has fewer long-term effects than NGO aid with a longer-term horizon and which is distributed by local immobile actors.[12] Therefore, it is important to bear in mind that there are clear limits to the horizontal generalization of the suggested economic geography to non-profit organizations.

Conclusion

This chapter has highlighted the unequal spatial distribution of NGO aid and sought to provide a theoretical approach to explain this. Traditional theories on the location choice of NGOs have nearly exclusively focused on supply and demand and have therefore been unable to explain the current high degree of concentration. This chapter proposes an evolutionary economic geography approach for non-profit organizations. The evolutionary economic geography of non-profit organizations developed in this chapter assigns a prominent role to increasing returns to aid, labour mobility and path dependence, while paying due attention to contextual factors.

The chapter compares two case studies: Tanzania and the Central African Republic. It has attempted to show that the abovementioned evolutionary economic geography factors contributed to the concentration of NGOs in Tanzania. These findings suggest an endogenous growth process among NGOs in Tanzania, in particular the Arusha region, in which self-reinforcing processes lead to the further concentration of NGOs. Factors that can explain the rise of Silicon Valley, could also be used to understand the rise of 'Serengeti Valley'. The case studies also highlighted various contextual factors that played an important role in the concentration and stagnation of the involvement of NGOs, indicating clear boundaries to what the evlutionary economic geography factors developed in this chapter can explain.

There is clearly a flipside to this concentration coin. International NGOs spend 60 times more in Tanzania than in the CAR. This is problematic if one considers that Tanzania is largely on track towards reaching the Millennium Development Goals (MDGs), while a country such as the CAR is still at the bottom of the bottom billion (Collier 2007). The NGO effectiveness in poverty reduction is thus at stake as strong geographical concentrations may be counterproductive for reaching the MDGs.

Next to elements at the level of recipient countries, which have been analysed in this chapter, also factors at other levels in the aid chain can play a role in stimulating concentration. The next chapter will move somewhat up in the aid chain and will focus on a factor at the level of international NGOs that contributes to geographic concentration. That factor is called the 'country image effect' and will shown to be of significant importance in explaining the emergence of NGO donor darlings and donor orphans.

5 Do country images affect the concentration of NGOs?*

Introduction

Chapters 2 to 4 showed that the activities of international NGOs are unequally distributed and there are strong patterns of concentration in the provision of international NGO aid. Chapter 4 focused on the Central African Republic, where four of the 61 international NGOs were active, and on Tanzania, which houses 37 of them. Tanzania received about €70 million in development aid from international NGOs in 2005, while this was approximately €1 million in the same year for the CAR. This chapter elaborates further on their differences in international NGO popularity.

The previous chapter highlighted various evolutionary economic geography arguments and argued that the country choices of international NGOs display self-reinforcing patterns. Chapters 2 and 3 demonstrated that the country choices of international NGOs often resemble the country choices of their back donors. The effects of the preferences of back donors are also felt in Tanzania and the Central African Republic. Bilateral donors, too, have shunned the CAR, while both international NGOs and bilateral donors are heavily engaged in Tanzania. In addition, Chapter 4 indicated that the 'NGO aid climate' is better in Tanzania than in the Central African Republic. The primary focus of this chapter, however, is another potential factor in clustering in and exclusion of certain countries from international NGO aid: country images.

When personnel from international NGOs shared their first associations on the Central African Republic, these included reactions such as 'hell hole', or 'isn't that the country with that cannibal as their emperor?' or simply question marks. It was for this reason that the decision was made to focus on the importance of country images. This chapter asks the question whether international NGOs are susceptible to prevailing, arguably partially incorrect, country images when making geographic choices. These negative country images can contribute to an explanation as to why international NGOs shy away from becoming involved in the CAR.

The structure of this chapter is as follows. First, 'country image' will be defined, drawing on insights from the international business, marketing and consumer behaviour literature, and applying them to the non-profit sector. The methodology section indicates that three steps will be taken to analyse whether country images mattered for geographic decision-making. The subsequent results section shows outcomes of those three steps. First, a comparison is made between the perceptions of cognitive elements of the country images by outsiders and by insiders. Outsiders are for instance personnel of international NGOs that are engaged in making geographic decisions, but whose NGOs are not active in the countries. Personnel from international NGOs that are active in the country are less outsiders. Local NGOs[1] and independent local experts can be considered insiders. Second, an analysis is made of whether these country images feed into the country selection process. In the third step, an analysis is made of how the country image is constructed. These stages will make it possible to answer the question whether it is the CAR's – potentially excessive – negative image which holds international NGOs back from becoming involved in the country, and whether the reverse is happening in Tanzania.

Constructing 'country images' – an overview of the literature

The 'country of origin' effect or the product-country image is a popular research subject in the fields of international business, marketing and consumer behaviour. Armington (1969) was one of the first to recognize that consumers may distinguish between apparently identical products by their country of origin. The country of origin is the country of manufacture or production: where an article or product comes from (Peng and Zou 2007). Two decades ago, Tan and Farley (1987) called the country of origin or the country-image effect the 'most researched' issue in international buyer behaviour analysis (Peterson and Jolibert 1995). A more recently developed database uncovers over 750 major publications written on the subject over approximately the last 40 years (Papadopoulos and Heslop 2002).

Although some aspects of the country of origin effect still need to be researched more thoroughly, such as changes due to recent globalization (Baughn and Yaprak 1993; Zhang 1997), there is a consensus that consumers' product evaluations and purchase intentions are influenced by their country-image stereotypes (Al-Sulaiti and Baker 1998; Papadopoulos and Heslop 2002). This is not restricted to the consumption of goods; services, such as tourism and foreign direct investments have also been shown to be affected. Paswan *et al.* (2002) investigated the exchange of higher education services and indicated that loyalty towards the country of origin is stronger than loyalty towards the service provider. Kotler and Gertner (2002) conclude that countries compete in the market for tourists, factories, businesses and talented people. This chapter aims to show that this could also hold for aid from international NGOs. Papadopoulos and Heslop (2002) argue that the idea that countries act like brands is common among marketers, politicians and economists.

Country images are the sum of beliefs and impressions people hold about those countries. Images represent a simplification of a large number of connotations and data associated with a place. Most country images are, in fact, stereotypes – simplifications of reality that are not necessarily accurate. They may be dated, based on exceptions rather than on patterns, on impressions rather than on facts, but they are nonetheless pervasive (Kotler and Gertner 2002). In this research country images are viewed as a halo-construct (Han and Terpstra 1988). A halo-construct is a mental tool that allows people to make inferences about product quality by means of simplified assumptions, in this case a country image. The effects of this halo are likely to be larger when there is less objective information present (Laroche *et al.* 2005).

Such country images can be persistent and difficult to change (Kotler and Gertner 2002). Country images can on occasion shift quickly because of intervening events, as research on the (positive) effects of the Olympic Games on the image of South Korea (Jaffe and Nebenzahl 1993) and (negative) effects of the Tiananmen Square Protests on China (Brunner *et al.* 1993) has shown. However, without these exceptional events, country images are resistant to change; they may shift over time, but very slowly (Papadopoulos and Heslop 2002). Bhinda *et al.* show how stubborn images on Africa have reduced private capital inflows into the continent, and how these negative images can lead to a vicious circle (Bhinda *et al.* 1999). This is because people are sloppy cognitive processors. They resist changing or adjusting their cognitive structures or prior knowledge. Their perception of what they see is adjusted in a way that it is line with what they already 'know'. They may fill in information that is not presented or distort reality to fit their mental representations. People are also more likely to pay attention to information that confirms their expectations. They disregard information that challenges their knowledge structures in a process known as confirmation bias. They avoid the effort necessary to reconstruct their cognitions, unless misrepresentations have a cost for them or they find utility in the revision of their schemas (Kotler and Gertner 2002). Chisik (2002) writes about country-of-origin reputations as self-fulfilling reputations that influence the pattern of international trade. Bourdieu and Eagleton (1992) would equate certain strongly downbeat country images as *doxas*: fundamental, untaught beliefs accepted as self-evident universal truths which inform an agent's actions and thoughts. *Doxas* tend to favour current social arrangements, thus privileging the dominant and taking their position of dominance as beyond question and universally favourable.

As mentioned above, the country of origin effect is not only applicable to consumer goods, but also to services and attracting foreign direct investments. It is not only consumers that are affected, but also multinational enterprises when they are involved in decision processes about where and how to invest, for example (Chisik 2002). Verlegh and Steenkamp (1999) conclude that, although industrial buyers are generally held to be more 'rational' and better informed than the average consumer, the country of origin effect on purchase decisions for industrial and consumer goods appears comparable in magnitude. This research is interested in the question of whether the same applies to decisions on the part of international NGOs and their personnel.

Laroche *et al.* (2005) suggest a three-dimensional construct for analysing perceptions of countries of origin, comprising: (1) a cognitive component which includes consumers' beliefs about the country's industrial development and technological advancement; (2) an affective component that describes consumers' affective response to the country's people and institutions based on past experiences; and (3) a 'conative' component, consisting of consumers' desired level of future interaction with the sourcing country. This research uses this distinction between cognitive and emotional (affective and conative) components.

If country selection processes of international NGOs were rational, one would expect cognitive elements to predominate. Cognitive elements include issues like local NGO legislation, security situation, levels of corruption, the absence of other NGOs and local absorption capacity. International NGOs are assumed to be professional organizations that work in an efficient and effective way to alleviate poverty. Affective elements (e.g. does the decision-maker happen to know people from the country concerned?) or conative elements (e.g. does the decision-maker enjoy making field visits to the country concerned?) are assumed to take a backseat to cognitive elements when deciding about which countries to intervene in.

The objective of this literature review has been to demonstrate that 'country image' is a highly researched subject, though not within the field of development studies. This research applies conceptualizations of 'country image' and their underlying theories, which were primarily designed for the for-profit sector, to the non-profit sector.

Approach

The main aim is to determine whether country images contribute to the uneven distribution of international NGO aid, and second, if this is the case, how these potentially inaccurate country images emerge. This chapter uses two case studies, one of the Central African Republic and one of Tanzania. The preceding chapter already highlighted similarities and differences between the two countries, and also showed how these evolved over time. Tanzania disposed over more of an enabling environment for international NGOs. There were more international donors present and there were higher levels of urbanization. In addition, there are other factors that make the NGO climate in Tanzania more attractive: there was slightly less corruption (Transparency International 2008) and people were better educated as higher literacy rates indicated. Furthermore, the infrastructure conditions were much better in Tanzania, with three times as many internet and mobile phone connections per capita (United Nations Development Programme 2006a) and the percentage of paved roads was six times as high (World Bank

2006). The aim of this chapter is thus not to determine whether international NGOs have differential cognitive ratings of Tanzania as opposed to the CAR. The main aim of this chapter is to determine whether country images of outsiders, who make decisions regarding involvement in those countries, corresponds to those who have a more insider's perspective.

The main data source is a Q-questionnaire of international NGOs based in OECD countries on their involvement in those two countries. This questionnaire was discussed in detail in Chapter 4. Additional data sources were interviews with local organizations and experts in the Central African Republic.

The sample of international NGOs for the questionnaire was based on extensive web-based research. The same selection criteria were used as in Chapter 2 of this research. In total 100 international NGOs were asked to participate, with an average annual turnover of €93 million. The response rate was 43 per cent. There is no reason to believe that any sample selection bias occurred.

To arrive at the research aim of this chapter, three logical steps are taken. The first step is to measure differences in perception between insiders and outsiders when it comes to the cognitive elements of the 'country images' of the two countries. The second step was to gauge whether the outsiders' views played a role in the international NGOs' geographic decisions. The latter step focused on how the country image is constructed.

Step 1: Differences between insiders and outsiders regarding cognitive aspects of country images

Figure 5.1 shows that in this section two methods are employed to determine whether the cognitive element of the country image as perceived by outsiders corresponds to view of the insiders.

First, the sample of OECD-based respondents within international NGOs is split into those whose organizations were active and those whose were not active in the respective countries. A hundred policy advisors from major international NGOs were invited to asses the cognitive aspects of the two countries

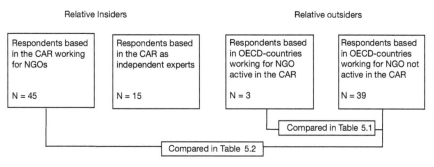

Figure 5.1 Overview of respondents in Chapter 5

images in the so-called Q-questionnaire by scoring various aspects related to the 'investment' climate for international NGOs (response rate 42 per cent). These aspects included issues such as the security situation, the capacity of the local organization, local fundraising possibilities, NGO legislation, corruption situation, stability situation and enabling environment for NGOs.[2] The representatives of these international NGOs responsible for and involved in country allocation decision-making were contacted, such as managers of the Africa unit, heads of strategy units or general managers. Splitting the sample into organizations that were and were not active in Tanzania and the Central African Republic enabled a verification of whether there was a *difference in differences* (cf. Abadie 2005). Table 5.1 presents the results.

Second, the views of the respondents based in the recipient country working for local NGOs are compared to the Q-respondents based in OECD-countries working for international NGOs that are not active there. Various reasons explain why this was only done for the CAR. First of all, there was no difference of opinion between the two categories of international NGOs regarding Tanzania (Table 5.1). In addition, the number of international NGOs active in the CAR was relatively low, making it impossible to draw statistically sound conclusions if drawing exclusively on those international NGOs.[3] An extra field-level check in CAR was therefore deemed necessary to test the robustness of the results.

Forty-five organizations in the CAR were asked to rate the local NGO situation.[4] A marginal sample selection bias was possible since both the number of organizations on the lists from more remote districts as well as their response rate might be lower. However, extensive field research outside the capital took place in the CAR.[5] These scores were validated by checking them with independent experts, who were not dependent on funds from abroad and might therefore provide less socially desirable answers. These experts included representatives from locally represented donor agencies, consultants that had carried out research into the local NGO sector and civil servants at the Ministry of Planning (the ministry responsible for NGOs). These results were further validated by discussing them during focus group discussions with all respondents.[6] In sum, Table 5.2 compares the views of the outsiders (Q-respondents based in OECD countries working for international NGOs not active in the relevant recipient country) with insiders (respondents based in the recipient country working for local NGOs).

Step 2: Do country images affect country choice?

To determine whether country images actually mattered when international NGOs decided on countries of intervention, Step 2 commences with a description of the role of international NGO staff and management in making those decisions and how they went about making those choices. Consequently, to assess whether the cognitive elements of the country image as assessed in Step 1 actually fed into the decision-making process, the Q-methodology is

Table 5.1 Differences in differences for cognitive elements of country images

(1 = very positive, 5 = very negative)	CAR (N=43)					Tanzania (N=43)					
	Outsiders		Insiders		Significance	Outsiders		Insiders		Significance	
	N	Mean	N	Mean		N	Mean	N	Mean		
NGO legislation	9	3.56	3	2.5	0.036	8	2.25	23	2.22	0.908	
Corruption situation	14	4.29	3	3.33	0.052	9	3.33	22	3.18	0.658	
Stability situation	15	4	3	2	0.021	9	2.22	24	1.96	0.362	
Enabling environment for NGOs	13	3.69	3	2.67	0.045	10	2.1	25	1.92	0.357	
Security situation	20	3.85	3	3.67	0.747	10	1.8	25	1.56	0.247	
Local organization capacity	18	4	3	3	0.058	10	2.3	25	2.12	0.548	
Local fundraising possibilities	14	3.79	3	4.67	0.127	8	2.88	22	2.82	0.883	

Source: Koch, own data.

Table 5.2 Contrasting the cognitive element of the CAR country image between outsiders and insiders

	N	Local NGO representatives (CAR-based)	N	International NGO representatives (OECD based)	Significance
Corruption situation	44	2.91	14	4.29	0.000***
NGO legislation	44	2.05	9	3.56	0.000***
Security situation	44	3.39	20	3.86	0.234
Enabling environment for NGOs	44	2.05	13	3.69	0.000***

Source: Koch, own data.
Note: *** means significant at the 1% level.

used. Such a methodology provides insight into the perceptions of respondents through relative visual ranking. As explained in Chapter 4, it is an excellent method of extracting subjective opinions, and therefore well suited for country-image research. Respondents could list various elements that were assumed to be relevant for their involvement or non-involvement in the two countries. The same respondents who participated in Step 1 were invited to rank which arguments played a role in decisions on their (non-)involvement in the two countries. Respondents were given the choice between 12 pre-fabricated arguments,[7] but if they had the feeling that the cards available did not include all the relevant arguments, they could also fill in additional cards themselves and include these in the rankings. In the previous chapter the Q-methodology is explained in greater detail.

Step 3: How are country images constructed?

The third step was to determine which factors contribute to the potential divergence of view between insiders and outsiders. The inclusion of questions in the Q-questionnaire relating to, for instance, the respondents' desire to visit the country and whether the respondent knew people from the country, makes it possible to determine whether emotional components overshadow the cognitive elements of an image. This step also indicates which, if any, pressures exist to ensure that country images remain fixed.

Results

Step 1: A negative image of the CAR

Table 5.1 demonstrates that there was not a significant difference regarding Tanzania between the OECD-based respondent of international NGOs that were and that were not active there. Both types of organizations had a similar perception of Tanzania; the difference did not exceed 0.3 (on a five-point Likert scale) for any of the indicators. With respect to the CAR, on the other hand, there were substantial differences between the ratings of those that were and were not active in the country. Organizations active in the CAR were significantly less pessimistic than those who were not active there on all but two items. Those that were not active in the CAR were more negative with respect to the items of corruption, local organizational capacity, NGO legislation and the enabling environment for NGOs. The only element on which respondents active in the CAR were more negative (not significant), was 'the possibilities for local fundraising'. It seems that this exception confirms the rule that outsiders to the CAR are less enthusiastic about it than the insiders. This is in stark contrast to the findings regarding Tanzania, where the perceptions were comparable among both those who were involved and those who were not.

Table 5.1 needs to be interpreted with caution due to the low number of international NGOs that were able to respond with respect to the CAR. To address this shortcoming, additional data were gathered for the CAR, which are reported below. The most important check involved juxtaposing the perception of the representatives of international NGOs to the experiences of the representatives of local NGOs themselves.

Confirming the findings of Table 5.1, Table 5.2 shows that international NGO representatives that were not based in the CAR were more negative about the situation than local NGOs. The local NGOs were either national or international in scope, but all locally active. The differences were remarkable. Whereas organizations involved in the CAR were actually mildly positive about the corruption situation (< 3), thus indicating that it did not affect the NGO sector in the CAR negatively, this was not the case for the outsiders, who rated the corruption situation very negatively (> 4). With respect to the local NGO situation, the local NGOs were clearly positive, but the international NGO representatives were rather negative. The same was true with respect to the ratings on the general enabling environment for NGOs; whereas the local NGOs were of the opinion there was such an environment, their Northern colleagues took the contrary opinion. Local NGOs were also more positive about the security situation, even though the difference was not statistically significant. Local NGOs claimed that there were indeed two insecure provinces, whereas the rest of the country was relatively safe. Outsiders did not appear to view these regional nuances, and tended to brand the entire country as unsafe.

To ensure the validity of these results, various checks were carried out. A first bias may have occurred due to a different conceptualization of the definitions by the OECD-based and CAR-based respondents. There is a danger that local NGOs have for instance a different definition of what constitutes 'corruption' to that of international NGOs. To verify this, the term 'corruption' was discussed at length during the focus group discussions with local NGOs, and it became clear that participants had used the same concept as their Northern counterparts when considering this item.[8] The focus group discussions revealed that they did not deny the existence of corruption in the CAR, but that there were efficient ways to circumvent it. The same procedure was followed with other key definitions in the research.

A second potential bias among the CAR-based respondents concerned the interest they may have had in promoting a positive image of the CAR, as they were dependent on external funds. Therefore, an extra validity check is made to determine whether local NGOs had a positive bias. Independent CAR-based experts on the situation regarding NGOs in the CAR, such as representatives from international organizations and external consultants, were also asked to shed light on the items rated above.[9] Their responses provided an interesting way to triangulate the results. The independent experts were more positive about the local situation than the OECD-based NGOs, but less positive than CAR-based NGOs (Koolwijk and Koch 2007).[10] In sum, compared to the opinions of both the local NGOs and the CAR-based experts (the insiders), the international NGOs (the outsiders) had a more negative view of the CAR. The international organizations that were not active in the CAR, which are outsiders *optima forma*, had the most negative view.

Step 2: The importance of country images

After establishing that the cognitive aspects of the country image as perceived by outsiders (who make decisions regarding involvement there) was more negative than the views of insiders, and maybe disproportionately so with respect to the CAR, Step 2 of the research considers the question of whether this actually matters.

The country allocation processes of these international NGOs are quite distinct, yet all organizations interviewed for Chapter 6 indicated that managers of the organizations played a role in making the country decisions. However, the relative weight of the managers in influencing geographic choices differed between organizations. For instance, since the American government earmarks their funding for certain countries, managers of Americans organizations have less influence. By contrast, the Dutch and German government give a block grant to the most important organizations, which increases the influence of their managers. The interviews showed that the allocation process of international NGOs can be divided into two stages. First is a selection process of countries, followed by the actual allocation decision.

Forty per cent of those interviewed stated that their organization had a formalized country selection process, meaning that the organization makes an official decision regarding the countries where it is active. It was only considered a formal selection system if the selection process was a regular event, in which objective indicators were employed. The majority of the organizations with a formal selection procedure undergo a country-selection exercise every 3–4 years when the international NGO submits a major grant proposal to the back donor. Typically, the highest administrative level of the international NGO is involved in the decision-making process. Many organizations start the process by selecting some relevant international poverty indicators, such as the human development index for general organizations, or child welfare indicators for agencies focused on children. Often, in addition to poverty indicators, other criteria are consequently included, such as whether the international NGO was already present in a country and how successful its programmes have been. The remaining 60 per cent of the international NGOs does not have such a formalized selection system.

Also, 60 per cent of the interviewees stated that their organizations did not have a formalized country allocation process (the level stage). Asked why these organizations did not have a formal system, they responded that they were not in a position to make these choices, as they depended financially on back donors who made those decisions. In some organizations with a formal allocation system, it was obvious that employees at lower administrative levels were responsible for actual country allocations within a certain bandwidth. If the agency had regional desks, as most do, various regional departments were allotted predetermined shares of the total budget, which they distributed among the countries on that particular organization's 'list'. The specific share of the budget is often based on the region's previous level of funding.

This indicates that 60 per cent of the organizations did not have a formalized country selection system and 60 per cent did not have a formalized country allocation mechanism. This 60 per cent did not make use of objective indicators, which related to for instance governance levels and infrastructure conditions. Consequently, in that 60 per cent, staff had relatively more discretion in making geographic choices and it can be assumed that they relied on subjective information, such as country images, to make them. Hence, the arguments and views of the respondents mattered for the geographic decisions of international NGOs.

Table 5.3 summarizes the findings of the Q-questionnaire of CAR, and shows exactly which arguments the staff of international NGOs used when deciding on interventions in the Central African Republic. Table 5.3 shows that the elements on which the perceptions of the outsiders did not square with the views of the insiders played a prominent role in decisions regarding

Table 5.3 Arguments of International NGOs for (non-)involvement in the CAR

Considerations used by international NGOs when deciding on involvement in the CAR	*N = 30*
Local corruption	53%
Security situation	50%
Local organizational capacity	57%
Enabling environment for NGOs	50%

Source: Koch, own data.

involvement in the CAR. Outsiders rated these elements, such as perceived levels of corruption and the security situation, much more negative than the insiders.

The following section will deal with how negative country images might come about, but before turning to that section an analysis of the qualitative aspects of the questionnaire of international NGOs can provide more insight in how the respondents feel about the two countries of this research. The country images of the CAR were clearly negative, as a qualitative analysis of the open-ended questions shows. When asked what their first impression was when hearing the word 'Tanzania' respondents often noted down positive connotations, such as 'beautiful country, lovely people, and calm without political tensions' (Q-questionnaire 30) and 'beaches and wildlife' (Q-questionnaire 34). When the same question was asked about the Central African Republic, respondents were much more negative and noted down statements such as 'Conflict-torn country, very poor and not very much hope [...]' (Q-questionnaire 1) and 'Dark – the Emperor' (Q-questionnaire 17). These answers to the open-ended questions suggests that the outsiders, the decision-makers with respect to involvement in either of the two countries, had a negative connotation when thinking about the CAR.

Chapter 3 described at length the geographic choice pattern of Oxfam Novib, the largest Dutch NGO. This was an interesting case, since Oxfam Novib succeeded in reducing the importance of subjective and emotional elements in country selection processes. They show how Oxfam Novib introduced a transparent and formalized selection system for its 'core countries'. This means that all desk officers are obliged to rate all developing countries according to various objective indicators that relate to the opportunities for Oxfam Novib to become effectively involved in them and the presence of other actors. This increases the objective information available to decision-makers, thereby reducing the scope for stereotyping. Consequently, Oxfam Novib came to realize that in some countries, too many other international NGOs were already active, and in some countries too few were active. As a consequence, they initiated identification missions to two countries where relatively few organizations were active, Niger and Nigeria, and found that there was ample room for more effective involvement. They subsequently selected these two countries as 'core' countries. The rationalization process, which included a formalized rating and allocation system, thus led to audacious country choices, which would not have been made if Oxfam Novib had continued to rely on their traditional methods of making geographic choices, in which personal and emotional considerations were key determinants.

In sum, taking into consideration the informal nature of the majority of the country selection and allocation processes of international NGOs, as well as the importance of the considerations on which the views of decision-makers did not correspond to those in the field, indicate that the negative image of the CAR appears to act as a brake on the involvement of international NGOs there.

Step 3: The construction and reconstruction of country images

Having asserted the relevance of images in the allocation decisions of international NGOs, Step 3 explores the origins of distorted cognitive aspects of country images. The theoretical framework provides some points of departure, notably that the cognitive part of a country image can be influenced, and even overshadowed, by other parts of the county image, such as the 'conative' and 'affective' components, especially when little objective information is available. The second relevant point highlighted in the theoretical section is that country images are often rigid and only change when there is an obvious need to do so.

To test whether the 'affective' component, sentiments based on personal experiences, and the 'conative' component, elements based on desired future interaction, have influenced the perceptions of international NGOs, this research contrasts the case of the CAR with Tanzania. This chapter has shown that the cognitive elements of Tanzania's country image are similar to both insiders and outsiders, which is not the case for the CAR. The CAR and Tanzania provide therefore interesting comparison material. Consequently, if it is found that the affective and conative elements of the country image of the CAR are rated lower than those elements for Tanzania, this may suggest that those components might also have contributed to the distortion of perceptions of the CAR.

The previous chapter showed that the CAR fell outside of the network of international NGOs. Staff of international NGOs had hardly ever been in the CAR, nor did they know people from there. Furthermore, they heard only occasionally from and about the CAR.

Table 5.4 reiterates the findings of the previous chapter on this low score on the 'affective' component of the country image of the CAR, and adds findings with respect to the 'conative element' of the country image. Table 5.4 shows that there are also marked differences with respect to the conative component of the country image. International NGO staff would rather visit Tanzania than the CAR.[11] Reading these comments, it might not come as a surprise that more of the international NGO staff wants their organizations to start/expand activities in Tanzania as compared to the Central African Republic. Consequently, the disconnect between the insiders' and the outsiders' perspective on the cognitive elements of the country image of the CAR might be related to a lack of emotional attachment towards it. This is in line with the theory on the strength of the 'halo effect', as proposed by Laroche *et al.* (2005). He argues that the less objective information that people possess and the more they identify positively or negatively with a country, the more their cognitive assessment will be blurred. In the case of the CAR this appears to have contributed to a downward bias in the rating of the cognitive aspects of the country image of the CAR. The saying 'unknown makes unloved' appears to be rather adequate to describe the situation in which the CAR finds itself.

Table 5.4 Affective and conative aspect of country image of the CAR

	CAR		Tanzania		
	N	% positive response	N	% positive response	Significance
Affective component					
Have you ever been (not in present capacity)?	40	3%	38	67%	0.000***
Do you know somebody from?	40	16%	39	88%	0.000***
Do you hear at least regularly something about ...?	34	31%	36	68%	0.001***
Conative component					
Would you like to visit?	38	56%	37	92%	0.002***
Would you like your organization to be more active?	39	29%	38	44%	0.196

Source: Koch, own data.
Note: *** means significant at the 1% level.

The theoretical framework suggests that the negative public image of the CAR will persist, since people's 'mental shortcuts' are hard to break. Country images only change when there is an actual need to do so. The respondents' answers demonstrate this: when asked what their first association with the CAR was, 21 per cent spontaneously mentioned Bokassa, the former president of the country who crowned himself emperor. This is remarkable since Bokassa was deposed over three decades ago and suggests that indeed, as there is no need to alter the country image, an image will remain strong and may even reinforce itself. Actually, a negative country image could even be useful as it could serve as a justification for continued non-involvement. International NGO staff could use their negative ratings of the CAR to explain away the cognitive dissonance that emerges when asked to explain why their organization is not active in this poverty-stricken country.[12]

The reverse has happened in countries with a strong country image and concomitantly large aid revenues. There are signs that donors maintain excessively positive country images for their 'donor darlings'. Whether this is just a portrayed image or whether organizations and aid agencies truly believe in it is debateable, but the effects remain the same: certain countries retain the status of donor darling, even though the conditions that lured donors into that county have long since subsided. A poignant example was Uganda, which was at one point engaged in an illegal war outside its own territory and whose president was becoming increasingly autocratic. Still, the country remained one of the largest recipients of foreign aid and was constantly cited as a success story (The Economist 1999).[13] In sum, there are forces which maintain country images, whether these images are positive or negative. This corresponds to what Bourdieu terms a *doxa*. This stipulates that people internalize certain stereotypes which enable them to make sense of the world around them, and that these stereotypes often tend to reinforce the existing status quo.[14]

Discussion

This chapter has shown that without major modifications the country brand literature can be transposed from the for-profit to the non-profit literature. The construction of country images as perceived by consumers and firms, also appear insightful to explain the perception within international NGOs. The remainder of this discussion focuses on the limits of the country image approach.

What is the scope of the findings? Undoubtedly, other factors than a lack of emotional connection could contribute to an inaccurate negative country image of the CAR, such as, for instance, its very low level of economic development. Schooler (1971) shows that consumers in developed countries rate the quality of a product lower when they know that a certain product comes from a developing country. Subsequent research confirms that the poorer a country, the worse its products are rated, even when the products are of similar quality (Han and Terpstra 1988; Barnabas and Elimimian 1999; Peng and Zou 2007). Staff in international NGOs could hypothetically reason along similar lines, namely that since the country is so desperately poor, the opportunities for effective intervention by international NGOs (in terms of local partners for instance) must be low. Yet these other factors complement rather than contradict the evidence presented here on the importance of the lack of emotional affiliation towards the CAR.

What is the relationship between these findings and those of Chapter 4? Chapter 4 focused on evolutionary economic geography elements such as increasing returns to scale, labour mobility and path dependence to explain the concentration of international NGOs in Tanzania, based on the work on geographic choices of international NGOs from Bebbington (2004) and Bielefeld and Murdoch (2004). That research revealed that there were real advantages to operating in Tanzania, as compared to the CAR. This chapter complements that one and argues that in addition to those real and existing differences, there is an additional factor that leads to exclusion, namely the image of a country. Both the country image and the evolutionary economic geography approach highlight the self-reinforcing nature of the processes of concentration and exclusion, and underline the fact that the geographic choices of international NGOs tend to lead to divergence rather than convergence. Therefore, inaccurate country images are only one of the factors that lead to more inequality of international NGO aid. It is complicated, or even impossible, to make any substantiated claims on the relative importance of the various driving forces of concentration; the ultimate consequences are clear, however: a skewed pattern of international NGO aid, resulting in the neglect of certain countries.

How general are the findings of this research? The findings suggest that the CAR may well be a victim of harmful stereotyping. Other countries, such as Guinea, Yemen and Côte d'Ivoire, are largely bypassed by international NGOs as well. It would go beyond the scope of this chapter to provide a thorough analysis on this; yet tentative hypothesizing is always possible. Do these countries suffer from the same problem? Other constraints play a role as well, such as a lack of interest from official aid agencies and the fact that they are non-Anglophone and non-Christian states (see Chapter 2). Nevertheless, there are indications to assume that these countries might have a similar country-image problem. These countries appear also rather isolated, which reduces objective information available to decision-makers in international NGOs. The international media plays little attention to these countries (Observatoires des Médias 2008). This lack of emotional affiliation, coupled with few sources of objective information, could prove to be a fertile ground for differential perceptions between insiders and outsiders.[15]

This chapter has shown that the concept of country image provides an interesting additional angle to explain the unequal choice pattern of international NGOs. The importance of this approach comes to the fore when contemplating potential policy implications. If one were to focus exclusively on the role of geographic economics, for example, policy recommendations would focus on issues such as providing incentives for NGOs to locate in more isolated areas. The concept of country images highlights the role played by subjective and emotional elements in decision-making processes, and consequently policy recommendations based on this approach ought to take this into consideration.

Conclusion

Many agree with the statement that a strong country image can influence how consumers perceive the quality of the products they buy. Fewer would think that commercial entrepreneurs are guided by these simplified constructs in the same way, even though there is now ample evidence that this does occur. Even fewer would think that non-profit professionals would make allocation decisions based on stereotypical images of certain countries. There are indications that this may be happening in the international NGO sector.

This chapter found that relevant decision-makers in international NGOs have a negative country image of the CAR, and maybe disproportionately so: (1) international NGOs that are not active in the CAR rate the enabling environment for NGOs in that country more negative than those that are; (2) local NGOs rate the enabling environment for NGOs more positive than international NGOs that are not based there. Conversely, these differences did not exist for Tanzania. This chapter has attempted to show that the informal and unsystematic way in which most international NGOs make their geographic decisions provide a fertile ground for these stereotypes to surface and have an impact on country choices of international NGOs.

This chapter also sought to show how these negative country image of the CAR were constructed and reconstructed over time. It was found that personnel from international NGOs have less contact with the CAR, know fewer people from there, and are less eager to go there. Negative country images and low levels of involvement mutually reinforce each other, as perceptions prevent organizations from becoming operational in these countries, and this, in turn, hampers an emotional rapprochement between international NGO personnel and the country. This could feed into future allocation decisions, perpetuating the marginalization of these countries. In addition, a negative country image of the CAR could justify continued non-involvement of international NGOs. These findings correspond to those of Chapter 4 that also noted circular causation with respect to the country choices of international NGOs. Taken together, these findings yield a bleak picture for the future distribution of international NGO aid, namely that current unbalanced distribution is likely to persist.

The policy relevance of this chapter is that it shows that simply creating an enabling environment for NGOs, as suggested in Chapter 4, will not be enough to attract more international NGOs. These agencies were shown to mostly make geographic choices on the basis of stereotypes and personal preferences and not on more objective indicators. Therefore it is important for NGO umbrella organizations and governments in recipient countries that would like to entice more involvement of international NGOs, to also market the opportunities for them in their country.

6 Back donors' influence on concentration
Marketization or slipstream?*

Introduction

> The sentiment predominates within the international NGOs that the government is stimulating competition without taking into consideration the consequences of it (...). The increased focus on results has led to a growing bureaucratisation and technocratisation. The tendency to tender everything needs to be examined critically: although it can have beneficial effects, it can lead to – among other things – to risk-averse behaviour.
>
> (ECDPM 2004a, p. 4; author's translation)

This was the conclusion of an intensive policy dialogue between Dutch NGOs and the Netherlands Ministry of Foreign Affairs regarding the future support to international NGOs. Such a critical stance towards tendering is widely shared in academic circles. Many leading authors on the topic criticized what Cooley and Ron call 'the marketization of aid' (Kuhn 2005; Bebbington 2004; Cooley and Ron 2002; Fowler 2000; Wallace 2000; Edwards and Hulme 1997).

This chapter attempts to provide an answer to the question how back donors affect the country allocations of 'their' NGOs, in particular their concentration. While several studies explain that increased governmental funding influences international NGOs operations (Brooks 2000; Frumkin 1998; Sogge *et al.* 1996; Wang 2006), little empirical research addresses the impact of diversity in co-financing systems. Chapters 2 and 3 showed that back donor preferences were an important determinant for the geographic choices of NGOs. This chapter moves beyond that general finding and draws attention to two potential specific mechanisms through which back donors have an effect on the geographic choices of the NGOs in their home country: the marketization hypothesis and the slipstream hypothesis. Particular attention is given to the effects of back donor behaviour on the geographic concentration of NGO efforts.

The marketization hypothesis postulates that back donors affect the choices of NGOs through the level of competition that they impose on them. Marketization, above referred to as the 'tendency to tender everything', is defined as the extent to which back donors attempt to simulate markets in their co-financing systems.[1] The more back donors induce competition between their 'contracting agencies', the higher the level of marketization. When back donors increase the level of marketization this reduces risk-taking behaviour of NGOs, according to the critics of the marketization. This reduced level of risk-taking manifests itself in a focus on 'easy' countries; countries that are not extremely poor and fragile, and where already many other actors are active. This is relevant since an increasing number of donors – such as the European Commission and the Dutch government – started to issue short-term, renewable contracts for discrete aid projects on the basis of competitive tendering (Schulpen and Hoebink 2001, p. 173).

The second hypothesis is that the geographic choices of NGOs are not related to the type of contracts that NGOs have with their back donors, but on the relative size of the contracts. NGOs tend to replicate the geographic choices of their back donor in this view and even more so if they are heavily financially dependent on them. Some initial evidence that supports this hypothesis was already found in Chapter 2 and 3 of this research, but this chapter studies this question in more depth, by making use of, among other things, financial dependence rates of NGOs.

Three donor countries that provide a significant amount of funding to international NGOs, yet are markedly different otherwise – Germany, Norway and the United States – were selected. The three cases vary substantially with respect to the degree of marketization and their back-donor dependence and hence provide excellent material to test the hypotheses. German organizations are generally financially heavily dependent on their back donor, yet operate in an uncompetitive environment (Sadoun 2006). Norwegian organizations are rather financially dependent, and operate in a somewhat more competitive environment (Ebrahim 2003a). American organizations are less financially dependent on their back donor, but do face competitive pressures (McCleary and Barro 2006).

The remainder of this chapter includes the following components. The analytical part of this chapter explains the 'Multiple-Layered Principal Actor' framework, which informs the two hypotheses. The analytical framework continues by expounding the two hypotheses. Hereafter, the research methodology will be outlined. The chapter continues by showing the results with respect to the hypotheses and subsequently discusses them at length.

Analytical framework

Multiple-Layered Principal Actor Framework

First a brief explanation of the Multiple-Layered Principal Actor (MLPA) framework will be given, enabling a better understanding of the theoretical underpinnings of the key hypotheses of this chapter. International NGOs tend to operate as part of the aid chain and they mostly act as an intermediary between official donors and the public on one hand, and local NGOs on the other hand. Therefore, this chapter relies on a Multiple-Layered Principal Actor model to understand some part of international NGO behaviour, as they are acting both as a principal (vis-à-vis their Southern partners) and as an agent (for the Northern donors).

Following Ebrahim (2003b) and relying on the work of Bourdieu (1984), this research takes as starting point that relations within the aid chain might be more equal than predicted.[2] One of the central concepts in Bourdieu's work is symbolic capital. With capital, he means the capacity to exercise control over one's own future and that of others. Symbolic capital stimulates to look beyond organizational interactions based on funding and to include other resources such as information, reputation, status and prestige in the calculus of organizational exchange and interdependence. Consequently, back donors need international NGOs nearly just as much as international NGOs need back donors. Moreover, international NGOs need local NGOs just as much as local NGOs need international NGOs. The examples provided by local NGOs of successful projects are essential for international NGOs to convince donors to fund them. The loss of reputation and consequently of income for international NGOs that occurs when local NGOs defaults on their obligations are momentous, indicating the importance of symbolic capital in this sector.[3]

International NGOs are thus considered as intermediary organizations: they exchange economic capital for symbolic capital, meaning that donors provide an international NGO with resources as they expect to receive success stories, a strong reputation, and or other proofs of developmental returns. International NGOs provide in their turn resources to local NGOs as they expect to receive success stories, a strong reputation, and the like. International NGOs will look for local NGOs that deliver most symbolic capital for their economic capital and seek the back donor that demands least symbolic capital for their economic capital and/or attempt to get a better economic-to-symbolic capital deal from their standard donor. Since international NGOs are involved in exchanging economic capital for symbolic capital, the MLPA framework predicts donors to discontinue funding if they do not deliver enough symbolic capital for the economic capital.

Hypothesis 1: Marketization simulates concentration

New Public Management thinking forms the basis of the marketization of aid (Hood 1995, p. 95). The main thrust of New Public Management thinking is that state-related organizations need to face an incentive structure: without regular competition, organizations are not encouraged to perform effectively and efficiently (Page 2005, p. 713). Public choice theory provides the analytical foundation of marketization of aid: organizations will pursue their self-interest and become inert unless they are stimulated by competition (Downs 1957). In a non-market environment, donors consider international

NGOs as partners where discontinuation of funding does not occur easily. But when aid is marketized, the back donor is operating more as a customer who – if no longer satisfied – will finish purchasing the 'product'. This implies that there is an increased (perceived) chance of donor default. This provides an incentive to international NGOs to generate more symbolic capital for the economic capital they receive. Potential surpluses of international NGOs are reduced, as nearly all capital is used in the exchange process. This reduces possibilities for accumulation of symbolic and economic capital for NGOs. Presumably, this is where marketization leads to efficiency and effectiveness gains: competition between agencies ensures that international NGOs deliver a high symbolic to economic capital ratio. A subsequent effect on country allocations, according to the proponents, is that international NGOs will focus on countries where their added value is highest: in countries where few other NGOs are active (Fruttero and Gauri 2005).

Drawing from the insights of New Economics of Organizations, the key criticism of the marketization of aid is that uncertain environments create risk-averse behaviour. These critics argue that when an organization's survival depends on making strategic choices in a market environment characterized by uncertainty, institutional means shape its interests. International NGOs then turn into organizations that operate strategically and opportunistically in order to secure funding (Cooley and Ron 2002). They argue that insecurity and competition often encourage international NGOs to behave in a rent-seeking manner. When placed in competitive, market-like settings, non-profit groups are likely to behave like their for-profit counterparts. Thus, donors, international NGOs and recipients perform in manners consistent with agency theory, e.g. not reporting failures and engaging in shirking, precisely because they are involved in contractual relations and thus have disparate preferences (Cooley and Ron 2002).

These critics consequently claim that it will drive international NGOs out of the economically and politically poorly performing countries, and towards those countries where already many other NGOs are active. According to them, marketization and its concomitant drive for fast and measurable results will lead to a focus on areas where symbolic capital is relatively cheap (Bebbington 2004; Wallace 2000). Fearing donor withdrawal, they will attempt to show quick results. Aiming to reduce overhead costs, they will focus on programmes that require little attention and guidance. As a result they will not allocate their resources in the socially, economically and poorly performing countries. On the contrary, they will prefer to work in those countries where already many other actors are active. This will enable them to claim the victory of others, and blame failures on others (Easterly 2002).[4]

Hypothesis 2: NGOs operate in the slipstream of their back donors

A second hypothesis claims that not the 'marketization' of aid stimulates the concentration of NGOs, but rather the preferences of bilateral back donors.

This can be voluntarily, if international NGOs make their country decisions independently, or involuntarily, if bilateral donors earmark contributions to their priority countries.

The slipstream view refutes an exclusive focus on the contractual relations between the organizations and their back donors. The gist of this 'slipstream' view is that the behaviour of the back donor is important for a variety of reasons. The MLPA framework postulated that NGOs are engaged in exchanging symbolic for economic capital. The examples of their success value more in those countries where their back donors also have their embassies. The MLPA framework predicts that the lack of visibility of NGOs in those countries where bilateral donors are absent drives them away from there (Takala 2005; Ilon 1998; Zetter 1996;). Zetter found that international NGOs that were working with refugees in Mozambique were more likely to focus on areas that were strategic 'communication routes'.

The predictions from the MLPA framework are strengthened by insights from neo-institutional theory that argue that when non-profit organizations are subject to external scrutiny and regulation, they gravitate to isomorphic transformation (Frumkin 1998). This homogenization occurs as the non-profit sector adapts its practices because of perceived expectations of public authorities. International NGOs that depend more on the government will thus also concentrate more in the priority areas of the government (Morena 2006).[5] Although most NGOs are independent to choose where they are active, and claim that the government has no direct or indirect impact on their country allocations, there may thus be more subtle processes at work. Neo-Marxists argue that these processes are not so subtle at all, and that donors use their NGOs generally to achieve foreign policy objectives, such as to stabilize important export regions or to brush up their image (Petras 1997). They claim that back donors force NGOs into certain geo-strategic important countries.

The slipstream hypothesis stipulates that even if the marketization effect exist, back-donor preferences – if the international NGO depends significantly on the bilateral donor – dominate international NGO behaviour. Consequently, back-donor country explanations could have a greater predictive power for international NGO country allocations than the degree of marketization of contracts. Since bilateral donors have their donor darlings and their donor orphans (e.g. Levin and Dollar 2004; Marysse *et al.* 2007), these choices will consequently permeate into the choices of NGOs that depend significantly on them for funding. Also, if the country allocations of the bilateral donors are skewed towards poorly performing countries, and international NGOs depend significantly on the bilateral donor, the country allocations of their NGOs reflect this.

Summarizing, if the first hypothesis proves to be correct – that is, if marketization leads to more concentration of NGO efforts and reduced poverty targeting – this indicates that the costs and benefits of marketization need to be considered. Conversely, if the second is accepted and the first hypothesis rejected, showing that country allocations of the back donors influence those of international NGOs, and levels of marketization do not have an influence, then the criticasters of the marketization of aid can be considered to be misguided in this respect. Instead, more financial independence of NGOs might then be needed to reduce concentration.

Methodology

The hypothesis of the critics of marketization predicts international NGOs to allocate progressively less aid to countries where fewer other international NGOs are present and in the less poorly performing countries, as the degree of marketization of their contracts increases. The slipstream hypothesis states that the country allocations of donors determine the country allocations of international NGOs. To test which of these two views is most likely to hold, a sample of major NGOs from Norway, Germany and the United States has been composed, subject to the same criteria that were used in Chapter 2. The only difference is that NGOs that did not accept any funds from their natural back donor, such as Oxfam America, were excluded as their degree of marketization could not be calculated. The total sample consists of data from 15 organizations.

The research was conducted through structured interviews with the programme heads of each of the selected organizations, complemented with overviews of their country resource allocations. The three co-financing systems for international NGOs reflect the three different traditions of welfare provision in each of the countries. Conventionally, many consider the United States as the archetypal example of a liberal welfare regime and Germany as the example of a corporatist welfare regime, whereas the Nordic countries are part of the social democratic tradition (Esping Andersen 1999). The classical liberal welfare regime confines the state to a residual social welfare role. A typical social democratic welfare regime assigns the welfare state a powerfully redistributive role. The corporatist welfare regime sees the welfare regime as primarily a facilitator of group-based mutual aid and risk pooling (Goodin *et al.* 1999).[6]

To make the theoretical framework operational, this research developed various indicators that highlight different aspects of the marketization of NGO aid. The five elements all focus on different elements of the contracts: (1) duration; (2) specificity; (3) the competition for them; (4) stability; and (5) the costs involved. This Marketization Index is the first of its kind and is therefore still rather tentative. These five elements are selected as they surface regularly in the literature on definitions and measurements of the marketization of public services (Evans *et al.* 2005; Eikenberry and Kluver 2004; Harris 2000; Rhodes 1999; Hood 1995). In line with the definition of marketization, the indicators reflect that the more international NGOs think that their back donor operates as a 'customer' who is buying 'products', the higher the marketization scores become.

The five sub-indicators that constitute the Marketization Index are the following:

1. Duration of contracts: The longer the timeframe of a contract, the lower the degree of marketization of aid (following Eikenberry and Kluver 2004).
2. Specificity of the contracts: The more specific the contract, the higher the degree of marketization (following Rhodes 1999).[7]
   - The number of contracts between the international NGO and the donor (e.g. the more contracts an international NGO has with its principal donor, the higher degree of marketization).
   - The flexibility the contract provides (more specific contracts goes hand in hand with a higher degree of marketization). Project funding is the least flexible way of funding, programme funding as a medium form and institutional funding as the most flexible.
   - The donor's focus on quick and measurable results (score from one to five).
3. The competition for the contracts: more competition indicates more marketization (following Hood 1995).
   - The presence of competitive bidding or a closed shop.[8]
   - The perception of the level of competition between the international NGOs (score from one to five).
4. Stability of contracts: The higher the stability, the lower the degree of marketization (following Harris 2000).
   - The presence of a guarantee for more funding after the contract has expired.
   - The presence of a drop of more than 20 per cent in funding from the major donor over the last decade.
   - The donor's focus on the learning capacity of the international NGOs (score from one to five, the higher the score the higher the marketization).
   - The donor threatens to withdraw funding in case of underperformance (score from one to five).
5. Cost of the contract: the more time and energy international NGOs spend to obtain the contract, the higher the degree of marketization (following Evans *et al.* 2005).

Organizations rated themselves on those indicators and provided arguments to substantiate the answers. If there was a perceived inconsistency between the argumentation and the ratings, the researchers asked for clarification. The Marketization Index brings the scores of the five indicators together, in which one stands for the lowest and five for the highest level of marketization. For each of the five categories (duration, specificity, competition, stability and costs of the contracts) unweighed averages are calculated per organization. The unweighed averages of the five categories together represent the Marketization Index.

The first hypothesis will be tested in two ways. First, the relationship between marketization and concentration is gauged.[9] The NGO Concentration Indicator plays a key role in this endeavour and indicates how many other NGOs are on average active in the countries in which the NGO is active. The highest score is for an organization that is active in countries in which on average 38 organizations are active, the lowest score is about 14, indicating that this organization operates in countries in which on average 14 NGOs are active (of the sample of Chapter 2, consisting of 61 organizations). This NGO Concentration Indicator is plotted against the marketization index to examine whether a relationship exists between the two. This will provide insight in the question whether those organizations that operate in a more competitive environment are more inclined to keep a low profile (and thus concentrate their activities).

Second, the relationship between marketization and a focus on the poorest countries is assessed. The international NGO country allocations are presented as a graphical distribution, which shows the aid concentration curve as cumulative shares, using a method forwarded by Baulch (Baulch 2003).[10] The statistical representation of this aid concentration curve is the Suits index.[11] This measure summarizes the progressivity or regressivity of a distribution. It varies between -1 and $+1$. A Suits index of -1 corresponds to the situation in which a donor gives all its aid to the poorest country in the world. A Suits index of $+1$ corresponds to the case when a donor gives all its aid to the richest countries in the sample. A Suits index of zero corresponds to the situation in which a donor distributes its aid in exact proportion to the number of poor people, with no reference to different countries' living standards.

The second hypothesis will be tested by analysing whether NGOs that depend financially stronger on their back donor display a stronger copycat behaviour than those that are less financially dependent on their back donor.

Results

Marketization Index

Table 6.1 presents the marketization scores and broadly confirms the predicted outcomes. American NGOs score highest on all marketization indicators, resulting in a Marketization Index of 3.9 out of five. Germany is scoring lowest on many indicators, such as the duration of contract, the flexibility of it, the perception of competition and the threats of the donor to withdraw. This leads to the conclusion that German organizations are operating in an environment with relatively low levels of marketization (Index: 1.9). The Norwegian organizations score on average in between and can be considered to be operating in a medium-level marketized environment. The coefficients of variance are in brackets.

The German Protestant (EED) and the Catholic development agency (Misereor) receive around 50 per cent of their budget line embedded in long-

Table 6.1 Summary table of the marketization of aid for each of the three countries

N = 14	Germany	Norway	United States
Duration of contract			
Average duration of contract	Indefinite/3 years	4 years	2.7 years
Specificity of contract			
Number of contracts	Mostly 1	1	47
Flexibility of contract	Mostly institutional	Mostly program	Mostly project
Donor focus on results (1–5)	3.1	3.3	3.8
Competition for contract			
Closed shop	Mostly closed	Mostly closed	Open tender
Perception of competition (1–5)	1.8	3.5	4.6
Stability of funding			
Guaranteed funding	Mostly yes	Mostly not	Not
Significant decrease in funding	No	No	No
Donor focus on learning capacity	3.0	4.0	2.4
Donor threats withdrawing (1–5)	1.8	2.8	3.6
Costs of contract			
Cost of contract (1–5)	2.3	2.5	3.4
Marketization Index (Mean and Standard deviation)	1.9 = low (0.7)	2.6 = medium 0.5)	3.9 = high (0.3)

Source: Koch, own data.

lasting agreements, thus reflecting a low level of marketization. Another example is that the number of seats in the Bundestag determines the funding of the political foundations such as the Friedrich Ebert Stiftung. Contracts are not country-specific. There is however a clear distinction between the political foundations and church organizations which receive the lion's share of the money from public resources and other German NGOs that are more market-dependent. The high coefficient of variance reflects this diversity.

The US-based NGOs operate in a much stronger market environment with short-term and smaller contracts that provide far less security. On average the American organizations have 47 contracts with their back donor. Those contracts are specific with respect to the countries where the funds can be used. The standard deviation for American organizations is very low. This reflects the absence of privileged relationships between the American government and certain (groups of) organizations: all organizations face a similar competitive environment.

Norway – with a Marketization Index of 2.6 – scores between Germany and the United States. Norwegian organizations state that the back donor focuses more on the learning capacity of their organizations than on direct tangible results. They operate more in a market like environment than the German organization as they have neither guaranteed nor institutional funding. The Norwegian organizations finds themselves in a less competitive environment than the American ones, as they have mostly only one contract with their back donor and the donor does not threaten to withdraw funding if they occasionally fail to deliver on agreed results.

The critics of the marketization of aid predict that organizations from Germany – other things being equal – take most risk and target the poorly performing countries. With long-term, unspecified, low-competition, and stable contracts they have a lower chance of donor withdrawal. They can therefore invest in countries where results will take more time to materialize – the poorly performing countries where few other organizations are active – without having to fear for their existence. They would also predict that American organizations – other things being equal – focus more on donor darlings and well-performing in a rush to show results.

Results for hypothesis 1: Marketization leads to risk-averse behaviour

To assess the relationship between marketization and concentration, Figure 6.1 depicts a scatter-plot of the Marketization Index against the Donor Concentration Indicator. The graph shows a parabolic relationship between the two. When competitive pressures rise, NGOs first become more active in countries where many other NGOs are active, but when competitive pressures are very high, they tend to focus more on those countries where fewer other actors are active. This figure is a first indication that the first hypothesis, marketization leads to concentration of NGOs by stimulating risk-averse behaviour is, likely to be rejected.

Aid concentration curves provide a graphical device to show whether donors target the poorest countries (see Figure 6.2). The diagonal line shows what the allocation would look like if aid were allocated in direct proportion to the share of the world's poor living in each country. If most of a donor's aid goes to the poorest countries, then its aid concentration curve will lie above the diagonal (and vice versa). The aid concentration curve plots the cumulative percentage of some measure of aid (in this case aid from the NGOs in 2004) against the cumulative percentage of some population variable (in this case the number of people living below the $1-a-day poverty line).[12] The ranking of the recipient countries on the x-axis of Figure 2 is based on their Gross National Income per capita (PPP average 1995–2004). The sample consists of 86 of the DAC recipient countries for which poverty data exist. The lines in the figure represent the three donor countries.

The sum of funds (both government and own funding) in the sample is €334 million for Germany (four organizations), €178 million for Norway (four organizations) and €1,376 million for the United States (six organizations). The data cover the disbursements of the year 2004.

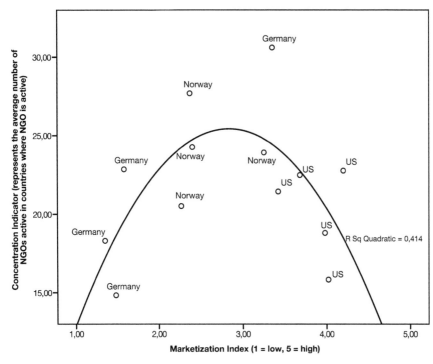

Figure 6.1 Marketization scores plotted against Concentration Indicator
Source: Koch, own data.

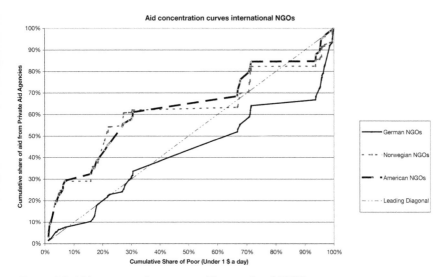

Figure 6.2 Aid concentration curves of international NGOs
Source: Koch, own data.

When analysing this curve, the most obvious observation is that the German international NGOs exhibit a quite different aid allocation pattern compared to the Norwegian and American organizations, which follow roughly a similar tendency. The German curve even has a Suits index of +0.15 – indicating a regressive distribution – whereas the Norwegian and the American curves both have an index of −0.22, which makes them progressive. In the Norwegian, German and American lines, three rather flat parts represent – from left to right – Nigeria, India and China. It indicates that poor people in those countries receive little aid. Other ways of measuring the Suits index, e.g. when the Human Development Index is used as the rank for the x-axis, show similar results, with the Norwegian international NGOs being slightly more poor-country-oriented.[13] This pattern of country allocations runs counter to the prediction of the marketization critics, as this hypothesis states that the NGOs that face more competition would avoid working in the poorest environments. In sum, it appears that the German organizations are spending their money in countries that are relatively rich and relatively well governed as compared to the American and Norwegian ones.

To create more insight in the relation between the marketization of aid and the targeting of poorly performing countries, Figure 6.3 compares the Suits and marketization Indices for each of the selected international NGOs.

Country aid allocations display a clear downward sloping line. The higher

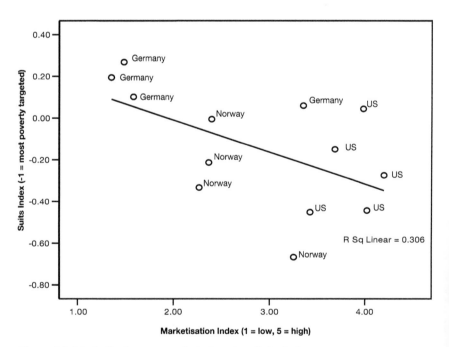

Figure 6.3 Marketization scores plotted against Suits Index
Source: Koch, own data.

organizations score on the marketization index, the more targeted their resources are towards poorly performing countries. Three different clusters can be distinguished: one for each country. Germany has a low score on the Marketization Index (1.9) and scores highest on the Suits Index (+0.15). The US, on the other hand, has a high score on Marketization (3.9) and scores lowest (together with Norway) on the Suits Index (−0.22). The correlation between the Suits Index and the Marketization Index, −0.55, significant at the 5 per cent level (N = 13), is consistent with the results shown so far: the higher the level of marketization, the more organizations focus on the poorest countries and vice versa. These findings, especially when considered jointly with the findings on the relationship between marketization and concentration contest hypothesis 1.

Results for hypothesis 2: Slipstream behaviour stimulates concentration

A scatter-plot can illustrate the relationship between on one hand the correlation coefficients of country allocations of international NGOs with those of their back donors, and the dependence rate on the other hand. This will demonstrate whether NGOs that depend for a larger share of their funding on back donors are more inclined to mimic their behaviour. Figure 6.4 depicts this relationship; the clear upward sloping line demonstrates that there is a significant and positive relationship between the level of financial dependence and the degree of conformity in country allocations. A positive correlation of 0.56 (significant at the 5 per cent level) exists between the dependence rate and the correlation between bilateral and international NGO country allocations. The German NGOs, which also depend most on their back donor, have on average the highest correlation coefficients (51 per cent), while the American NGOs, which depend on average least on their back donor, have the lowest average correlation coefficients. In sum, the more an organization depends on the bilateral donor, the more the organization will follow their geographic priorities, which is consistent with the slipstream hypothesis.

Proponents of the slipstream hypothesis appear thus correct when predicting the importance of the country allocations of back donors. This is pivotal when attempting to explain the concentration of NGOs, as official donors also display an unequal distribution of aid. The Gini coefficient of official aid was 0.78 (own calculation). Sixty per cent of the people that live in DAC countries that receive least per capita ODA receive 5 per cent of total ODA. The 20 per cent of the people that live in the DAC countries that receive most ODA, receive 81 per cent of the ODA. By mimicking the choices of their back donors, international NGOs end up reinforcing the existing divide between the donor darlings and donor orphans.

To illustrate the importance the level of financial dependence on back donors, it is instructive to compare the poor country targeting of back donors with those of the international NGOs. The Suits Index of Norway as a bilateral

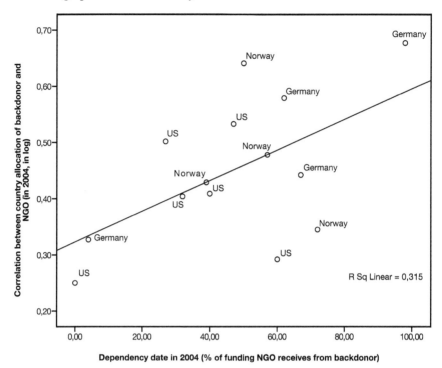

Figure 6.4 Dependence rates plotted against correlations of bilateral and NGO aid
Source: Koch, own data.

donor is -0.29, which means that Norwegian bilateral aid targets the poorest countries. The German and US bilateral aid are regressive (Suits indices are respectively: +0.18 and +0.14) as these donors do not target the poorest countries. When comparing the three bilateral Suits indexes with the three respective international NGO Suits Indexes (Figure 6.2), it becomes clear that the German and Norwegian NGO Indices do not differ from their bilateral curves, while the American Suits Indices differ substantially. While US bilateral aid is regressive (Suits index +0.14), the international NGOs in the US are quite progressive (Suits index −0.22). This means that the American NGOs are – compared to their government – more active in the poorest countries. This divergence is in line with predictions of the slipstream hypothesis: American organizations depend least on their back donors and therefore have the possibility to deviate from back-donor preferences.

Other actors and factors

As stated in the Introduction, many different factors influence country allocations of international NGOs. It would be methodologically unsound to attribute all differences between NGOs on differences in co-financing systems and dependence rates. Interviews were used to gain in a systematic way more insight in other actors and factors that influence country allocations.

Interesting similarities and differences occur in the answers of the organizations regarding the importance of other actors in determining country allocations. Besides the needs of the intended beneficiaries, which all claim to be most important in determining aid allocations (4.0 out of five), the geographic preferences of the donating public are considered quite important for the United States (2.8) unlike for the German organizations (2.0). In Germany the managers of the organization and their members/constituency are quite important (both 2.8), while these appear to be less relevant for the American and Norwegian organizations (1.8 and 1.6 respectively). As expected, the German organizations rate themselves low on the influence of the major donor on their country allocations (1.8), while the American organizations rate the influence of the major donor at 3.8. This higher perceived importance of the back donor in driving country allocations of the American organizations does, however, not automatically lead to isomorphism between back donor and international NGO, as has been shown.

In the interviews, organizations also rated the importance of factors that influence country allocations, which provided an interesting pattern of convergences and divergences. The needs of beneficiaries and the opportunity to achieve results were rated highest on average by all at 4.0. For the American organizations, the presence of local funding (3.6) and the need to reach rapid and tangible results (2.8) were more important than for others, indicating that these factors are therefore not inconsistent with a focus on countries where few other actors are active. The German organizations rate the importance of capacities of local personnel higher (4.2) than the Norwegians (4.0) and the Americans (3.4). The majority of the German organizations is working only through local partners and has field offices only in exceptional cases. The Norwegian organizations maintain quite a few field offices, but hardly execute any programmes themselves. Many American organizations operate via their own field offices, and tend to execute more of the programmes themselves, whereas German organizations depend most on local capacities. There thus appears to be some kind of trade-off between donor orphan and poor country targeting on one hand and hands-off operational modalities on the other hand.[14]

Discussion

The critics of marketization fail to predict the country allocations. Organizations that operate in more competitive environments are not displaying more risk-averse behaviour. Instead of the American organizations with their short-term performance-based contracts, the German organizations with long-term and secure contracts target the poorly performing countries least, and even display a regressive pattern. The prediction that organizations operating in an environment with high levels of marketization seek to work in those countries where symbolic capital is cheap to obtain, proved incorrect. Organizations that did not face competitive pressures did not focus on those countries where fewer other NGOs were active. These results are in line with the conclusion of Harrow (2002, p. 156) who claims that 'the case that New Public Management approaches have excluded social justice goals is 'non-proven'.[15] This is not to say that those who claim that New Public Management will enhance social justice are right, as the Norwegian example shows that medium levels of marketization can be combined with high levels of poor country targeting.

New Public Management thinkers appear to have a point that the discretion that organizations obtain by accumulating symbolic and economic capital in environments with low levels of marketization might not be used to make riskier and more pro-poor decisions. Organizations operating in a market-like environment are less likely to have predetermined shares allocated to various (sub)-regions than those operating in non-market environments. One of the largest German organizations maintained a 1/3, 1/3 and 1/3 distribution between Latin America, Africa and Asia for decades, even though poverty increased significantly in Africa, decreased significantly in Asia and remained more or less stable in Latin America during this period. These results are consistent with findings from Schmid (2003, p. 320) who argues that non-governmental agencies can ignore equity when delivering services. The argumentation is as follows: while government agencies have to be universalistic, non-profit agencies can be particularistic. Governments need to have clear criteria for targeting, while non-profit agencies do not need to serve all people in their target group and can choose clients on the basis of a group characteristic, e.g. place of residence (Lipsky and Smith 1990). Support for this proposition was already encountered in Chapter 2.

The slipstream view appears to be more informative as NGOs that depended more on their back donor copied to a larger degree their country choices. This chapter has shown that Norwegian organizations – being rather highly dependent on their bilateral donor – target the same countries as their back donor, which are in the case of Norway the poorest countries. Norwegian organizations claim that – although the direct influence of the bilateral donor is low – the indirect influence is rather strong. They all confirm that NORAD – their major donor – held discussions with them about country allocations and stimulated them – by means of discussion and not financial incentives – to focus on poorer countries. The slipstream view also explains the German distribution consistently: there is a strong correlation with bilateral allocations even though German organizations consider themselves rather autonomous in determining country allocations. The divide between the geographic focus of American international NGOs and those of the US government does thus not contradict the slipstream hypothesis. On the contrary, it suggests that lower dependence rates translate in less isomorphic transformations. This finding is even more striking since the geographic strings that the US government attaches to its grants are much more stringent than those for German and Norwegian organizations.

Even though the results are quite robust, there are some caveats that warrant caution when interpreting the results. First, there are many factors that affect country allocations. Even though there are many similarities in those factors between the three countries, there are also some differences, which reduce the comparability of the cases. These other factors could have induced the geographic differences. In the results section these differences have been highlighted. The 'local capacity constraint' received special attention. This constraint is more pronounced for German organizations, as they work most with local actors. Nevertheless, as the Norwegians rate local capacity nearly as important as the Germans (4.2 vs 4.0) this is not likely to be the major factor in explaining the large differences in targeting of the international NGOs.[16] Second, although the response rate to the questionnaires was high (77 per cent), the sample size is relatively small. The sample covers roughly 63 per cent of the expenditures of the German government to international NGOs, 43 per cent for the Norwegian government and 22 per cent for the American government. This reflects the fragmentation of international NGO aid in the three countries. As the organizations were randomly selected, there is no reason to believe that there is a bias.[17]

Conclusion

Many scholars are strong opponents of the marketization of aid. Wallace (2000, p. 28) asserts that: 'When insisting on measurable impact within two to three years, what happens to risk taking, to working on the difficult, sometimes intractable problems which often underpin the causes of poverty for some groups of people?' Fowler (2000, p. 38) suggests, after warning for increased competition in aid, measures to improve aid quality to international NGOs: 'They include greater flexibility, a longer term perspective, greater attention to process over outputs, more merit to qualitative changes and measures (...)'. Edwards and Hulme (1997) state also that donors must be encouraged to move toward funding arrangements which provide stability and predictability in the long term.

This chapter has shown that organizations operating in the most competitive environment do not shy away from operating in countries where few other actors are active, nor from intervening in the poorly performing countries. Quite to the contrary, international NGOs in the countries subject of this research that were operating in an environment characterized by long-term, flexible contracts (as proposed by Fowler 2000; Edwards and Hulme 1997), spent considerably less on operations in poorly performing countries. Reducing marketization in foreign aid is thus not likely to have a substantial effect on increasing aid to donor orphans by international NGOs.

The slipstream hypothesis provided a useful framework for understanding the country allocation of international NGOs. With higher dependence rates of international NGOs on their government, they are increasingly mimicking the country choice priorities of their back donor. Since bilateral donors distribute their resources unevenly, this slipstream behaviour contributes to concentration

Part I of this research showed that there was strong process of concentration among international NGOs. Subsequently Part II presented various causes of this concentration. The next chapter will focus on the consequences of concentration of international NGOs on cooperation between local NGOs.

Part III

Analysing implications of geographic choices of international NGOs

7 The consequences of concentration of NGOs

Does it affect cooperation?*

Introduction

The previous chapters have highlighted the processes of concentration that characterize the geographic choices of international NGOs. After having established some of the causes of this concentration, this chapter focuses on the consequences of concentration, notably on the effects on cooperation between local NGOs.

The consequences of concentration are little understood: does it simulate cooperation, or does it lead to competition among NGOs? Authors such as Cooley and Ron (2002) argue that increased concentration of local organizations turns them into strategically and opportunistically operating entities aiming to secure their own survival. Consequently, NGOs tend to put more time and effort into obtaining funding, rather than directly assisting the poor. Yet, other authors stress the benefits that the local population may gain from cost-sharing between NGOs, referred to as complementarities, when NGOs are located close to one other (Barr and Fafchamps 2005). The first aim of this chapter is to assess whether the concentration of NGOs is likely to lead to strategic and unproductive behaviour or will lead to better outcomes for the target population. This could inform the future decisions of donors regarding their policies on geographic targeting.

The second objective of this chapter is to review the usefulness of game simulation as a research methodology. While there is ample experience with surveys and questionnaires as research tools, experimental methods have been used far less, particularly in the context of developing countries. The latter methods can, however, be especially useful for gaining insight into the behavioural consequences of where NGOs choose to locate. The specific game developed for this purpose was repeated eight times with different Tanzanian NGOs. The game was played in Tanzania, in the Arusha region, as this is a country where many international and national NGOs are active (see Chapters 4 and 5). To check the validity of the game simulation the results are juxtaposed with those of a survey conducted among the same local NGOs. While a number of similarities in the outcomes of the two research methodologies exist, also some consistent discrepancies manifested themselves. The research uses these overlaps and contradictions to engage in a critical discussion of the merits and demerits of game simulation as a research methodology.

The remainder of this chapter is structured as follows: first it will be explained how collective action theories address cooperation among NGOs, in particular the relationship between concentration and cooperation. Then the choice of game simulation as a research method will be justified and it will be explained how the game is developed in practice. Thereafter the results of the NGO GAME will be presented. This chapter will continue by comparing the results of the game with the survey. These outcomes are used to discuss the advantages and disadvantages of both research methods.

Theoretical approach

Collective action theory and its predictions on the relationship between concentration and cooperation form the basis of the theoretical framework of this chapter. 'Cooperation' in this chapter means the practice of NGOs to engage in joint activities so as to improve the quality of these activities and expand the impact of individual operations, organizations and the sector as a whole. Collective action theory makes certain predictions about the conditions under which cooperation is likely to occur. Olson (1967, p. 36) argues that 'the larger the group, the less it will further its common interests'. Since the NGOs in the Arusha region belong to the same sector, are member of the same umbrella organization and operate in a restricted geographic area, they can be considered as a group. Fewer collective goods will be produced in larger groups because contributions and the individual benefits they produce become less noticeable. This reduces selective incentives[1] for individuals and thus threatens cooperation. In addition, the costs associated with reaching and enforcing a contract for collective action become prohibitively high when many actors are involved (Olson 1967, p. 46). In areas with high levels of concentration (i.e. areas with many NGOs), the large group size should – according to this theory – lead to reduced cooperation. Olson's theory, depicted in Figure 7.1 with the declining line, would thus predict a downward slope when cooperation is plotted against concentration.

While Olson reasons from a political-economy perspective, social psychologists reach similar conclusions. Supporters of the 'power approach to hostility' (Giles and Evans 1986) argue that increased concentration is likely to enhance competition. They argue that individuals and organizations are involved in ongoing competition to gain control of economic, social and political structures. In geographic areas with high numbers of NGOs, these structures will be more constrained than in areas where only few NGOs are present. Cooperation among NGOs will therefore probably be inversely related to the number of NGOs.[2]

Alternatively, Wade (1988, p. 207) argues that another factor co-determines outcomes in cooperation. Even without selective incentives, cooperation can emerge if the collective benefits are high enough. Following Barr and Fafchamps (2005), it can be assumed that the collective benefits are limited in areas with a low density of NGOs (i.e. areas in which few NGOs are present).

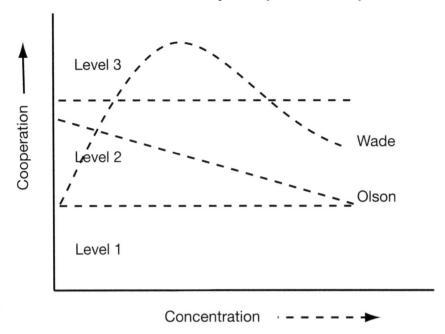

Figure 7.1 Predicted levels of cooperation in market intermediate groups

This implies that the opportunities for sharing learning possibilities and joining marketing opportunities are limited in those areas. Wade (1988) argues that in these circumstances little cooperation will take place. In a similar vein, it can be assumed that with rising concentration, collective benefits could increase, as opportunities for NGOs to complement each other's activities arise (Barr and Fafchamps 2005).[3] When the number of NGOs operating in a specific geographic area increases further, there is increased competition for funding and for promising target groups. This theory therefore predicts that after a certain point, the opportunities for cooperation and the willingness to cooperate may decrease. In sum, Wade's theory would suggest that rising concentration causes an initial increase in cooperation which levels off and then decreases after a certain level of concentration is reached (depicted in Figure 7.1 by an inverted U-shape curve).[4]

This research distinguishes analytically between three levels of cooperation:

1. cooperation with high selective benefits for individual NGOs, but not necessarily for the target group;
2. cooperation with selective benefits for both individual NGOs and the target group;
3. cooperation without selective benefits for individual NGOs but high benefits for the target group.

The first level of cooperation refers to activities related to joint fundraising by NGOs. These activities relax the funding supply constraint, but do not necessarily increase the effectiveness of their work. This type of cooperation provides selective incentives for NGOs, but does not necessarily benefit the target group. Examples of such shared marketing and fundraising efforts are joint fundraising websites or fundraising proposal-writing workshops. Both Olson and Wade argue that this type of cooperation can take place between groups. Social psychologists also claim that if the interests of various groups are concordant, as is the case with this level of cooperation, it is likely to occur (Brown 2000).

The second level of cooperation refers to activities such as joint training centres for staff and a mutual quality control system. These types of activities stimulate the operational quality of the work of individual organizations and increase the quality of the overall product. Some selective benefits exist, but most of the benefits accrue to the common good. For example, organizations that provide training to individuals may lose them to other organizations, but quality rises among all the organizations as a group, not just for their own.[5] Hence, this kind of cooperation is the maximum kind of cooperation that Olson predicts in small intermediate groups. As the group size increases and thus concentration effects occur, Olson predicts that decreasing selective benefits are likely to lead to diminishing cooperation. In large groups, therefore, only cooperation with selective benefits will continue to exist (level 1).

The third level of cooperation (no selective benefits and collective benefits only) refers to activities such as the coordination of regional and thematic priorities. These types of activities are good for the target group because the overlap between organizations is reduced and resources are more equitably distributed. Brett (1998) argues that this type of cooperation is difficult to obtain as NGOs 'are independent agencies, which defend their autonomy jealously and compete for funds and contracts. This makes coordinated action difficult, producing duplicated services in some areas and nothing in others' (p. 11). Wade argues that third-level cooperation can nevertheless occur if the collective benefits are high enough. The collective benefits are highest with medium levels of concentration because complementarities between NGOs exist and competition for funds and target groups remains modest. This theory would therefore argue that this level of cooperation exists when neither too few nor too many NGOs are active within a particular area. Olson argues that this kind of cooperation will not take place between market-groups because organizations do not benefit individually from it.[6]

Figure 7.1 shows that, according to Olson, there would be no level 3 cooperation. Type 2 cooperation is the maximum level of cooperation and only specific types of intermediate groups obtain this. Wade views this differently; for him level 3 cooperation is possible if collective benefits are high enough. This is the case in situations with neither too little nor too much concentration. In regions where NGOs are too sparse, too few complementarities exist for cooperation to come about, whereas in regions with concentration, there is too much competition.

To sum up, this research attempts to discover whether Olson's prediction (that increasing concentration leads to decreased cooperation) or Wade's prediction (that increasing concentration leads initially to increased cooperation, but after a certain point it leads to decreased cooperation) holds in the case of development NGOs in Tanzania, Arusha.[7]

Methodological approach

This section employs game simulation as its main research method. Game simulation provides an interesting experimental environment for studying strategic behaviour in complex systems because: (a) it enables to monitor and measure strategic behaviour as it occurs; (b) participants can report various patterns of strategic behaviour conducted or experienced during the game without repercussions; (c) during debriefing it is possible to discuss with participants the similarities to and the lessons for real life (Kuit *et al.* 2005). Other research shows that stakeholders actually enjoy participating in games, and that game simulations can provide insight for both researchers and participants alike (Meijer *et al.* 2005). The results are triangulated by comparing them with those of a survey among the same NGOs.

The NGO Game

The NGO Game covers three fictive years (rounds) and is thus a repeated interaction game. The NGOs have to balance two conflicting interests in the game. On one hand they compete against other NGOs in order to maximize their own operating budget. On the other hand, a team (a group of NGOs) wins a prize if it succeeds best in serving their target group by cooperating. A team of NGOs consists of four to six representatives from different NGOs, and in each game three teams of NGOs are participating. It is made clear from the start that NGOs compete on these two fronts, and that two prizes can be won. The individual NGO that succeeded in ending with most tokens wins one prize, and the team that succeeds in gaining most joint projects 'for the community' wins another. These two prizes represent the dilemma faced by NGOs every day: do they secure their own financial situation, or do they cooperate and achieve more for their target communities? Participants were asked to represent their own organization and act accordingly.[8] Figure 7.2 provides an overview of how the game is played.

In the three rounds, the three levels of cooperation are tested. In the first round, the first level of cooperation is tested, followed in the second round by the second type and so on. In every round NGOs face the same dilemma: they either invest in joint projects (cooperate) or invest in individual projects (compete). The rates of return are generally higher if NGOs chose to

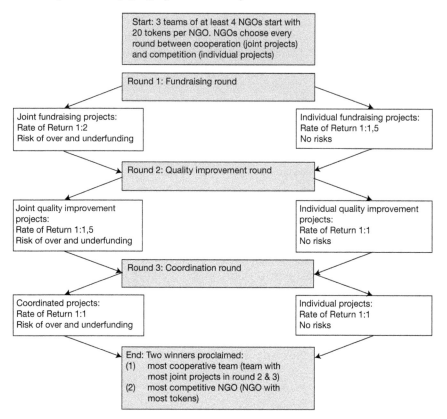

Figure 7.2 NGO Game
Source: Koch, own material.

cooperate, but there are clear risks involved in cooperating: projects can become overfunded or underfunded. If NGOs overfund a certain project (that is, spend two tokens more than necessary on the project), they will all lose five of their tokens; the project will nevertheless be executed. If NGOs underfund a certain project (spend less on the project than the amount that is needed to have it executed), they will all lose half of their money and the project will not be executed. Clear communication is thus quintessential for successful cooperation. NGOs can discuss how much money they will invest and can suggestively place the number of tokens they are willing to invest on the board for all players to see; however, they also need to note down their actual decisions without sharing them with others. Only projects in which more than one NGO participates are executed.

In the first round, NGOs need to invest their money in projects that have benefits for their NGO, but have no effect for the target population. They can spend their money on the various projects indicated on the board (they receive 20 tokens at the start of the game). They can either spend their tokens on projects such as shared fundraising trips and a joint workshop on proposal writing, or invest in their own fundraising projects. NGOs receive a higher return when they invest in joint fundraising projects (rate of return 1:2) as opposed to individual projects (1:1.5). All participants have this information. Since projects need at least two donors, cooperation is necessary. There is a risk associated with investing in joint projects, as tokens can be lost due to over- and underfunding. At the end of the first round, the game leader adds up all the amounts that NGOs have written down, and informs the participants which projects have been executed and which have not. The game leaders finish the first round by taking tokens from – or distributing them to – participants, depending on whether joint projects were executed and whether over- and underfunding occurred.

In the second round of the game, the second type of cooperation is tested. In this round, both NGOs and the target group can benefit. NGOs can invest their tokens in either joint projects that are beneficial for both themselves and the public good, such as joint assessment missions, joint training centres (rate of return 1:1.5) or in individual projects (1:1). The same rules and procedures apply as in round one. Projects that are jointly executed in this round count as 'community projects', and are thus included when calculating the total cooperation score of the various teams.

The third round shows whether NGOs can coordinate their activities (third-level cooperation). In this round, no benefits for NGOs can be obtained, but there are benefits for the target population. Again two types of projects exist: joint projects and individual projects.[9] Only joint projects deliver tangible results for the target group and are considered 'community projects' (and count when calculating the cooperation score of the team). The rules and procedures of previous rounds also hold for this round.

After this third round, the game leader calculates how many tokens every player has ended with and calculates the value of all the joint community projects. The game leader then shares this information with the overall game leader. The game ends when the overall game leaders hand over the prizes to the 'team' that has cooperated best (as determined by the total value of their joint community projects), and to the individual NGO that has ended with most tokens.

After this, a debriefing in an informal setting can be organized, in which the game leaders can solicit for reflections of the participants on the game. Debriefings with the participants took place after the official games in an informal setting, with the aim of stimulating the participants to reflect openly about the game and their behaviour. They were particularly asked to hint at how there might be a difference between real life and the game situation. Few criticisms were raised during these debriefing sessions with the participants. The only complaint arose after the first session of the game and concerned the time allotted to their team, which was allegedly shorter than for the other teams. The debriefing with game leaders confirmed this, and appropriate action to remedy this shortcoming in the next sessions of the game were adopted. A number of the participants mentioned, without being asked, that they had appreciated the learning component of the game. Various participants said that the game had made them realize that, to progress jointly, they needed to share more information. This learning component emerged thus as one of the unintended consequences of the game simulation. The international staff of NGOs present confirmed this and suggested that the game could serve in other countries as well, and that it could have positive effects on cooperation between NGOs. To conclude, the game leaders hold a debriefing session among themselves.[10]

The teams are not composed in a random fashion. To test the hypothesis, it is ensured that teams differed significantly with respect to the level of concentration. For example, there were some teams in which all the participants worked on the same theme in the same district (e.g. HIV/AIDS in the regional capital), and some teams in which all the participants worked on different themes in different regions.

Various control variables that could affect the behaviour of NGOs were included when analysing results. First, individual level controls were included, as individuals can influence game simulations (Hofstede 2005). Barreteau and Daré (2007) argue that the designers of games in Africa should consider the social status of players. Therefore, control variables were included for the position of the participant in the organization, his/her nationality, and his/her sex. Second, NGOs are often assumed to be more outward-looking, and thus more likely to cooperate, when they are more mature (USAID 1999). Consequently, the age of the NGO was included as a control variable. Third, the debriefings made it clear that in some instances game leaders affected the course of the game simulation, a control variable was included for the three different game leaders. Other ways of ensuring a streamlined behaviour of game leaders are explained in the following section.

The attributes of the game include one poker-set of tokens and a dynamic playing surface (which could be adjusted for the various rounds and for varying number of players). To ensure that negotiation is inevitable, the value of all joint projects combined is always 25 per cent more than the amount of tokens in the game.

With hindsight there are two potential ways to further refine the design of the NGO game. First, to avoid results being influenced by 'learning by doing' it is advisable that in future sessions the various 'rounds' are not played always in the same order. This will enable establishing whether participants learn to cooperate better as the game unfolds and correct for it. Second, in the current game design more concentrated teams have some additional benefits to cooperate, as they can share the costs of joint projects among more participants. Economies of scale are thus a certain extent addressed. However, there are some doubts if these reduced marginal costs of concentrated teams are fully reflected in the current set-up of the game.

Figure 7.3 Pictures of the NGO Game (Arusha, 2 April 2007)
Pictures by Annelies Claessens

The reduced transaction and transport costs of more concentrated teams could ideally be reflected in the prices of their joint projects. For this game it is assumed that players incorporate these considerations when playing the game, as they had to play themselves in the game. Taken into consideration these potential refinements of the game, the results presented below need to be interpreted with appropriate caution.

Results

The results can be analysed at two levels: at the team level and at the individual NGO level. More attention is paid to individual-level results, as the number of observations is more amenable to statistical analysis (N = 37 for individual NGOs and N = 8 for teams), yet for illustrative purposes this section starts with a scatter-plot on the group level results. Hence, in Figure 7.4 a 'group concentration indicator' is scattered against the group 'cooperation index' for illustrative purposes.

The 'group concentration indicator' consists of two elements: (1) the average of the NGO concentration indices of the NGOs in the group; (2) a group size corrector. The group concentration indicator is the product of the average NGO concentration index and the number of players in the team (the group size corrector).[11] A higher score on the group concentration indicator reveals that many NGOs are in the team and that they are active on the same themes and in the same districts.

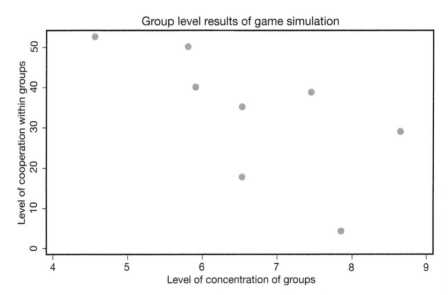

Figure 7.4 Cooperation results of game simulation at the team level
Source: Koch, own data.

The 'cooperation index' was derived by dividing the value of all joint projects that contributed to community development by the number of players in the team.

Figure 7.4 shows that the more concentrated teams (teams that worked on the same theme and/or in the same district and/or had more players) scored lower on cooperation. They succeeded in funding fewer joint projects that benefited the community. This graph suggests that the downward sloping line of Olson in Figure 7.1 resembles more the outcomes of the game simulation, than Wade's inverted U-shape. To analyse whether these results hold when scrutinized in a more systematic way, the remainder of this chapter explores the behaviour of individual players.

The dependent variables in the following regressions in Table 7.1 are individual propensities to cooperate in the three different rounds and the average individual propensity to cooperate. This propensity is calculated by dividing the number of tokens invested in joint projects by the total number of tokens a player owns. To recap, in the first round the aim was shared fundraising – type 1 cooperation (regressions 1 and 2). This shifted to shared quality improvement, type 2 cooperation, in the second round (regression 3 and 4) and to coordination, type 3 cooperation, in the third round (regressions 5 and 6). Regressions 7 and 8 depict the average propensity to cooperate. An 'Ordinary Least Squares' regression model is used to test the relationship between concentration and cooperation. Two different functional form specifications exist: the Olson specification and the Wade specification. In the Olson specification, the individual concentration index enters the model. In the Wade specification, a squared function of the concentration index is also included to test non-linear concentration effects (the supposed inverted U-shape).

The results of the regressions in Table 7.1 indicate that in the Olson specifications there was a significant (at the 1 per cent level) negative relationship between concentration and cooperation in two rounds, namely round two (quality improvement) and round three (coordination). This is consistent with predictions of Olson, who noted that when supply is fixed and there is increased concentration, intermediate groups will reduce cooperation. In round one, supply is not fixed as this round creates opportunities to relax the funding supply constraint. When supply is not fixed, groups will cooperate to further their common interest. In rounds two and three, where the concentration variable is significant, its size is quite significant: a one-unit increase in the concentration index (which ranges between one and two), leads to a reduction of 0.32 – 0.41 units in the propensity to cooperate (which ranges between zero and one). Overall cooperation regressions show a similar pattern.

The concentration indicators have the predicted signs in the Wade specifications, namely positive for the linear concentration index and negative for the squared index, but they both lack significance. This suggests that the results of the game simulation are not in line with Wade's inverted U-shape relationship between concentration and cooperation.

Table 7.1 NGO propensity to cooperate

	Round 1: Cooperation in Fundraising		Round 2: Cooperation in Quality improvement		Round 3: Cooperation in Coordination		Average cooperation	
	Olson	Wade	Olson	Wade	Olson	Wade	Olson	Wade
N	33	33	33	33	33	33	33	33
NGO Concentration	−0.046 (0.662)	0.871 (0,496)***	−0.405 (0.008)***	1.078 (0.534)	−0.319 (0.002)***	0.172 (0.883)	−0.254 (0.016)**	0.697 (0.563)
NGO Concentration-squared		−0.019 (−0.472)		−0.506 (0.392)		−0.167 (0.674)		−0.325 (0.430)
NGO director at game simulation	−0.006 (0.930)	−0.019 (0.807)	−0.012 (0.904)	−0.032 (0.758)	−0.319 (0.629)	0.026 (0.711)	0.006 (0.936)	−0.007 (0.922)
Female participant at game simulation	0.040 (0.595)	0.031 (0.686)	0.032 (0.754)	0.018 (0.865)	0.032 (0.858)	0.008 (0.915)	0.029 (0.685)	0.020 (0.786)
International staff at game simulation	0.043 (0.645)	0.060 (0.533)	−0.046 (0.713)	−0.018 (0.893)	0.012 (0.811)	0.030 (0.738)	0.007 (0.936)	0.025 (0.780)
Maturity of NGO (year of foundation)	−0.004 (0.321)	−0.005 (0.304)	−0.007 (0.269)	−0.007 (0.248)	0.020 (0.283)	−0.005 (0.279)	−0.005 (0.222)	−0.005 (0.207)
Game leader 1	0.058 (0.436)	0.046 (0.547)	0.051 (0.615)	0.032 (0.759)	−0.004 (0.762)	0.014 (0.840)	0.040 (0.566)	0.028 (0.697)
Game leader 2	0.171 (0.064)*	0.183 (0.063)*	0.259 (0.049)*	0.278 (0.039)**	0.020 (0.877)	0.020 (0.823)	0.144 (0.11)	0.157 (0.091)*
R^2	0.265	0.28	0.342	0.362	0.343	0.348	0.342	0.362

Notes: (1) p–values between brackets (2)*** indicates significance at 1% level; ** indicates significance at the 5% level;* indicates significance at the 10% level. Multi-collinearity is not a problem as there is no significant correlation between various regressors (except for the Wade specification, where concentration and concentration are highly correlated, which could explain the lack of a concentration effect in the Wade model). The Breusch–Pagan/Cook–Weisberg tests for heteroskedasticity show that there is none. There is no significant autocorrelation in the residuals, as shown by the results of the Durbin Watson test between 1.9 and 2.4. Lastly, reverse causality and endogeneity are not problems as the dependent variable is measured after the independent variables and independent variables are theoretically exogenous. The robustness of results was checked by running regressions without including a constant and also by clustering the standard errors at the team level. The results were virtually the same.

The dummies for the different game leaders show the importance of game leaders. NGOs that were in a game supervised by game leader two were significantly more prone to cooperate in two of the three years. In three of the four Wade regressions, the game leader is the only significant variable that can explain the propensity to cooperate. Still, despite this, the concentration results remain significant in the Olson specification. This indicates that when controlling for 'the game-leader effect', concentration continues to have a negative effect on cooperation. The goodness of fit of the overall Olson model is about 34 per cent, ranging from 26 per cent in the second year to 34 per cent in rounds one and three.

Discussion and conclusion

Validity

How valid are the game simulation results? The concept of validity can be split into two parts: internal validity and external validity. Internal validity, roughly speaking, addresses the extent to which a simulation functions in the intended manner (Feinstein and Cannon 2002). Internal validity refers to the approximate validity with which a relationship between two variables can be inferred to be causal or that the absence of a relationship implies absence of cause. External validity asks whether this internal functioning corresponds to relevant phenomena outside the simulation. External validity refers to what extent it can be inferred that the presumed causal relationship can be generalized to and across alternate measures of cause and effect, and across different types of actors, settings, and times (Cook and Campbell, cited in Feinstein and Cannon 2002).

Internal validity was ensured by having various test games and incorporating comments into the game design. To tackle the issue of external validity, this research takes a hermeneutical perspective. Within a hermeneutical approach, data are considered relative to specific purposes and conventions that are set in context. Expert modellers and other stakeholders should be called on to make design decisions, bringing all their expertise to bear on the specifics of the situation. Thus, simulation models must be validated in much the same way as a judicial court system operates. Defendants are not proven guilty through the mere induction of empirical facts or relativistic presumptions. They are found guilty only when the prosecution has proven the case to a jury of peers beyond reasonable doubt (Feinstein and Cannon 2003).

Both experts and practitioners designed the game, which enhanced external validity. However, discussions with stakeholders and experts after the game simulation provided insight into some of the doubts they had about the external validity of the game. One of the game leaders put it as follows: 'To what extent does the game measure whether participants are just good at playing games instead of measuring whether they truly cooperate in real life?' Another game leader concurred, the results of the game simulation show that international staff-members cooperate more successfully than local staff in the game. Is this really true, or does it just reflect that the game was conceived by international staff and that the game designers and those international participants operate with similar mindsets?

These are valid queries that merit discussion.

The incentives that NGOs had in the game were based as much as possible on the incentives they would have faced in the real world. This implies incentives that encourage or discourage cooperation, and incentives that encourage or discourage strategic behaviour. When analysing the results, individual-level controls considered relevant by game leaders were included, such as the nationality of the participants. The inclusion of these control variables did not make the negative concentration effect insignificant. In line with the herme-neutical perspective, external validity is not only assessed in terms of whether stakeholders agree that the design resembles the real world, but also whether outcomes in the game bear a resemblance to real-life outcomes as perceived by other stakeholders. Therefore, this discussion continues by high-lighting some interesting convergences and divergences between the results of the game simulation and the survey results.

The survey consisted of 47 structured interviews with local NGOs in the Arusha region. This constituted a response rate of 67 per cent. The survey consisted of 42 questions on the background and activities of the local NGO, and focused on passive benefits arising from the concentration of NGOs and on the active behaviour of organizations to capitalize on them. The survey gave substantial insight on cooperation among NGOs and their concentration. All NGOs that were interviewed for the survey were invited to participate in the game simulation. Various parallels between the results of the game simulation and the survey can be drawn, although there are also some divergences. These will be used to highlight strengths and weaknesses of the game simulation as a tool for research, and propose some measures to mitigate potential weaknesses.

Various striking similarities between results of the two research methods are found. A first similarity is the type of cooperation among NGOs that occurs in the Arusha region of Tanzania. Aggregates from the survey show that level 1 cooperation (cooperation that only benefits the organization itself) is reasonably high (69 per cent), the second level of cooperation is slightly lower (57 per cent), but the third level is extremely low (9 per cent) (Laan 2007). Also, the network of NGOs in Arusha, ANGONET, focuses on cooperating on marketing and fundraising (level 1 cooperation) and not on quality control (level 2 cooperation) and coordination (level 3 coopera-tion). This corresponds to the results of the game simulation, which showed the highest propensity to cooperate (> 85 per cent) in round one (the fun-draising round). A second similarity exists with respect to cooperation in an area with a high level of concentration. The survey showed that organizations in Arusha city cooperated significantly fewer hours per week with other organizations than those that were based in other, less concentrated, parts of the Arusha region. A third similarity is that international staff, who cooperated more successfully in the game simulation, also cooperated more in real life, as measured by the number of hours Arusha-based international NGOs work with other NGOs, for instance.

Differences

Despite these similarities, a number of differences between the outcomes of the game simulation and the survey also become apparent. The results of the survey were more in line with Wade's prediction than with Olson's prediction. For instance, NGOs working in very remote districts and in the capital worked fewer hours per week together than NGOs that operate in semi-remote regions. Thus, the survey results indicate that cooperation rose with increasing concentration but decreased when concentration reached a stronger level. The game simulation results were more in line with the downward-sloping curve of cooperation on concentration, as Olson suggested. This is an important difference as it deals with the core of the research question this research is trying to answer.

It appears that various factors contribute to an overestimation of the extent of cooperation among isolated NGOs in the game simulation. In real life, information asymmetries and higher transaction costs hinder cooperation, especially for NGOs in more remote regions. For example, in the actual situation, some organizations face high negotiation costs due to the cost of transport. However, in the game simulation, NGOs are all sitting at the same table and have the same information. They are invited to do this by external actors and do not take this initiative themselves. The transport costs involved in participating in the game simulations were reimbursed by the researchers. In short, the artificial situation that is created when playing the game influences the willingness and ability to cooperate for NGOs that normally work outside the concentration. In future versions of the NGO GAME it might be interesting to explore more opportunities to incorporate transaction and transport costs into the game design.

There are also reasons to assume that the level of cooperation in the game is overestimated for NGOs that operate in areas with a high level of concentration. This is assumed because in the game simulation, the maximum number of participating NGOs was capped at six, while this is not the case in the real-life situation, where sometimes dozens of NGOs work on the same theme in the same region. This cap was inevitable because of game set-up. The theoretical framework predicts that with higher number of participants, cooperation is more difficult to materialize. Most likely, therefore, the game simulation overestimates the extent of cooperation among NGOs that operate in those areas characterized by high levels of concentration.

The shortcomings of the game simulation appear intrinsic to the method: it is impossible to replicate exactly the incentives structures that organizations face in real life. This, and the consequent strain this puts on making inferences on the basis of results of game simulations, has been described at length by Levitt and List (2007). Also in this game real life was not perfectly simulated. The transport costs and information asymmetries were almost inevitably lower in the game simulation than in real life. By further refining the set-up of games, these discrepancies could be further reduced, but never totally eliminated. Levitt and List emphasize consequently of embedding experimental research findings in a sound theoretical framework, something that was done in this chapter.

In the game simulation, a number of examples of strategic behaviour were recorded. Some of the players went to great lengths to secure funding for their own organization, including promising to work in other themes than those in which they had actually any experience of interest in, and reneging on those promises once the funding was confirmed. Such manifest strategic behaviour was not recorded in the survey. How can this be explained? Are the results of the game simulation biased, or those of the survey, or both? It is believed that game simulation results are more reliable with respect to strategic behaviour and suffer less from a social desirability bias. The control questions in the survey showed that in a number of cases, NGOs had replied in a socially desirable and donor-pleasing way. For instance, when organizations were asked whether the presence of other NGOs stimulated innovation, nearly all replied positively. When organizations were consequently asked to provide a specific example, this number dropped significantly. Participants in the game simulation clearly experienced less need to display socially desirable behaviour than in the survey. When NGOs were confronted with this type of strategic behaviour in the debriefing, they commented that 'it was just a game'. Socially desirable behaviour was not restricted to the survey; in the game simulation, too, this was probably also to a certain extent present. After all, the game leaders were, in the eyes of the players, arguably potential donors, which created an incentive for them to show that they were actually good at cooperating. As strategic behaviour was more prevalent in the game simulation than the survey, it appears reasonable to assume that levels of socially desirable behaviour were lower in the game simulation than in the survey.

Interestingly, during the debriefing the participants stressed the value of the game simulation as a learning method. Participants stated that the game simulation enabled them to cooperate better in the future. Thus, game simulation appears to have a clear advantage in action-research, since it facilitates learning for participants as demonstrated succinctly by for instance Starkey and Blake (2001) and Shellman and Turan (2003) with respect to gaming and simulation in international relations. How effective it was in this respect falls outside the scope of this research.

Conclusion

The aim of this chapter was twofold: to create insight in the relationship between the concentration of NGOs and cooperation among them and into game simulation as a research tool.

The critical discussion on game simulations presented in this chapter revealed certain strengths and weaknesses of the game simulation as a research method. The reduced socially desirable behaviour on the part of the participants in a game simulation as opposed to the survey was considered a strength. Furthermore, participants of the game simulation claimed that the game simulation had contributed to organizational learning, while this was not the case for the survey. Conversely, the inherent artificial nature of game simulations, which involves bringing people together and excluding other people, influences research results. Thus, just like other social science research methods, game simulation has its flaws and biases, too. This chapter suggests, therefore, that game simulations could become an interesting additional device in the toolbox of social scientists. By combining various methods – triangulation – the risk of bias decreases. That is exactly the approach of this chapter; by combining two research methods it attempts to be able to draw firmer conclusions.

This chapter concludes by answering the second research question: does the concentration of NGOs reduce cooperation among them? The findings of the NGO GAME and the survey make it clear that high levels of concentration tend to reduce cooperation. Fundraising is the only domain in which local NGOs continue to cooperate when high numbers of them are operating on the same theme and in the same location. The findings suggest that local NGOs are only willing to cooperate when it benefits their own organization, and cease to do so when those benefits are not guaranteed. This is in line with Olson's theory of collective action and consistent with the predictions of social psychologists. The survey and game simulation show different results with respect to NGOs that operate in remote regions and on less popular themes. Whereas in the game simulation, cooperation between these organizations flourished, the survey results indicate that cooperation is highest in areas with a medium level of concentration. Despite this particular divergence, both research methods suggest that a strong concentration of NGOs has a negative influence on cooperation among them. Taking this implication with regards to concentration into consideration, it is now time to turn to the academic and policy implications of the ensemble of the research findings.

8   Implications of the research findings

The previous chapters have mapped the geographic choices of international NGOs and explained why those choices are made the way they are. This chapter assesses the potential academic and policy implications of these findings. It also discusses to what extent the determinants of cross-national geographic choices of international NGOs identified in this research can explain some of their other geographic choices. This concluding chapter is more evaluative than scientific and ought to be read as such.

This research focused on five potential determinants of the geographic choices of international NGOs: poverty and governance levels in recipient countries, back-donor preferences, concentration and NGO-specific missions. Based on the results of Probit regression, it has been found that, in 73 per cent of the cases, the five determinants combined correctly predict whether an international NGO will be active in a recipient country or not. This suggests that they cannot account for all geographic choices of NGOs, but can certainly help to explain the majority of them. The Introduction and Chapter 2 referred to some other factors that could have an impact, such as the local security situation and the strength of the local civil society, but these were not analysed systematically in this research.

This chapter discusses the implications of these research findings. It focuses on four of the five potential determinants of geographic choices; findings on the fifth determinant, the NGO-specific mission, will not be discussed in depth since they were unsurprising and have few practical implications. There is one implication, however, that merits attention. The research found that it cannot be assumed that international NGOs, if given the choice, will allocate their resources equally among poor nations. Unlike governments, non-profit organizations do not have to provide transparent justifications for their selection of target groups and hence can exercise much more discretion in selecting target groups based on certain, for instance geographic, characteristics (Lipsky and Smith 1990). This has an impact on the equity of the distribution of international NGO aid. The research found, for example, that international NGOs with a Christian background invested significantly more in countries where the majority of the population is Christian and that organizations were much more engaged in countries that are former colonies of their home country. It can thus not be assumed that international NGOs automatically will be equitably spread among poor countries, as the relatively limited presence of international NGOs in the Middle East and Francophone Africa exemplifies.

Poverty

Main findings on poverty

Chapter 2 showed, by means of a cross-sectional statistical analysis, that the level of expenditure of international NGOs in a particular country is negatively influenced by the country's level of economic development, as measured by GDP per capita. A country's level of human development, which encapsulates the social dimensions of poverty and is measured by the Human Development Index, is a significant determinant of expenditure levels. A country's relative level of poverty, as measured by the Gini-coefficient, does not influence the geographic choices of international NGOs.

Using a panel analysis of Dutch NGOs, Chapter 3 showed that changes in poverty levels do not affect country allocations. The finding that only two of the top ten recipients of Dutch NGOs are classified as Least Developed Countries, according to the standards set by the Development Assistance Committee of the Organisation for Economic Co-operation and Development, suggests that they are insensitive to poverty levels when making country choices.

Throughout this book, drivers of the difference in poor-country targeting were identified, scrutinized and occasionally dismissed. The research showed that many academics and NGOs claim that increased 'marketization' of international NGO aid limits their opportunities to become involved in the most difficult countries. However, the empirical analysis failed to find statistical support for this. In fact, the opposite appears to be true. The international NGOs that operate in the most protected environment are actually least active in the poorest countries. One explanation is that international NGOs are path-dependent: once they become active in a country they tend to stay active, even if the country becomes significantly richer. The research findings suggest this path dependency is stronger in less 'marketized' environments (e.g. Germany and The Netherlands) than in more competitive ones. Back-donor preferences were also found to influence the pro-poor targeting of international NGOs. It appears that the stronger the pro-poor focus of the back donor, the more likely it is that the international NGOs support the poorest countries.

Chapter 3 analysed how one major Dutch NGO, Oxfam Novib, strengthened its pro-poor focus. It demonstrated that this shift was mainly driven by two factors: the commitment of organization's senior management and exogenous shocks, such as grant reductions.

Discussion of main findings on poverty

Does it matter that international NGOs do not focus on the most poverty-stricken countries? International NGOs are divided on the issue. Some argue that they focus on the poor and that the poor are entitled to equal financial support from international NGOs, regardless of where they live.[1] Others argue that for ethical reasons, relatively more NGO aid should be targeted towards the poorest countries. In line with this latter view, it will be argued here, that it would be ill-advised, from a financial point of view, to support the poor in middle-income countries to the same extent as the poor in least developed countries. This claim is based on premises on the following factors: (1) costs of alleviating poverty; (2) access to other forms of finance; (3) type of support.

The costs of alleviating poverty are higher in the poorest countries. Put differently, it is more expensive for international NGOs to support them. First, their overhead costs are higher because travel expenses to and within the poorest countries are higher (Chapter 4). Second, in the poorest countries, it is not enough to target just the health care system, or to improve only access to justice. All these problems merit attention (United Nations Development Programme 2003) Therefore, the necessitated scope of NGO interventions is wider, and these are, as a consequence, more expensive. Third, the chance that poverty reduction results will be sustained is lower in the poorest countries, since many of them are caught up in a conflict or other trap (Cordaid 2005; Collier 2007). For these three reasons, it is more expensive for international NGOs to support the poorest countries (the consequent trade-off between equity and efficiency will be discussed later in this chapter in the section 'Discussion on main findings on concentration').

Local NGOs in the least-developed countries are dependent on international NGOs for funding and are less able to tap local funds than their peers in middle-income countries (Bailey 1999). In middle-income countries, local NGOs can, for example, solicit funds from the government, which may able to respond to such a request because it has a sufficiently large tax base. Local NGOs can also tap private funds from the elite or the middle class or they can enter into partnerships with private companies. Such options are not available in the poorest countries.

The poorest countries require different types of support than middle-income countries. The types of support that are generally provided by international NGOs tend to fall in three categories: 1) direct poverty alleviation; 2) civil society building; 3) lobby and advocacy.[2] The poorest countries are most likely to benefit relatively more from service delivery support. There are, after all, fewer opportunities for effectively lobbying a country's government, if that government is so ill-resourced that it is unable, even with the best will in the world, to carry out its most basic functions. By contrast, in middle-income countries, poverty is largely a distributional problem. This calls for a political solution, which is more likely to be achieved through lobby and advocacy (Bailey 1999). The challenge is to include marginalized groups in the social system, not to build a new system. Since this is less capital intensive than direct service delivery, it makes sense for international NGOs to channel more aid to the poorest countries.

For the three reasons outlined above, international NGOs could allocate a disproportionate share of their budgets to the poorest countries, while taking purchasing power parities into consideration. However, as the introduction and subsequent chapters have shown, this is currently not the case. Poor people in the middle-income countries received more aid (purchasing power corrected) than poor people in the poorest countries.

Policy and academic implications of main findings on poverty

Certain back donors, particularly the Dutch and the German, could do more to ensure that the international NGOs they fund better target the poorest countries. Back donors in Norway and Ireland set the example for this. For example, NORAD, the implementing agency of the Norwegian government, invested substantial effort in influencing the funding decisions of the organizations it supports:

> Through having discussions with NGOs we convinced them that they should spend at least 50 per cent in the least developed countries. It has taken us years, but our NGOs— because of our active policy towards them—have reached this percentage.
>
> (Interview with the head of the Civil Society Unit on 11 September 2006)

In terms of academic implications, the research brought to light that there is a quantitative void in the research on international NGOs. The most prolific authors on the topic, such as Edwards, Fowler and Howell, base their findings only on qualitative data and refrain from subjecting their ideas to statistical scrutiny. Although their work and other similar work provided the material on which the hypothesis of this research was based, anecdotal evidence (such as Tendler 1982) has long indicated that such qualitative findings may not be valid and that the poverty focus of NGOs needed to be put in perspective. However, the idea that NGOs are 'closer to the poor' never lost traction (Fowler and Biekart 1996; Steering Group 2002). This study provides empirical evidence across countries, which demonstrates that the assumption that international NGOs automatically target the poorest countries needs to be reconsidered.

The findings and the discussion also suggest that the quantitative work that was conducted for this research could be expanded to test other assumptions, for example that the portfolio of international NGOs differs between middle-income countries and the poorest countries and whether NGOs with field offices focus more on the poorest countries. Such assumptions are put forward in the literature (e.g. Bailey 1999), but have not been tested empirically.

Governance

Main findings on governance

The empirical evidence in Chapters 2 and 3 indicated that international NGOs are not gearing their efforts towards the poorly governed countries. To the contrary, there are signs that international NGOs are more active in more democratic countries. The assumed distribution of labour between international NGOs on one hand and official donors on the other hand, in which the former focus more on the poorly governed countries and the latter more on the well-governed countries, is not taking shape.

Discussion of main findings on governance

Whether the lack of attention from international NGOs for countries with bad governance should be a cause for concern depends on whether such aid is viewed as a substitute or as a complement to official aid. This section presents a substitute/complement analysis between international NGO aid and bilateral aid to explore this issue (following Koch 2007a).

In economic terms, a good is considered a substitute for another good insofar as the two can replace each other in at least some of their possible uses. The demand for the two goods is linked because consumers can decide to substitute one good for the other when it is advantageous to do so. Thus, an increase in the price for a certain product (e.g. butter) will result in an increase in demand for its substitute (e.g. margarine), while a drop in price will have the inverse effect (more demand for butter, less demand for margarine). Here 'demand' refers to the preferences of government aid agencies in OECD countries for different aid-distribution channels. Theoretically, they have two choices: government-to-government (bilateral) or through international NGOs. If international NGO aid is a substitute for bilateral aid, then 'demand' for it will rise if the 'price' or cost of using the government-to-government channel increases, and vice versa.

The World Bank publication *Assessing Aid* (1998) was the first to suggest that bilateral aid should go only to countries that already enjoy good governance. Based on statistical research, Levin and Dollar (2004) conclude that this policy selectivity began to take shape in the 1990s, when a clear relationship emerged between the level of bilateral aid and the quality of governance in recipient countries. This selectivity is based on the claim of aid agencies and academics that international NGOs have a comparative advantage in countries with low levels of democratic governance and in stimulating democratic governance. In economic terms, this means that the relative 'price' of bilateral aid is high in countries with poor democratic governance because the price–quality ratio of such aid is low, e.g. monitoring costs are high and general budget support is not possible, and demand for international NGO aid will therefore be stronger in such countries. Conversely, in countries with high levels of democratic governance, the 'price' of bilateral aid is low (e.g. DFID 2006b) and hence the 'demand' for international NGO aid weak.

A complement good is the opposite of a substitute: if demand for a good increases then the demand for its complement increases as well (e.g. bikes and bike-locks). If international NGO aid is a complement to bilateral aid, then it follows that the higher the level of government-to-government aid to a particular country, the higher the level of international NGO aid to that country will be.

Viewing international NGO aid as a complement to bilateral aid casts doubt on two of the main tenets of the substitute theory, namely (i) that bilateral aid is more effective in countries with good governance than in countries with bad governance and (ii) that international NGO aid can be effective in countries with poor governance. The complement view further implies that the work of bilateral agencies and international NGOs in a country is mutually reinforcing; official donors are effective at the macro-level, international NGOs are effective at the micro-level and so together they can adequately bridge the micro–macro gap in a country (Netherlands Ministry of Foreign Affairs 2006). According to the complement theory, international NGOs do have comparative advantages, for instance in supporting civil society and testing innovative development solutions, but these are country-neutral and do not depend on whether a country is well or badly governed.

Supporters of the complement theory claim that bilateral aid is not necessarily more effective in countries with better governance. They argue that it depends on the type of bilateral aid provided. General budget support, for example, will only be effective in countries with good governance, whereas sectoral support and/or project support can be provided to countries with weak governance, where only certain ministries are functioning properly. Those favouring the complement theory also increasingly challenge the assumption that good governance is a prerequisite for development (e.g. Khan and Jomo 2000).[3] They argue that countries with poor governance that are falling behind in the battle against poverty should not be abandoned by bilateral donors (Netherlands Ministry of Foreign Affairs 2007).

The proponents of the complement view reject the claim that international NGOs can be effective in countries with poor governance. First, if international NGOs were to receive significant amounts of financing and local governments were not, then unaccountable parallel structures would emerge that would lead to an unbalanced society (DFID 2006a). Second, international NGOs point out that in countries with poor governance they have difficulties finding good partners. This is consistent with theories on state formation and civil society, which argue that badly governed countries or those with a weak state often have an underdeveloped civil society (Chabal and Daloz 1999). They argue that the conceptualization of the countervailing power of civil society and its disciplining effects on states are theoretically unsound. One of these theories, the state-in-society approach, postulates for example that states often reflect the struggles within a society at large and that poorly performing states often coincide with weak civil societies (Migdal 2001). This approach argues that it may seem appealing to support local NGOs as a countervailing power vis-à-vis states, but that in reality civil society may be to weak to play this role (Kalb 2006). Financing weak local organizations from abroad can even be counterproductive, as the centre of accountability gravitates towards external donors and away from their constituency (Heaton Shrestha 2008; Pelkmans 2005; Biekart 1999).

The debate on whether international NGOs should focus more on countries with poor governance continues. The following section proposes a way out of the impasse.

Policy and research implications of main findings on governance

It could be useful to approach the question of whether international NGOs should focus more on countries with poor governance through the lens of the three intervention strategies that they can use: 1) direct poverty alleviation; 2) civil society building; 3) lobby and advocacy. This shows that, in poorly governed states, international NGOs have a comparative advantage in the area of 'direct poverty alleviation' but not in the other two areas. When supporting poverty alleviation, international NGOs can work with local organizations or in their absence through the subsidiaries of international NGOs. They can thereby bypass the state. However, international NGOs should ensure that such parallel structures do not weaken the role of the state.

While there is thus a case to be made for a substitute approach considering the 'direct poverty alleviation' intervention strategy, this case is absent with respect to 'civil society building' and 'lobby and advocacy'. The need for international NGOs in these latter two domains is not contingent on whether donors are also active in those countries, and does not depend on the levels of governance in a country.[4] In all instances, the role played by international NGOs, with their specific networks and bottom-up approaches, is unique and cannot easily be taken over by other actors.

Is there any information on the distribution of NGO aid over the various intervention strategies in various types of recipient countries? The evidence presented in among others the introduction, which showed that the ratio of international to official aid remained stable across different governance levels in recipient countries, indicates that the two are across the board behaving as complements. Unfortunately, a country breakdown of international NGO expenditure by intervention strategy is lacking. This makes it difficult to determine whether international NGO support to 'service delivery' is a substitute to bilateral aid or not. Yet, the absolute majority of international NGO aid goes to service delivery.[5] Therefore, if international NGO aid and bilateral aid were indeed substitutes, this should have shown up in the data, which was clearly not the case. All in all, this section has indicated that while the presence of international NGOs and bilateral donors is important in all different policy environments, it would be recomended that direct service delivery activities of international NGOs should focus relatively more on the poorly governed states. This is currently not happening and this reasearch suggests that this deserves more attention in policy discussion.

The academic implications of the findings with respect to governance mirror those in the section above headed 'Policy and academic implications of main findings on poverty'. The findings indicate that the 'conventional wisdoms' that guide the policies of the largest donors of international NGOs, do not hold when empirically tested. Mosse (2005) argues that the gap between policy and practice in development aid does not stem from certain implementation difficulties, but that policy primarily functions to mobilize and maintain political support; that is, to legitimize rather than to orientate practice. He claims that development interventions are not driven by policy but by the exigencies of organizations and the need to maintain relationships. Mosse has shown that ethnographies of aid can be insightful in bringing to light how these gaps emerge; this research has indicated that also quantitative studies can be useful in challenging the primacy of policy. This highlights the potential importance of investing more in quantitative studies dealing with international NGOs. One potential avenue for further research is to test whether one of the assumptions that exist these days – namely that international NGOs are relatively less engaged in service delivery in well-governed states than in poorly governed states – will be proven correct when analszed statistically (e.g. Capacitate 2007; DFID 2006b).

Back-donor preferences

Main findings on back-donor preferences

Chapters 2, 3 and 6 showed that the autonomy of international NGOs is by no means a given. Chapter 2 demonstrated that the allocations of international NGOs are driven by the allocations of their back donors. Chapter 3 used case studies of Dutch NGOs to show how this works. Chapter 3 found that, while the Dutch government did not exercise direct influence over country choices of Dutch NGOs, various other informal mechanisms, such as general policy message or promises of financial opportunities, did push them in certain directions. Since Dutch NGOs depend for 85 per cent of their funds on the Ministry of Foreign Affairs, it is not surprising that they heeded these policy messages.

Chapter 6 showed a correlation between the extent to which international NGOs follow the country preferences of their back donors and what percentage of their budget is provided by back donors. Country allocation processes were found to be quite heterogeneous. The American government earmarks funds for certain countries and thus directly influences the country allocations of the organizations it supports. This is not the case for international NGOs from other countries. For example, the governments of The Netherlands and Germany give block grants to the largest organizations which, in theory, reduces their influence on country allocations. The system in Norway lies somewhere in between; according to Norwegian organizations, the government does not influence their country allocations directly, but it does impact them indirectly through discussions. Paradoxically, although the American government is clearly the most prescriptive, American NGOs are the least affected by back-donor preferences because they are the least financially independent of the government.

Discussion of the main findings on back-donor preferences

Should international NGOs be given more freedom to allocate their resources? In policy dialogues with their back donors, international NGOs consistently aim to maintain their autonomy and to be seen as independent 'development actors in their own right' (e.g. Better Aid 2007; Concord 2008). They also claim that reporting requirements to back donors hamper their effectiveness rather than increase their transparency and consistently demand leaner reporting requirements (e.g. Opheusden 2007). This claim is supported by many academics, who claim that these requirements prevent organizations from becoming demand-led and poverty-driven (e.g. Porter 2000; Wallace 2000; Townsend et al. 2002). Furthermore, political preferences of official donors are often capricious. The high levels of funding that have suddenly become available as of late for civil society work in Iraq exemplify this (Pratt et al. 2006).

However, the 'Multiple Layered Principle Agent' framework developed in Chapter 6 actually warns against the optimistic assumption of altruism on the part of international NGOs. This framework portrays international NGOs as intermediary agencies that engage in elaborate bargaining processes with their back donors, whereby back donors attempt to gain as much symbolic capital (evidence of success and success stories) as they can for the economic capital (resources) they deliver, and international NGOs attempt to do the opposite. For the more symbolic capital they promise to deliver, the less likely they are to meet their obligations. This would have negative repercussions on their track record with their back donor and increase the chance that the donor will stop or reduce funding in the future. With more flexible contracts and relaxed reporting requirements, international NGOs can accumulate symbolic capital without starting to work more efficiently or effectively. The persistent calls from international NGOs for looser reporting requirements and more flexible grants thus needs to be viewed with healthy scepticism since it is international NGOs themselves who stand to gain from a potentially more favourable symbolic-to-economic capital exchange rate.

It is not a given that the increased freedom for international NGO managers to make country choices will automatically lead to increased poverty performance of NGO aid. First, as shown in this research international

NGOs have specific missions, which translate themselves in preferences for specific types of countries. These preferences, which are not necessarily pro-poor, engrain themselves within organizations. The subsequent organizational inertia is likely to prevent automatic increased autonomy to lead to more pro-poor and demand-led choices. Second, power imbalances between international NGOs and their Southern partners are too large to assume that the geographic distribution would automatically be more tilted towards where the demand is greatest if back donors reduce their interference in the country choices of international NGOs. The literature on the relationship between Northern and Southern NGOs is clear on the extent to which the former dominate the latter's agendas (e.g. Townsend *et al.* 2002; Wallace 2000). This imbalance can be illustrated by an analysis of the governing bodies of international NGOs, such as their boards. An analysis of such bodies for a representative sample of 55 of the largest international NGOs worldwide shows that they have a total of 693 members, of whom a mere 42 – 6 per cent – come from developing countries (Koch 2008b). The imbalance also surfaces when contrasting the contracts that international NGOs sign with their back donors with those they sign with local NGOs. One study of Dutch co-financing agencies, for instance, showed that while Dutch NGOs often receive core grants (institutional subsidies, which organizations can spend on overheads and programmes), they do not give core grants to their partners (CIDIN 2006). Also, while the contracts of international NGOs with their back donors are often for about four years, they sign shorter contracts with their Southern partners. The unwillingness of international NGOs to finance the organizational development of local NGOs is well documented (Bornstein 2003; Cooley and Ron 2002; Low and Davenport 2002). Often, international NGOs appear more interested in executing their own projects than in strengthening the capacity of Southern organizations (CIDIN 2006). A broken feedback-loop has been shown to exist in international aid (Martens *et al.* 2002). Hence, even if the support international NGOs receive from their back donors would cease to be geographically tied, it is not clear whether this would automatically lead to country choices that are more demand-led and poverty-oriented.

Policy and research implications of main findings on back-donor preferences

There is evidence that the geo-strategic considerations continue to influence aid allocations of official aid agencies and even more so since 2001, when aid became seen as an instrument for combating terrorism (Ritzen 2005). For instance, French and American official aid is known to be highly influenced by political considerations. Consequently, the official aid that American and French NGOs receive is mostly tied to specific countries, and therefore relatively supply-driven. Even though, as argued in the previous chapter, more autonomy for international NGOs does not automatically lead to more need-led behaviour, it can be assumed that in these particular cases of supply-driven aid, more discretion for international NGOs could translate into more demand-led behaviour.

However, optimism regarding the pay-offs to this approach ought not to be overestimated, as this research has also shown that NGOs tend to follow the behaviour of their back donors, even if they are not legally obliged to do so. Besides, because of the natural tendency of NGOs to mimic the behaviour of their major donor, bilateral donors tend to ensure that NGOs become active in those countries where they are active themselves. Pratt *et al.* (2006) demonstrate this by pointing out the number of attempts on the part of official agencies to align NGO support with their own priorities in terms of country funding. However, since those donors that are most interested in politics and least interested in poverty, are also the most reluctant to actually provide their NGOs with any extra room for manoeuvre, greater financial independence from those back donors appears crucial. This is in line with the advice of many authors who have studied international NGOs (e.g. Klees 1998; Edwards and Hulme 1996).

What are the academic repercussions of the findings outlined above? The findings suggest that those who view international NGOs as implementers or subcontractors, of the state have a case in point (e.g. Kalb 2005; Chandhoke 2002; Tvedt 1998). Back donors seek to influence the choices of NGOs in a myriad of ways, and in numerous instances they are successful. However, it would be going too far to view international NGOs exclusively through this lens. Howell and Pearce (2001) classify NGOs as part of civil society, and argue that civil-society organizations are in a constant process of contesting the space they can occupy. This classification comes closest to the findings of this research. For instance, international NGOs also have their own resources; they are often involved in struggles with their donors to maintain their freedom of choice, and regularly succeed in this respect. This research has aimed to show that international NGOs are neither necessarily need-driven organizations, nor merely implementing agencies in an increasingly neo-liberal world. Organizations were found to have the possibility of carving out some autonomous space from which to operate, but often choose not to do so, especially when they are financially dependent on back donors (Michael 2004). Empirical research that analyses the varying degrees to which NGOs succeed in creating this autonomous space remains much needed. This research suggests that 'financial dependence rates' could be an interesting angle from which to examine this, as those came to the fore in this research as relevant determinants of the behaviour of international NGOs.

Concentration

Main findings on concentration

Chapter 2 indicated that international NGOs are more likely to become active in and allocate more aid to a country in which other international

NGOs are already active. Consequently, the numbers of international NGOs active in recipient countries differ widely. In some countries, such as Ethiopia, five of World Vision's organizations, seven of Oxfam's, six of Care's and 12 of Save the Children's are active, the latter mostly with their own offices. Even in smaller countries such as Guatemala, Sri Lanka and Zimbabwe, more than 40 of the 61 largest international NGOs have a presence. This is in stark contrast with Gabon, Guinea, Moldova or Uzbekistan, where less than ten international NGOs operate. Chapter 3 demonstrated that 'families' of international organizations (e.g. the Oxfam alliance or the Protestant alliance, Aprodev) regular map which organization is active where, but do not use joint planning to ensure a more rational and equitable division of labour.

Chapter 3 suggested that geographic choices are historically determined and that significant changes are piecemeal. Exogenous shocks, such as significant reductions in back-donor grants, are the main cause of change. Chapter 4 confirmed those findings and demonstrated that the geographic choices of NGOs are self-reinforcing processes. Past involvement of international NGOs increases the absorption capacity of local NGOs, which stimulates a further influx of international agencies. Chapter 5 corroborated the finding that the geographic choices of international NGOs are self-reinforcing processes. International NGOs without a presence in the Central African Republic, hold more negative views about opportunities for involvement in the country than those already active there. This divergence between the views of insiders and outsiders does not exist for Tanzania. The, potentially disproportionate, negative image of the Central African Republic discourages international NGOs from getting involved. The chapter also found that only 40 per cent of the international NGOs have formal country selection and allocation systems in place, allowing for the possibility that inadequate country perceptions influence geographic decisions. These findings combined suggest that the unequal distribution of international NGO aid is likely to persist in the future.

Discussion on main findings on concentration

What degree of concentration of international NGOs is desirable? Within the aid allocation literature there are broadly speaking two schools of thought on this: a utilitarian and an equal opportunity view (Llavador and Roemer 2001; Cogneau and Naudet 2004). The utilitarian view stipulates that aid is distributed so as to maximize the sum of utilities. It postulates that the success that can be achieved in terms of poverty reduction, and not the needs observed, should drive allocation. Consequently, for utilitarians, projections of optimal aid allocations would show a high level of concentration since results are easier to obtain in countries where many other international NGOs are involved. As a result, many countries do not receive any aid (cf. Collier and Dollar 2002). Rawls (1973) is one of the most influential critics of utilitarianism. He challenged the utilitarian principle by focusing on the prospects of the worst-off person rather than on overall social welfare. Rawls argues that inequality resulting from differences in natural advantages and social circumstances are unjust.

An equal opportunity approach to aid allocation follows Rawls' principles. It seeks to equalise aid across types of country, compensating for structural factors. If an equal opportunity approach guides the allocation of international NGOs, a dominance of need based criteria can be expected (cf. Cogneau and Naudet 2004). For people in every country have an equal right to assistance, no matter how difficult the environment, no matter how impoverished the population, no matter how limited the opportunities. For proponents of the equal opportunity approach, optimal aid allocation projections would not show any concentration at all.

This research does not support either of these views and argues for a middle-of the road approach that balances equity and efficiency considerations (for a more elaborate discussion on this, please consult Koch 2006). According to this approach, one can speak of over-concentration if clear opportunities in the neediest countries are foregone and if levels of concentration are so high that signs of decreasing marginal returns are emerging. Since the distribution of international NGO aid shows both, as argued below, a shift to a less concentrated form of international NGO aid seems warranted, even though this might initially reduce the efficiency of their support.

For this research, potential opportunities for the involvement of international NGOs in one of the poorest countries, the Central African Republic, were assessed during a four-month period of field research which resulted in the research report '*Où sont les ONG internationales de développement en République Centrafricaine?* [Where are the International Development NGOs in the Central African Republic?]' (Koolwijk and Koch 2007).[6] The elements researched were the organizational and institutional capacity of local civil society organizations, as well as their current dependence on international agencies. These elements were selected because they are normally indicative of the strength of a civil society (e.g. Anheier 2004; Heinrich 2005). Since the strength of the civil society and in particular of Southern partners is considered a vital determinant of the involvement of international NGOs in a country, it is important to assess those factors to determine the potential for increased international NGO support.

The findings of the research indicate that there are clear possibilities for an expansion of international NGO involvement in the Central African Republic. Despite a fairly strong dependence on international donors, there are large numbers of semi-formal small-scale organizations in the Central African Republic that receive no support, even though they are well embedded in society. However, given their limited human resources and their semi-formal nature, such organizations would require labour-intensive support that would combine financial support with capacity development. The statements of certain NGOs that in certain countries 'civil societies need to be built up from scratch (e.g. Somalia, Sudan, Afghanistan, Angola)' (Borren 2007, p. 2) appears to say more about the lens through which international NGOs view local civil societies than about the existence of civil societies in these countries. Informal structures and solidarity groups exist in the poorest and most vulnerable countries in the world, as the 'Civil Society Index' and academic case studies show (e.g. Civicus 2005 and 2006; Trefon 2004; Kassis 2001). Such organizations may not have formalized accounting procedures and may not be able to handle large sums of money, yet they could benefit from increased labour intensive involvement of international NGOs.

The first signs of decreasing marginal returns, which is one of the parameters of over-concentration, are showing. Chapter 7 indicated that in the Arusha region, the high-density area where field research was conducted for this research, cooperation declined with rising levels of concentration. Organizations working in the same region and on the same theme cooperated less with each other than organizations that were operating in different regions or on different themes. Examples of excess supply of international NGO aid can be found in both emergency aid and regular aid situations (Laan 2007; Tsunami Evaluation Coalition 2006). Consequences of excess supply include increased corruption, soaring levels of dependence on foreign donors and the duplication of aid efforts.[7] These consequences have been observed in India (Kudva 2005), Sri Lanka (Harris 2005) and the Balkans (Karajkov 2007).

Policy and research implications of main findings on concentration

According to the 'middle of the road option' outlined above, which seeks to balance equity and efficiency considerations, international NGO aid is seemingly suffering from over-concentration.[8] This is undesirable and hence greater spatial dispersion of international NGO aid should be promoted. As this research indicates, this will not happen by itself.[9] Therefore, umbrella organizations of local NGOs, recipient country governments, international NGOs and their back donors should all take action into counter this trend.

Chapter 5 on country images illustrated that the country images that outsiders have do not correspond to the views of insiders. Local umbrella organizations and governments in low-density areas could play a role in marketing their local civil society actors better.[10] International NGOs could do much more with respect to coordinating their interventions: the efforts of the 'families' of international NGOs in these areas need to be strengthened. There is an urgent need for an up-to-date and easily accessible database on the programmes and expenditure of international NGOs by country and by theme.

Throughout this research, the pivotal role of back donors has been underlined. It is therefore important to sketch their potential role in stimulating the dispersion of international NGOs. International NGOs copy the country choices of their back donors. If official donors would show a more equitable distribution of aid, international NGOs would follow suit. If they focus more on forgotten countries, such as the Central African Republic, Côte d'Ivoire, Togo, Yemen and Moldova, so will international NGOs. There are, however, serious doubts whether official agencies are willing to spend their resources in such difficult environments. It is noteworthy that the European Commission has stepped up its efforts to address this collective action problem. According to the European Commission, official donors contribute to an increasing gap between the 'donor darlings' and 'donor orphans' (Commission of the European Communities 2007). The Council of the European Union adopted an EU Code of Conduct on Division of Labour in Development Policy in 2007. The sixth guiding principle is titled 'Address the "orphans" ' and stipulates that 'EU donors will strive to dedicate part of their aid budget to "underfunded" countries' (Council of the European Union 2007, p. 11). The efforts of the EU to coordinate the bilateral aid of its member countries and to address the problem of donor orphans will probably also impact international NGOs, if put into practice.

It would be risky, however, to rely too heavily on such changes in the fundamentals of the aid distribution architecture. Targeted solutions to address the inequality are possible and needed. The theoretical framework in Chapter 4 used an evolutionary economic geography approach to identify three factors that influence concentration: increasing returns to scale, labour mobility and path dependence. The chapter showed that there is effectively a coordination problem among international NGOs. Any policy suggestions to address concentration will need to look at coordination as well.

Scholars refer to this coordination problem also as a first-mover problem (Lieberman and Montgomery 1988). Organizations are not willing or able to invest the time and money to be the first to move into a region. Public agencies that succeed in addressing this first-mover problem do so by acting as a 'launching customer', a 'socializer of risk', and/or a 'credit generator' (Chang 2002; Evans 1995). Since coordination appears to be a problem for international NGOs, back donors could help address the first-mover problem with targeted interventions, such as political risk-insurance instruments and (subsidized) credit for capacity-development activities in neglected regions. Back donors could also provide a premium to organizations that can demonstrate that they coordinate their geographic choices with their peers. It is crucial that back donors provide incentives that mitigate the disadvantages for first-movers. For instance, donors now work often with fixed overhead percentages for international NGOs, regardless of the countries in which they are active. This reduces their involvement in difficult environments, as shown in Chapters 4 and 5. Lastly, promoting an environment that encourages risk-taking and openness could reduce another concentration-inducing factor: the blame-sharing effect (explained in Chapter 2). Instead of withholding finances from specific international NGOs because their projects were unsuccessful, donors could assess whether the organizations concerned had conducted a proper risk analysis and had taken precautionary measures and remedial action – steps that government agencies should applaud rather than punish. If back donors stimulate risk-taking behaviour, international NGOs will be more likely to venture into uncovered territory. Multilateral donors, who are increasingly funding international NGOs, are in a good position to solve this collective action problem.[11] Co-financing schemes of for instance the European Commission could focus their aid towards the 'donor orphans'.

The academic relevance of the findings and analysis regarding 'concentration' is that they have shown that analyses of the geographic choices of non-profit organizations could benefit from moving beyond a supply-and-demand framework. The location choices of non-profit agencies cannot be explained solely by considering 'needs' and 'funds'. Past geographic choices and those of their peers have a bearing upon the current geographic choices of international NGOs. Such factors therefore deserve to be integrated into theoretical and analytical frameworks on the geography of non-profit organizations. This research has done so by proposing an evolutionary economic geography approach to non-profit agencies. Its results indicate that this contributes to an enhanced understanding of the geographic choices of international NGOs.

This research has also attempted to show that the academic discipline of 'development studies' could benefit from taking better stock of developments in other academic disciplines. The theoretical basis for Chapter 4 on economic geography and Chapter 5 on country images came from the literature on business administration. This provided additional insight into the topic at hand. Many of the behavioural decisions of non-profit organizations could be analysed through the same lens as is used to understand their for-profit counterparts (e.g. Ruben 2007). This could lead to broader insights than would otherwise be the case.

Generality of findings for other geographic choices

A key question that remains is whether and to what extent the determinants of country choices of international NGOs also apply to other decisions. It was therefore decided to check the research findings against sub-national geographic choices and non-financial geographic choices of NGOs (e.g. network formation among international and local NGOs).[12] International NGOs consistently mentioned the importance of these other geographic choices in their response to the preliminary findings of this research. The a priori hypothesis is that there is no reason to assume that these other decisions are guided by different decision-making mechanisms. This section indicates, albeit tentatively, that other geographic choices follow similar patterns than those observed in this research. There may be additional factors that play a role, but the factors that affect geographic choices between countries also appear to influence other choices.

Some of those commenting on this research argue that more emphasis should be placed on sub-national choices, since 'We do not work for countries, we work for people, and we support those who are marginalized' (Ploumen 2007, p. 2). According to these critics, even in middle-income and well-governed countries there are marginalized groups and these also merit support (*ibid.*). The first two sections above assessed these claims and concluded that, even though intra-country targeting is important, choices between countries are equally so. Nonetheless, it is relevant to discover how sub-national geographic choices are made, to see if certain cross-country determinants are offset at the sub-national levels (e.g. do international NGOs have an equitable coverage within countries?). Do the determinants of the choices between countries also explain choices within countries, or are the latter dependent on different decision-making processes?

Non-financial geographic choices, such as decisions regarding joint lobby and advocacy activities with Southern partners, are viewed as increasingly important in the work of international NGOs. Reviewers of this research claim that the distributionalist perspective, which only focuses on the financial allocations of NGOs between countries, overlooks the fact that NGOs are increasingly addressing global inequalities, which also requires extensive work in richer countries, for instance. As the director of Oxfam Novib at the time put it (2007, p. 2): 'It is not only local and national but also global democracy that has to be achieved – because of the structural global injustice in trade, arms and aid distribution'. Their efforts in these areas, such as supporting networks, are not capital intensive, but labour intensive. This section examines whether geographic choices in these non-financial respects are similar to those that involve financial transfers. It equally deserves to be remembered, however, that other research suggests that international NGOs are still firmly operating within the financial-transfer resource paradigm and that analysing NGOs from this angle remains appropriate and even desirable (Koch 2008b).

Sub-national geographic choices

Sub-national geographic choices play out at different levels: regional, provincial, communal, inter- and even intra-household. Targeting can also take place on the basis of non-geographic characteristics, such as ethnicity. Since this research focused exclusively on the geographic choices of international NGOs between countries, conclusions about other geographic levels are, at best, tentative.

Since hardly any research was available on the choices of international NGOs between countries, in the beginning this research relied heavily on research on geographic choices within countries. The hypothesis put forward in this research regarding the concentration of international NGOs was informed, for instance, by research on Uganda (Barr and Fafchamps 2005), Bangladesh (Fruttero and Gauri 2005) and Ghana (CIDIN 2006; Population Council & Planned Parenthood Association of Ghana 2000). The hypothesis on the poverty targeting of international NGOs, or the lack thereof, was also based on studies at the sub-national level, such as the abovementioned studies on Uganda and Bangladesh, but also the work of Sharma and Zeller (1999) and Zeller *et al.* (2001) on Bangladesh and Bebbington (2004) on the Andes region. These studies clearly document clustering behaviour of NGOs, their neglect of the poorest segments of society and the complementary nature of their efforts. Annex 9 outlines the regional choices of NGOs within Tanzania and the Central African Republic. In these two countries clustering occurs and typically not in the poorest parts of the country.[13]

Non-financial geographic choices

There exists significant research on the non-financial geographic choices of international NGOs. Non-financial choices are for instance joint lobby initiatives of international and local NGOs. Various academic studies have mapped these networks of international organizations. Taylor's analysis of the interlocking civil-society network at the city level deserves special mention (2004), as well as the transnational social movement analysis of Smith and Wiest (2005) and the work of Beckfield on the structure of international organizations (2003). All three studies focus on the relationships between non-governmental organizations across countries. Though their methodologies differ, they all attempt to map the non-financial ties between non-governmental organizations and the determinants of these ties, using data from the Union of International Associations. These studies are some of the few well researched ones available on the non-financial links between non-governmental organizations and their findings the most indicative of the geography of non-financial aspects of ties of international NGOs.

With respect to levels of economic development, the authors reach divergent conclusions. Taylor shows that the capital cities of some poor countries are among the best connected NGO cities in the world, and argues therefore that 'these results support a positive interpretation for NGOs contributing to an emancipatory global agenda' (Taylor 2004, p. 266). The conclusions of the two other studies are less optimistic. Smith and Wiest (2005) reveal that richer countries are substantially better connected to transnational social movements than poorer countries. They therefore title their research the 'Uneven geographic of global civil society'. Beckfield shows convincingly that poorer countries have fewer international non-governmental ties. He states that 'the level of inequality in international NGO ties is as high as the level of world income inequality' (Beckfield 2003, p. 401). These contradictory findings are consistent with the inconclusive findings of this research on the poverty focus of international NGOs when it comes to choices between countries, as discussed in Chapters 2 and 3 and in the 'Poverty' section above.

Only Smith and Wiest (2005) research the influence of governance cross-country ties between non-governmental agencies. They show that countries with stronger democratic traditions, e.g. that are members of international organizations and signatories of international treaties on human rights, are better represented in transnational social movement organizations, such as international trade unions. This mirrors the findings of this research, which shows that international NGOs have closer financial links with organizations in more democratic countries.

The Smith and Wiest study focuses on the relationship between official aid and participation in transnational social movement organizations. They find that aid positively affects participation and attribute this to the fact that official aid generates multiple forms of transnational interaction – including ties among non-governmental organizations. This is in line with the findings of Chapters 2, 3 and 6 of this research, which demonstrated that official development assistance also determines the financial geographic choices of international NGOs.

The Beckfield (2003) study pays particular attention to other elements of interest to this research: the importance of past involvement and concentration. He shows convincingly that a country's level of connectedness with international non-governmental organizations in 1960 is an important determinant of its level of connectedness in the year 2000. He also shows that there is increasing inequality between countries that are linked up to international NGOs and those that are not.

The three studies cited above seem to substantiate the a priori postulation that similar factors as those that influence cross-country choices of international NGOs affect sub-national and other geographic ones.[14]

Conclusion

This three-year research project has attempted to map uncharted territory: the geographic choices of international NGOs. Its findings were sometimes in line with expectations and sometimes counter-intuitive, yet they always contributed to filling this blind spot on the aid map.

It covered a distinct area of research that turned out to be in rather high demand. Leading international think thanks on development issues, such as the Development Centre of the OECD, the World Institute of Development Economics Research and the Brookings Institution were interested in its findings, other academics, notably Nunnenkamp and Dreher, are expanding on this arguably pioneering research, and a number of other studies on the topic are being conducted (e.g. Nunnenkamp 2008). In the coming year, the Centre for Development Issues in Nijmegen (CIDIN) will launch an NGO expenditure tracking dataset that will capture data on the country and thematic choices of large international NGOs and will be updated annually. Future research will thus be able to use larger and better datasets to analyse the geographic and thematic choices of international NGOs.

This conclusion outlines the five empirical findings of the research and its theoretical and methodological contributions to the field of development studies. The five empirical findings concern the relationship between the geographic choices of international NGOs and the levels of poverty and governance in recipient countries, the strong influence of back donors on these choices, the patterns of concentration that characterize them and how they are influenced by the NGO-specific mission. This research has aimed to be theoretically innovative in that it adds to the development of an evolutionary economic geography approach to explaining the concentration of NGOs. Its potential methodological innovation is its combination of experimental and traditional research methods.

Poverty is not as strong a determinant of the geographic choices of international NGOs as was hitherto assumed. When calculated on a per capita basis, international NGOs actually spend more in lower-middle-income countries than in the least-developed countries. However, there are differences between NGOs from different donor countries. NGOs from The Netherlands and Germany, for example, are less influenced by poverty levels than NGOs from other countries.

The weak focus of international NGOs on the poorest countries appears not to result from competitive pressures but from other factors, such as historical relationships and religious connections. Colonial ties and choices of a generation ago are more important determinants of today's geographic choices than a country's current level of economic, social and human development. The view that international NGOs target the neediest countries and are not constrained to do so, needs to be nuanced. International NGOs have their preferred constituents and those are not necessarily the poorest.

This research found that international NGOs are not disproportionately engaged in countries with low levels of governance. It challenges the view held by many international aid agencies and academics that international NGOs enjoy a comparative advantage in difficult institutional environments and are more active there. It suggests that international NGOs can play an important role in countries with better levels of governance, for instance to support the voice of marginalized groups, but ideally could focus more of their service delivery efforts in countries where aid cannot be channelled through the government. Such targeting is, acording to this research, not yet sufficiently taking place. Consequently, countries like Côte d'Ivoire, the Central African Republic, Yemen and Nigeria do not receive any support through government channels and are neglected by international NGOs. This situation necessitates policy discussions and maybe a policy response.

A third empirical finding of this research concerns the observed lack of autonomy of international NGOs in their geographic choices. These choices were actually found to be rather *governmental,* that is, influenced by the preference of their back donors. Sometimes back donors influence international NGOs by attaching strict geographic strings to their financial support; sometimes they influence them more subtly. As a key determinant of the copycat behaviour of international NGOs, their financial dependence on their back donors came to the fore. The stronger this dependence, the more likely they are to mimic the geographic choices of their back donors, whether voluntarily or involuntarily.

This research intended to demonstrate that international NGOs tend to cluster in certain countries. 'Donor darlings', such as Tanzania, Kenya, Malawi, Sri Lanka and Uganda, receive per capita over 20 times more international NGO aid than 'donor orphans'. In absolute terms, 'donor darlings' receive more than US$100 million in international NGO aid per year, whereas countries like Congo-Brazzaville, Guinea, Papua New Guinea, Togo and the Central African Republic receive significantly less than US$10 million per year. It was found that this gap could be partly explained by the fact that geographic choices are generally made on the basis of outdated and subjective 'country images' rather than systematic and transparent procedures. Based on field research, this study found that there is ample opportunity for international NGO involvement in one of the donor orphans, the Central African Republic, and that cooperation between NGOs tends to decrease when they cluster in certain areas, as the case of the Arusha region illustrates. This situation will not change automatically, as indicated by the theoretical framework on the evolutionary economic geography of non-profit location choices and related fieldwork. There is thus a case for policies that encourage a more equitable spread of international NGO aid.

The envisaged theoretical contribution of this study lies in its development of an evolutionary economic geography approach to non-profit location theory. The literature on the geography of voluntarism and the non-profit sector notes that one of the salient characteristics of this sector is its unequal spatial coverage. However, it does not provide a clear theoretical framework to explain this concentration. This research provided some stepping stones to fill that void by developing a framework based on the principles of evolutionary economic geography. This is normally used to explain concentration in a for-profit context but turns out to be applicable to a non-profit context as well. The framework developed in this research is rooted in detailed empirical work on specific regions and stresses the social and institutional foundations of cluster formation. Increasing returns on investment, labour mobility and path dependence were found to be the elements from the evolutionary economic geography approach that contributed to the explaination of the concentration of international NGOs. This approach also helped explain the finding that the geographic choices of international NGOs are self-reinforcing processes in the sense that international NGOs prefer to work in regions where other international NGOs have already trained local personnel, strengthened local organizations and created a basic NGO infrastructure and so on.

Lastly, this research tried to make a methodological contribution to the field of development studies by developing and testing a game simulation with NGOs to gain insight into their propensity to cooperate. The game simulation was developed to reduce the influence of socially desirable behaviour on the research findings and was found to be rather effective in that respect. However, by juxtaposing the results of the game simulation with the results of a survey among the same NGOs, certain intrinsic shortcomings of a game simulation as a research method were highlighted, for example that real-life incentive structures cannot be replicated exactly. To illustrate, transport costs and information asymmetries were found to be inevitably lower in the game simulation than in real life. To reduce the risk of bias it is therefore suggested to use game simulations in combination with other research methods (triangulation). This research made use of qualitative, quantitative and experimental research methods in an effort to create such a mutually reinforcing combination of research methods.

Policy suggestions

Based on the findings of this research, several policy recommendations can be made. International NGOs could focus more of their efforts on:

- the poorest countries;
- countries with a poor governance situation;
- countries where few international NGOs are active.[15]

To facilitate this, they are advised to develop transparent and systematic procedures for their location and allocation decisions, based on objective indicators of a country's poverty levels, its governance situation and the number of international NGOs that are active in a country. They are also advised to coordinate their activities better among each other. To stimulate autonomous decision-making, international NGOs are proposed to become more financially independent from their back donors.

Back donors, in turn, should adjust their incentive structures to stimulate international NGOs to focus their service delivery efforts on the poorest and poorly governed countries and to improve coordination among them. However, they are advised to refrain from micro-managing the geographic choices of international NGOs.[16]

Local NGOs and governments of donor orphans are recommended to create an enabling environment for international NGOs and to market opportunities for their involvement.

Summary

The size and number of international Non-Governmental Organizations (NGOs), such as World Vision and Oxfam International, has been rising substantially in the recent years. They increasingly depend on official donors for funding and compete among each other for grants. Such trends bring a set of research questions to the fore: Do international NGOs coordinate their activities and complement the efforts of other aid actors? Do they maintain autonomy vis-à-vis their back donors? Do they focus on their core mission or do they behave strategically because of competitive pressures? This research answers these questions by analysing the geographic choices of international NGOs, in particular why they choose to work in one country and not in another. It thereby fills a blind spot on the map of aid allocations.

The underlying premise of the research is that the work of international NGOs can be beneficial for their target groups. The research does therefore not question the 'raison d'être' of international NGOs. Rather, it analyses the determinants of the geographic choices of international NGOS and the consequences of these choices. It also proposes tentative solutions to improve them.

The research is guided by three questions:

1. What are determinants of the geographic choices of international NGOs?
2. What explains the geographic concentration of international NGOs?
3. What are the analytical and policy implications of the research findings?

The Introduction (Chapter 1) explains why the research uses a combination of qualitative, experimental and quantitative methods (a mixed-methods approach) and how it searches for synergy between them. It also highlights the academic relevance of the research and its potential (1) empirical, (2) theoretical and (3) methodological contributions to the field of development studies. First, by creating two datasets on the geographic choices of international NGOs, and by making them publicly available, the study intends to facilitate more systematic research of these choices. Second, the study's envisaged theoretical contribution is its use of concepts and theories from other disciplines, especially business administration, which are normally used to explain the geographic concentration of for-profit actors. As this study shows, they can also be used to explain the concentration of non-profit actors. Third, the intended methodological contribution of the research is its development of a new game simulation, the NGO GAME, which can be used as a tool for gathering empirical data.

The introduction also outlines the structure of the research. The first part (Chapters 2 and 3) maps and tests potential determinants of geographic choices of international NGOs. It finds that international NGOs have a tendency to follow each other's geographic choices and hence end up working in a similar set of countries. The second part (Chapters 4 to 6) explains why this geographic concentration of NGOs is occurring. The last part (Chapters 7 and 8) analyses the analytical and policy implications of the research findings.

In Part I, 'Mapping and testing potential determinants of the geographic choices of international NGOs', based on a literature review, Chapter 2 proposes five potential determinants of the geographic choices of international NGOs. These determinants are: (1) the level of poverty in the recipient country; (2) the level of governance in the recipient country; (3) the country preferences of back donors; (4) the geographic choices of other international NGOs; and (5) the organization's mission. This research shows that these potential determinants together explain 73 per cent of the country choices of international NGOs. It finds that international NGOs generally follow the geographic choices of their back donors and that they are (more) active in countries where other international NGOs are present. Some top recipients, dubbed donor darlings, receive more than 20 times more aid on a per capita basis than so-called donor orphans do. Of the sample of 61 organizations included in this study, more than 40 are active in countries such as Sri Lanka, Uganda and Guatemala, while only a handful are active in countries such as Yemen, Côte d'Ivoire and Congo-Brazzaville. International NGOs are also (more) active in countries with a profile similar to their own, as a result of a shared colonial past or religion. Counter-intuitively, international NGOs are not more engaged in countries where governmental aid agencies find it difficult to work: those characterized by bad governance. The study's findings on the poverty focus of international NGOs are not conclusive. There is some evidence that NGOs are more likely to be active in countries with higher levels of poverty, but this depends on how poverty is measured.

Chapter 3 analyses whether the five determinants identified in Chapter 2 can also explain the geographic choices of Dutch NGOs. It introduces an innovative combination of research methods: in-depth interviews were held with representatives of Dutch NGOs, relevant government officials and experts, and a longitudinal dataset was compiled with a breakdown by country of the geographic choices of the largest Dutch organizations over nearly two decades. Using panel regression analyses, the research finds that for Dutch NGOs the level of poverty in recipient countries is not an important determinant of their geographic choices. This is exemplified by the list of top ten recipients, which includes just one Least Developed Country. The study also finds that, like their international peers, Dutch NGOs follow the geographic preferences of their back donor, the Dutch government, do not focus on countries suffering from bad governance, and tend to cluster in those countries where other Dutch NGOs are active. Moreover, Dutch NGOs are remarkably stable in their geographic choices; choices that they made decades ago still influence their current choices. A case study of Oxfam Novib, the largest Dutch NGO in terms of budget, helps explain why certain determinants of geographic choices are influential while others are not. It shows how the organization's leadership pushed for a formalized and transparent ranking and rating system of recipient countries, which resulted in more objective geographic decisions and a focus on poorer countries. However, this system was only used systematically in response to an exogenous shock that highlighted the need for more rational geographic choices.

The first part of the research demonstrated that international NGOs tend to concentrate their efforts in a limited number of countries. The second part explores how this concentration is brought about and how it evolves. It analyses these questions at three levels of the aid chain – recipient countries, international NGOs and back donors.

Chapter 4 develops an evolutionary economic geography approach to non-profit organizations. Evolutionary economic geography is normally used to explain the geographic concentration of for-profit organizations, but is used here to explain choices made by non-profit actors. It assigns a prominent role to increasing returns to aid, labour mobility and path dependence. This chapter focuses on the level of recipient countries, using case studies of the Central African Republic (CAR) and Tanzania. These two countries represent opposite ends of the spectrum. In the Central African Republic very few international NGOs are active while in Tanzania, and especially in the Arusha region where field research was conducted, they are heavily concentrated. This chapter analyses the stagnation of the foreign-funded NGO sector in the Central African Republic and its rapid expansion in Tanzania. The example of Arusha shows that increasing returns to aid, labour mobility and path dependence did indeed contribute to the influx of international NGOs. This suggests that local NGO sectors grow endogenously, and display a self-reinforcing process that leads to the further geographic concentration of international NGOs. This indicates that evolutionary economic geography complements current theories on the location decisions of international NGOs. Factors that can explain the rise of Silicon Valley could also be used to understand the rise of 'Serengeti Valley'.

Chapter 5 moves up the aid chain and looks at the level of international NGOs. The underlying assumption in previous chapters was that choices were based on objective indicators. This chapter shows that this might not be the case, as it intends to explain why international NGOs are concentrated in certain countries by analysing how their staff develops images of recipient countries. This chapter uses insights from management literature and applies them to the case of the Central African Republic and Tanzania. It finds that geographic choices of international NGOs are partly based on simplified country images. 'Outsiders' have a more negative image of the Central African Republic than those who work there, whereas for Tanzania no such difference is observed. Since country choices are generally made by 'outsiders' their negative country image appears to contribute to the lack of involvement of international NGOs in the Central African Republic. International NGO personnel have limited emotional attachment towards the CAR, which appears associated with a downward bias in their perceptions. This negative country image also serves a purpose, since it justifies continued non-involvement. This passivism hampers the chances of emotional rapprochement between the CAR and NGO personnel, sustaining a negative country image.

In Chapter 6 the attention shifts to the level of the back donor. It analyses whether factors at this level contribute to the concentration of international NGOs. The chapter finds that back donors indeed influence the concentration of international NGOs, but differently than expected. Many international NGOs state that they are willing to invest more in 'difficult' countries where few of their peers are active, but are unable to do so because they are under pressure to show quick results to their back donor. To test this claim, data on aid allocations of international NGOs and their competitive environment were collected from 15 international NGOs in Germany, Norway and the United States. The chapter finds that their geographic choices are not influenced by the level of competition among them. For example, the German NGOs included in this study, which operate in the least competitive environment, are also the least focused on difficult countries. This suggests that critics of the 'marketization of aid' may overestimate its negative effects on country allocations. Geographic choices are influenced, however, by the level of financial dependence that back donors create. Increased levels of financial dependence are related to increased levels of 'slipstream' behaviour. This means that international NGOs tend to mimic the geographic preferences of their back donors and stick to the same 'donor darlings' and 'donor orphans', even though they are supposed to make such choices autonomously.

Parts I and II of the research showed that international NGOs concentrate their activities in certain countries and explores possible explanations. Part III, 'Analysing the implications of the geographic choices of NGOs', discusses the analytical and policy implications of these findings.

Chapter 7 introduces an experimental gaming approach that was used in Arusha, Tanzania, to gain insights into the consequences of concentration. The approach built on a new game, the NGO GAME, which was developed especially for this research. Its results indicate that the willingness of local NGOs to cooperate with each other decreases when the level of concentration increases, that is when more of them work in the same area and on the same theme. To check the validity of the game simulation results, they were triangulated with the findings of a survey among the same local NGOs. The results of the survey generally confirm the findings of the game simulation; NGOs in highly concentrated areas operate on average more as competitors than as colleagues. Advantages of the game approach are that it permits one to control, to a certain extent, for socially desirable behaviour and that it has positive side-effects for participants, such as learning effects. A disadvantage is that it seems impossible to replicate real-life incentive structures precisely, leading to other biases. Consequently, a combination of various research methods is likely to provide the most robust results.

The last chapter, Chapter 8, reviews the findings of the research against the five determinants introduced in chapter two and discusses their academic and policy implications. It provides some indication of the extent to which these determinants of choices between countries can be used to explain other geographic choices of international NGOs, such as their location choices within a country. The findings of this research show that the field of development studies could benefit from making more extensive use of insights from other academic disciplines, notably business administration. They also demonstrate that there are various empirical lacunae in the research of international NGO behaviour that deserve attention.

Policy suggestions

Several policy recommendations can be made based on the findings of this research. International NGOs could focus more of their efforts on:

- the poorest countries;
- countries with poor governance;
- countries where few international NGOs are active.

To facilitate this, international NGOs are advised to develop transparent and systematic procedures for location and allocation decisions, based on objective indicators of a country's poverty level, its governance situation and the number of international NGOs that are active in a country. They are also advised to coordinate their activities better among each other. To stimulate autonomous decision-making, international NGOs are proposed to become more financially independent from their back donors.

Back donors, in turn, could adjust their incentive structures to stimulate international NGOs to focus their service delivery efforts on the poorest and poorly governed countries and to improve coordination among them. However, they are advised to refrain from micro-managing the geographic choices of them.

Local NGOs and governments of donor orphans are recommended to create an enabling environment for international NGOs and to market opportunities for them in their countries.

Annex 1
Overview of new datasets of this research

1 International NGO database on country expenditures

Coverage: 61 of 100 of the largest international NGOs
Year: 2005
Subject: overview of annual expenditures, broken down per DAC country.
Publicly available: http://www.ru.nl/cidin/about_cidin/staff/virtual_map/koch/
Used in: Chapter 2

2 Dutch NGO database on country expenditures

Coverage: the five largest Dutch international NGOs
Year: 1989–2005
Subject: overview of annual expenditures, broken down per DAC country.
Publicly available: http://www.ru.nl/cidin/about_cidin/staff/virtual_map/koch/
Used in: Chapter 3

3 Q-questionnaire among international NGOs

Coverage: 43 of 100 of the largest international NGOs
Year: 2007
Subject: Considerations regarding NGO involvement in Tanzania and Central African Republic
Used in: Chapters 4 and 5

4 Survey among local NGOs in Tanzania and the CAR

Coverage: 92 local NGOs in Tanzania and the Central African Republic
Year: 2007
Subject: Characteristics of foreign funded NGO sector in Tanzania and Central African Republic
Used in: Chapters 4 and 5 (and Tanzania findings also in Chapter 7)

5 Semi-structured interviews with international NGOs in Germany, Norway and the US

Coverage: 15 international NGOs in Germany, Norway and the US
Year: 2006
Subject: Marketization of NGO aid and country selection and allocation procedures
Used in: Chapter 6

6 NGO GAME simulation results

Coverage: Eight games with 37 local Tanzanian NGOs participating
Year: 2007
Subject: Cooperation and competition results of the NGO GAME simulation
Used in: Chapter 7

Annex 2

Table with top recipients of NGO aid

International NGO expenditures in Euro (2005)		International NGO expenditures in Euro per capita (2005)	
India	261,550,584	Palestine	12.3
Ethiopia*	174,638,922	Lesotho*	11.4
Sudan*	149,705,388	Zimbabwe	9.7
Indonesia	135,186,046	Nicaragua	9.1
Kenya	125,746,998	Haiti*	8.8
Zimbabwe	125,709,694	Swaziland	8.3
Bangladesh*	117,578,166	Zambia*	7.6
Uganda*	109,005,501	Malawi*	7.3
Sri Lanka	95,408,083	Honduras	6.7
Malawi*	92,567,876	El Salvador	6.6

Source: Koch, own data

Note: *Indicates that a country was labelled a Least Developed Country by the OECD/DAC in 2005.

Annex 3
Overview of the sample of NGOs

Action Aid International	South Africa (other)
ADRA	USA
Broederlijk delen	Belgium
Brot für die Welt	Germany
CARE Canada	Canada
CARE France	France
CARE Norway	Norway
CARE USA	USA
Caritas Switzerland	Switzerland
Catholic Agency for Overseas Development (CAFOD)	United Kingdom
Christian Aid	United Kingdom
Christian Childrens Fund	USA
Church of Sweden Aid	Sweden
Concern Worldwide	Ireland
Cordaid	Netherlands
Diakonia	Sweden
Evangelischer Entwicklungsdienst	Germany
Ford Foundation	USA
Friedrich Ebert Stiftung	Germany
German Agro Action / Deutsche Welthungerhilfe	Germany
Goal	Ireland
Handicap International	France
Hivos	Netherlands
ICCO	Netherlands
International Planned Parenthood Federation (IPPF)	United Kingdom
Kellogg Foundation	USA
Kindernothilfe	Germany
Konrad Adenauer Stiftung	Germany

Koordinierungsstelle	Austria
Mac Arthur Foundation	USA
Marie Stopes International	United Kingdom
Mercy Corps	USA
MISEREOR	Germany
Norwegian Church Aid	Norway
Norwegian Peoples Aid	Norway
OCCDP	Canada
Oxfam Australia	Australia
Oxfam Belgium	Belgium
Oxfam Novib	Netherlands
Oxfam USA	USA
PLAN International	United Kingdom
Population Services International (PSI)	USA
Redd Barna (Save the Children)	Norway
Rädda Barnen (Save the Children)	Sweden
Rockefeller Foundation	USA
Save the Children USA	USA
SNV	Netherlands
Soros International Foundations	USA
Swiss Catholic Lenten Fund	Switzerland
Swissaid	Switzerland
Swisscontact	Switzerland
Terre des Hommes NL	Netherlands
Terre des Hommes Switzerland	Switzerland
TROCAIRE	Ireland
Voluntary Services Overseas	United Kingdom
Vredeseilanden	Belgium
WaterAid	United Kingdom
Woord en Daad	Netherlands
World Vision Australia	Australia
World Vision Canada	Canada
World Vision USA	USA

Annex 4
Overview of variables

Sources of data in Chapter 2:

NGO aid: NGO aid from an individual NGO to a recipient country in Euros in 2005

GDP p.c.: GDP per capita in 2004 (constant 2000 US$), source: World Bank (2006)

Human Development Index: Human Development Index 2004, source: United Nations Development Programme (2006a)

Gini: Gini coefficient, source: United Nations Development Programme (2006a)

Polity: Polity 2 indicator from the Polity IV project. Source: Marshall and Jaggers (2004)

Freedom House: Freedom House political rights and Freedom House political liberties in 2004, source: Freedom House (2006)

Governance: Factor score of six Kaufmann indicators, source: Kaufmann *et al.* (2005)

Bilateral aid: Net bilateral aid inflows from the home country of the NGO to the recipient country in 2004 in million US$, source: OECD 2007

Other NGOs: The number of other NGOs in the sample that are active in the recipient country, source: see text

Expenditures of other NGOs:
Total expenditures in 2005 of other NGOs to a recipient country in Euros, source: see text

Population: Population in millions in 2004, source: World Bank (2006)

Colony: Colonial status. Source: Correlates of War 2 Project (2003)

Religion: Dominant religion, sources: Alesina *et al.* (2003) and annual reports of NGOs.

Recipients' share in total exports: Bilateral exports to a recipient country as a share of total bilateral exports to countries in sample, source: Comtrade (2007)

UNGA voting: Conformity in voting in United Nations General Assembly in 2004. Source: Dreher *et al.* (2006a)

	N	Min	Max	Mean	Standard deviation
NGO aid (Euro)	6891	0	47700000	577435	2065290
GDP/capita (dollar)	6466	88	7483	1425	1522
HDI	6588	0.31	0.86	0.62	0.15
Gini	5368	19	74.3	43.1	10.7
Polity	6039	−9	10	1.87	7.17
Freedom	6771	2	14	8.2	3.35
Governance	6893	−2.68	2.97	−0.04	0.98
Bilateral aid (million dollar)	6893	−57.46	3021.99	31.52	142.34
Number of other NGOs	6893	0	49	19.92	12.32
Expenditures of other NGOs	6893	0	2.62e+08	3.46e+07	4.12e+07
Population (millions)	6893	0.28	1296.15	44.05	158.4
Colony	7005	0	1	0.04	0.21
Religion match	6893	0	1	0.13	0.33
Export share	6465	7.15e−06	0.049	0.002	0.006
UNGA voting	6660	0.132	0.903	0.577	0.192

Annex 5

Overview of interviews

Borren, Sylvia. Oxfam Novib, Director (until Feb. 2008), interview in August 2007.

Bos, Jone. Former Director of ICCO (1965–81) and director of DPO (Department of Private Aid and Education), interview in December 2007.

Bouma, Theo. Oxfam Novib, Director of Projects, interview in October 2007.

Derksen, Harry. ICCO, Deputy Director of Research and Development Department, interview in January 2006.

Dijkstra, Jaap. Hivos. Currently advisor to the management team of Hivos, Director of Hivos from 1985 until 2002, interview in October 2007.

Gennip, Jos van. Director of Cebemo, predecessor of Cordaid from 1967–1984 and Deputy Director General of International Development Cooperation of the Dutch Ministry of Foreign Affairs, 1984–1991, interview in November 2007.

Hoebink, Paul. Previously chairman of the Project Pool Committee of Novib (1993–2002) and author of various articles on Dutch NGOs, interview in October 2007.

Hoogen, Hans van den, Oxfam Novib, Humanitarian Coordination, previously project leader of the focus discussion in 2001–2, interview in October 2007.

Huisman, Peter, Oxfam Novib, Research and Development Unit, interview in October 2007.

Konijn, Peter, Cordaid, Deputy Director, Head of the Quality, Policy and Strategy Unit, interview in January 2006.

Kruijssen, Hans. Former Director of Cebemo, predecessor of Cordaid, 1984–2003, and Head of Unit of the legal department of development cooperation at the Dutch Ministry of Foreign Affairs, interview in October 2007.

Leeuwen, Bram. ICCO, Project Leader of Project Implementation Service, interview in October 2007.

Pelgröm, Hans. Former Director of Projects of Novib 1983–94, interview in September 2007.

Ruyssenaars, Jan. Oxfam Novib, formerly member of the 'Geographic Resource Allocation Programme' team at Oxfam Novib, interview in December 2005.

Teune, Bastiaan. SNV, wrote previously MA thesis on geographic choices of Oxfam Novib and was consultant to other Dutch NGOs on this topic, interview in October 2007.

Verhallen, Pim. ICCO, policy adviser, interview in November 2007.

Annex 6
Summary statistics of total sample

Regions	Number of Countries	Life expectancy at birth	Total bilateral aid (million current USD)	GDP/cap (constant dollars)	Freedom House political rights	Population total (million)	Population share
Africa	44	48.9	9461	670.3	4.9	584	13.31%
Asia	28	65.4	5341	821.9	4.5	2947	67.21%
Middle East	10	68.5	1613	1738.9	5.8	173	3.94%
Latin America	23	69.9	2760	2605.8	2.8	370	8.44%
Europe	16	70.4	1518	2340.6	2.6	312	7.11%
Total	121	62.1	20694	1384.3	4.1	4384.8	100.00%

Regions	Total NGO aid (million current USD)	NGO aid (share)	Bilateral aid (share)	NGO aid per country (million current)	NGO aid per capita (current USD)
Africa	1425	37.1%	45.7%	32.4	2.44
Asia	1084	28.2%	25.8%	38.71	0.37
Middle East	69	1.8%	7.8%	6.91	0.4
Latin America	1172	30.5%	13.3%	50.94	3.17
Europe	88	2.3%	7.3%	5.47	0.28
Total	3838	100.0%	100.0%	26.9	1.33

Sources: OECD DAC, World Development Indicators and Koch (own data).

Annex 7
Overview of top recipients of total Dutch NGO aid

Overview of top recipients of total Dutch NGO aid (millions, constant US dollars)

1989–1995		1995–2000		2001–2005	
1. India	108.26	1. India	119.89	1. India	144.57
2. Brazil	91.9	2. Brazil	88.89	2. Peru	56.47
3. Peru	70.8	3. Peru	71.82	3. Indonesia	55.68
4. Philippines	54.25	4. South Africa	59.08	4. South Africa	55.17
5. Chile	52.84	5. Philippines	58.79	5. Brazil	54.68
6. South Africa	51.88	6. Bolivia	55.57	6. Uganda*	47.97
7. Indonesia	32.48	7. Bangladesh*	53.49	7. Bolivia	46.66
8. Zimbabwe	32.38	8. Tanzania*	35.12	8. Tanzania*	44.13
9. Bangladesh *	31.78	9. Uganda*	34.31	9. Afghanistan*	42.76
10. Congo, Dem. Rep. *	29.92	10. Kenya	33.37	10. Kenya	41.56

Overview of top recipients of NGO aid per capita (constant US dollars)

1989–1995		1995–2000		2001–2005	
1. Belize	13.9	1. Suriname	10.23	1. Suriname	11.98
2. Botswana*	7.53	2. Bolivia	6.99	2. Albania	5.63
3. Nicaragua	6.11	3. Nicaragua	5.87	3. Nicaragua	4.69
4. West Bank/Gaza	4.35	4. Belize	4.75	4. Bolivia	4.45
5. Guinea-Bissau*	4.34	5. Albania	3.9	5. West Bank/ Gaza	4.39
6. Bolivia	4.22	6. West Bank/Gaza	3.84	6. Belize	3.82
7. Chile	3.88	7. Guinea-Bissau*	3.18	7. Estonia	2.71
8. Costa Rica	3.69	8. El Salvador	3.18	8. Guinea-Bissau*	2.69
9. Namibia	3.62	9. Honduras	3.06	9. El Salvador	2.43
10. Uruguay	3.34	10. Peru	2.88	10. Guatemala	2.02

Source: Koch, own data.
Note: * indicates whether a country was a Least Developed Country according to the DAC (year 1996 for 1995–2000 and year 2002 for the period 2001{-}5). For the period 1989–1995 the UN list was used. Botswana graduated from the UN list in 1994.

Annex 8

Example of Q-questionnaire sheet

Considerations of your organization on involvement in C.A.R?

Major argument against involvement	Minor argument against involvement	Argument that works both ways (against and in favour)	Minor argument in favour of involvement	Major argument in favour of involvement

Please only drag the boxes to the columns when they are relevant according to you

Preference of general public	Local Corruption	Local climate for NGO operations	Capacity local partners	(no) informal network
Overhead concerns and spending pressure	Needs population	Potential for results	Others, namely	Possibilities for local funding
	Preference of donors	Local security situation	Others, namely	General image of country

Annex 9

Sub-national geographic and thematic choices

During the field research in Tanzania and the Central African Republic information was also gathered on the sub-national and thematic choices of the NGOs. In line with the other chapters dealing with the determinants of geographic choices of NGOs, the starting point here is the relationship with poverty. For the research in Tanzania, information was collected on the location of offices of NGOs in Tanzania and on the location of programme activities within the Arusha region.

The maps of Tanzania (Map A9.1) indicate that there is no correlation between the number of NGOs in a region and the level of poverty in a region. The highest levels of poverty are encountered in the Western parts of the country, but this is the region where fewest of the NGOs have offices. The Arusha region, which actually has one of the lowest incidences of

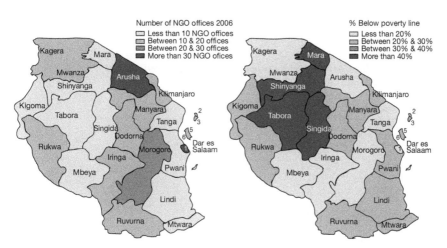

Map A9.1 Maps of Tanzania, NGO office density and poverty levels
Source: Koch and Laan (2007) (based on Tanzania Association of Non-Governmental Organization 2001; May and Magongo 2005; Zoete 2006; Devdir 2007; Umbrella NGO training project n.d.)

poverty, has one of the highest NGO densities. The coastal region is also low in NGO office density, but suffers relatively high poverty levels.

It could simply be that NGOs do not have offices in the poorest regions, but rather operate from their offices in Dar es Salaam and Arusha (city). Data was not available for Tanzania as a whole but was collected for the Arusha region. All NGOs in the sample were asked in which regions they intervened. In line with previous findings, it became clear that the region just around the capital of the region, the Arumeru district, was best served, though poverty levels were lowest in this region. The regions with the highest levels of poverty, the Nogorongoro and Karatu district, are actually least covered by NGOs. The maps look slightly more equitable when NGO density is calculated on a per capita basis, but the general theme remains the same: NGOs do not focus on the poorest geographic areas.

The findings for the Central African Republic (Map A9.2) are similar to those for Tanzania: the target areas of NGOs are not disproportionately

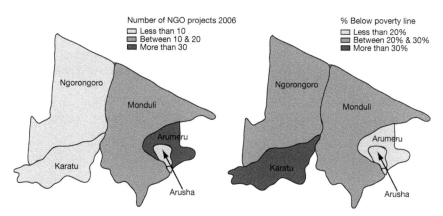

Map A9.2 Maps Arusha, NGO project density and poverty levels
Source: Koch and Laan (2007)

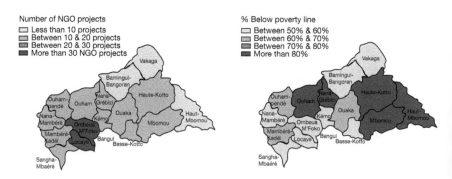

Map A9.3 Maps of the CAR, NGO target population density and poverty levels
Sources: Koolwijk and Koch (2007); UNDP (2006b)

poor regions. The capital and the areas around it are the best covered by NGOs, whereas poverty levels are higher in areas that are far away from the capital. The picture looks somewhat more equitable if population densities are taken into consideration.

With respect to the clustering of NGOs, Maps A9.1–A9.3 show that clear clustering patterns are also emerging within these countries, with significant variations in the density of NGOs. Historical relations are of significance in the distribution pattern of NGO aid in both Tanzania and the Central African Republic. The location choices of Catholic missionaries have shaped which regions in Tanzania have received large sums of aid from NGOs with a Catholic background. With substantial numbers of Catholic missionaries in Mwanza, for instance, this has been a popular destination for aid from Catholic organizations. The absence of Catholic missionaries in Zanzibar, for instance, which is still predominantly Muslim, reduces the amount of aid this region receives from international Catholic organizations.

The inequality of the thematic distribution of NGOs does not match the level of concentration in the geographic domain, though. This is corroborated by analysing a thematic breakdown of the expenditure of NGOs in the case study of Tanzania and the Central African Republic. Certain themes are clearly less prioritized, such as the environment and housing, than other themes, such as HIV/AIDS. Nevertheless, this rather dispersed thematic spread suggests that some kind of distribution of labour emerges between local organizations (Laan 2007).

Table A9.1 Thematic priorities of NGOs in the Central African Republic and Tanzania

	Central African Republic. N= 58	Tanzania (Arusha region). N = 49
Micro-finance	7%	7%
Agriculture	12%	9%
Human rights	13%	12%
Education	11%	18%
Health (general)	17%	11%
HIV/AIDS	16%	11%
Children and Women	19%	22%
Environment	5%	10%

Source: Koch, own data.

Annex 10
Thematic choices of NGOs

To what extent do the factors that influence the geographic choices of NGOs also affect other decision-making processes of NGOs, in particular thematic choices? There are both similarities and discrepancies between geographic and thematic choices. The most important difference relates to the level of concentration. The most important similarities relate to the importance of back donors and the importance of past choices.

Is thematic clustering by NGOs as pronounced as their geographic clustering? Traditionally, international NGOs have focused on social sectors, such as health and education. This has been reported in countries including Kenya (Oyugi 2004) and Bangladesh (Feldman 2003). There are also differences in thematic priorities within countries, sometimes depending on specific development challenges in certain regions, such as environmental protection around the Amazon region (Meyer 1995), or special historical developments, such as the ballooning of micro-credit NGOs in Bangladesh (Fruttero and Gauri 2005). In some instances, excessive thematic clustering has occurred, as is reportedly the case with respect to NGOs working on the theme of HIV/AIDS expense of other themes, such as agricultural development or general primary health care development (Lewis 2005). Annex 9 shows that as far as Tanzania and the Central African Republic are concerned there is some, but not excessive, thematic clustering.

It would be beyond the scope of this section to analyze in depth why NGOs succeed in better dispersing activities when gauged in thematic terms. The origins of many of the local organizations, which were often broad-based community development organizations (Korten 1990), appear to play a role. The thematic specialization of international NGOs is also something of a more recent development (Steering Committee for the Evaluation of the TMF-programme 2006).

There are also striking similarities between the underlying mechanisms of both geographic and thematic choices. Wallace (2003) describes at length how back donors influence the thematic choices of NGOs. The thematic priorities of donors, often reflections of problems in donor countries themselves, then permeate the thematic choices of local NGOs, such as environmental issues in the 1980s and security concerns in the aftermath of the attack on the United States in 2001 (Fowler 2005). Path dependence also plays an important role in thematic choices. The thematic priorities of NGOs in Bangladesh in 1995 were a good predictor of the thematic choices of NGOs in 2000 (Gauri and Galef 2005).

Notes

1 Introduction

1 Dijkstra (2007) is however more critical of what the impact of international debt relief has been.

2 'Concentration' is strictly speaking not a determinant of geographic choices, but a result of NGOs tending to become active in those countries where other NGOs are active. Thus, 'the preferences of other NGOs' might have been a more appropriate term when discussing potential determinants of geographic choices of NGOs. However, since the term 'concentration' is apt for the second part of the book, in which the spatial clustering of international NGOs is explained, this term is maintained throughout the book.

3 The number of poor is based on national poverty lines as reported in the World Development Indicators. The amount of aid is corrected for by the purchasing power parity index (to control for lower purchasing power parities in richer countries).

4 The 61 organizations do not comprise humanitarian aid agencies. They were excluded from this research as their geographic choices are guided by amongst others different determinants and a different intervention logic. That being said, certain international NGOs do have a humanitarian wing. This explains why in figure 1.4 certain countries, such as Sudan, receive more NGO aid than one would expect it one would only consider non-humanitarian aid.

5 More specifically, the research adopts a mixed-model approach and uses various research methods at *various stages* of the research process (Johnson and Onwuegbuzie 2004).

6 Interestingly, in the late 1990s quite a number of academics predicted that the era of the international NGO as a financial intermediary would soon come to an end, as they were becoming increasingly dependent on public donors whose aid budgets seemed set to dwindle further (Fowler 2000; Malhotra 2000; Biekart 1999). Nearly a decade later, it can be observed that the opposite has actually happened; the budgets of international NGOs have increased dramatically over the last decade. Most of them are still operating firmly within a financial resource-transfer paradigm. Assessing their choices by analysing their financial transfers is therefore a relevant endeavour.

7 This resulted among others in publications in 'Vox' (Dreher *et al.* 2008) 'the Broker', Koch (2007), and in an essay collection (Koch 2008a) interviews with the author in 'de Volkskrant' (Sloover 2007) and 'Transfer' (Visscher 2008) and on appearances in various radio shows.

2 What determines the geographic choices of NGOs – an exploration

* This chapter is loosely based on an article forthcoming in *World Development*, co-authored by Axel Dreher, Peter Nunnenkamp and Rainer Thiele.

1 http://www.oecd.org/dataoecd/52/11/1893159.xls
2 Bangladesh and Uganda received particular attention (e.g. Barr and Fafchamps 2005; Fruttero and Gauri 2005).
3 According to McGillivray (2003) as well as Dollar and Levin (2006), the poverty and policy orientation of several official donors has improved recently, but targeting by some major bilateral donors (e.g., France and the United States) still leaves much to be desired from a developmental perspective.
4 More specifically, some official donors tend to use aid to promote exports to recipient countries (see, e.g., Berthélemy and Tichit 2004; Canavire *et al.* 2006); others 'buy' political support by granting ODA (e.g., Kuziemko and Werker 2006; Dreher *et al.* 2006a; Dreher *et al.* 2006b).
5 Humanitarian organizations are excluded from this research. The potential determinants that guide their research would arguable be more related to the occurrence of, for instance, natural disasters.
6 It could alternatively be the case that international NGOs focus on the poorest groups within countries. This research focuses however on the cross-country choices of international NGOs and uses therefore national poverty statistics. Annex 9 displays the within-country poverty targeting of NGOs of the case studies of this research: Tanzania and the Central African Republic.
7 However, Chapter 6 will demonstrate that there is no empirical support for this proposition. For instance, German NGOs do not appear to take more risks (by allocating more aid to poorer and badly governed countries) than NGOs from the United States, even though the marketization of aid was much more advanced in the United States.
8 For similar concerns, see Smillie (2000, p. 127) and Robinson (1997, p. 61).
9 Organizations that spend more than 50 per cent of their budget on humanitarian aid are considered humanitarian organizations in this research.
10 For 21 NGOs the data refer to 2004; in addition, for a few NGOs the financial year deviates by some months from the calendar year 2005. It would obviously be advantageous to cover more than one year for all NGOs. However, insisting on data for several years would certainly have come at the cost of a significantly declining response rate, thus compromising the representativeness of the NGO sample. Chapter 2 will also demonstrate that the allocations of NGOs do not change much over time.
11 Those were excluded since many data for these small island states are missing and the levels of NGO aid that these countries received were significant outliers (calculated on a per capita basis).
12 See Annex 4 for exact definitions, summary statistics and sources of all variables.
13 It was also tried to include the poverty headcount, taken from the World Bank (2007). However, 90 per cent of the observations were lost because these data were only scarcely available, so the results are not reported.
14 All those indicators are based on a set of sub-indicators, which reduces the chance of biases. In line with the broad definition of governance applied in this research, it was ensured that the data representing governance both encompass political and technical aspects. Whereas the Polity IV index of democracy and the Freedom House index focus more on the political aspects of good governance, the World Bank indicators focus more on the technical aspects of good governance.
15 Few official donors report to the OECD a recipient country breakdown of aid to and through international NGOs. Hence, the risk is negligible that the OECD figures on aid from official donors, broken down per recipient country, comprise aid to and through international NGOs to any significant extent. Generally, the category sector '920 X support NGOs' only includes support provided by embassies directly to (local) NGOs, often bypassing international NGOs.

16 It could also be interesting to operationalize the NGO-specific mission with a variable that represents whether there are Christian minorities at risks in the countries concerned. I thank Prof. Dr. P. Hoebink for pointing this out.

17 In addition, the variable 'the number of other NGOs', could be endogenous. The left-hand side variable, the number of NGOs, could be influencing the number of other NGOs. Ideally, one would have introduced a lagged version of the independent variable, but this is not possible since all data on NGO activity are from the same year. Neither was it possible to find a suitable instrumental variable. There are thus some endogeneity concerns. In Chapter 3, in which NGO data for multiple years are present, the endogeneity concern is addressed by introducing lags. The statistical findings of chapter 3 come to the same conclusion with respect to the relevance of the presence of other NGOs.

18 The differences in the pseudo R-squared was 3 percentage points in the probit base regression (Table 2.1).

19 For this purpose the Emergency Events Database (EMDAT) was used. If a country was struck by a natural disasters that claimed more than 1000 lives in the three years prior to 2005, the variable was 1, otherwise 0.

20 Note, however, that the regressions also include bilateral aid, our preferred proxy for dependence on backdonors. Excluding bilateral aid from the regressions, the export share is no longer significant at conventional levels (not reported in the table).

21 The Heckman estimates of the split sample point in the same direction.

22 It might seem counterintuitive that American organizations, whose contracts with their back donor have specific restrictions with respect to the countries in which they are active, appear to display a more autonomous behaviour than other organizations in the sample. Chapter 6 indicates that this might be related to the relative low level of financial dependence of American organizations on their back donor, the United States government.

23 This does not hold for organizations from the UK, which could very well be a reflection of the fact that there is a significant and negative relationship between the religious match variable and the colony variable for the UK (as many former colonies of the UK are not Christian, and UK NGOs are still active in those former colonies). When including both simultaneously for the UK organizations the coefficient is indeed reduced significantly in size.

3 Geographic choices of Dutch NGOs: myths and realities

* This chapter is based on a chapter in the Dutch Yearbook of international cooperation (forthcoming, Hoebink ed.), which was co-authored by Bart Loman.

1 Oxfam Novib is one of the oldest and largest Dutch co-financing agencies. It grew continuously during its existence, and now has an annual budget of about US$200 million. It is part of the confederation of Oxfams and is after Oxfam GB its second largest member. Oxfam Novib is a secular organization and aims to create 'a just world without poverty' (Oxfam Novib n.d.). It finances local organizations to execute projects and is characterized by a broad scope of activities, from emergency aid to lobby campaigns.

2 e.g. Minister Pronk stimulated NGOs in the 1970s to become active in authoritarian countries, and Minister Bukman in the late 1980s in te newly democratised Latin American countries (with Cristian democratic presidents).

3 The interviewees stated, however, that if the authorities of the recipient country were not willing or capable to sign the letter of consent, the embassy could do that instead, which implies that embassies could have under certain circumstances an influence.

4 Besides these formal influencing processes, there could also be some more tacit co-evolution processes. Both officials from the Ministry and personnel from the NGOs operate within the same aid community, and they are consequently mutually influencing their preferences, contributing to a shared reference framework and preferences, also in the geographic domain.

5 Population variables as these are a standard procedure in aid allocation regressions (e.g. Dreher *et al.* 2007). Lastly, to assess year-specific and regionally specific effects dummies for all years and all regions were included. All independent variables were lagged, as decision-makers often have information from the previous year at their disposal when allocating their budget.

6 To prevent that the number of instruments becomes too large compared to the number of observations the maximum number of lags for the instruments was capped at two.

7 Ideally, also bilateral aid would be instrumented for by means of its lags, since there might be a chance that bilateral aid is not completely endogenous in this model even though it is lagged when included as a dependent variable. However, the number of instruments in the model becomes too high if these lags are included as instruments. Since the risk of endogeneity of the choices of other NGOs is higher, these are the ones that controlled for in the results presented here.

8 To test whether the indicator 'bilateral aid' is not absorbing many other effects, and to test whether 'bilateral aid' and 'NGO aid' are not moving simultaneously, the models were also ran with 'bilateral aid' without any lags. The bilateral aid variable became insignificant if included without lags, suggesting that indeed *past* bilateral aid indeed influences NGO aid.

9 Since the size of the coefficients is rather unstable, it is better not to comment on their sizes.

10 This suggests that also the themes on which organizations choose to intervene, and their underlying definition of poverty, affect the poverty focus of the organization. Hivos focuses on themes such as culture and gay rights, which could influence the percentage of aid they spend in the poorest countries negatively.

11 Assessed by breaking down the expenditure of the NGOs on the DAC-status of the recipient countries.

12 This number suffers from one important caveat, namely that also more affluent non-core countries receive significant amounts of funding.

13 Sometimes the government provided signals that 'complementarity' meant that organizations had to work in the same countries as the government did, and sometimes exactly the reverse.

14 However, annual reports do not show this aspect, since they do not disclose how much money is spent in each of the non-core countries. Therefore, the 'focus' is more limited than Novib would like to suggest.

15 The NGOs that the Steering Group was researching were organizations such as Woord en Daad, Solidaridad and Nederlands Instituut voor Zuidelijke Afrika. The findings do not hold for the thematic organizations engaged in specific themes, such as peace-building.

4 The concentration of NGOs: an evolutionary economic geography approach

* This chapter is based on an article that was published in the 'Papers in Evolutionary Economic Geography' series, and was co-authored by Ruerd Ruben.

1 Another reason to make use of the industrial district approach is that the composition of the researched NGO sectors bears resemblances to those analysed by the industrial district approach. Sforzi (2002) highlights that an industrial district is constituted by a set of small independent specialized organisms in different phases of the same production process. Recent inventarizations of NGO sectors in

developing countries make clear that the NGO sector also consists of many different small actors, that are all engaged in different aspects of the aid delivery process (Barr and Fafchamps 2005; Fruttero and Gauri 2005). The NGO sector is less characterized by vertically integrated supply chains but relies more on dense networks and consequently a post-Fordist approach appears well-suited.

2 In a similar vein, since international NGOs are active in a knowledge intensive sector, spreading resources thinly reduces the knowledge that can be accrued, which could hamper the efficiency of their operations.

3 Local staff are most mobile within the same country, as they may be restrained by visa and education requirements, for example.

4 One could argue that this aspect of labour mobility should fall under the category of increasing returns to scale (cf. Arthur 1994), after all the presence of better-trained personnel reduces personnel search costs and drives marginal costs down in a cluster. Labour mobility was nevertheless retained as a separate category since the labour mobility processes within the international NGO sector are extremely important, and arguably more so than in the international for-profit sector. International NGOs largely depend on expatriates to fill top-levels positions in local subsidiaries of their organizations. While for the majority of international firms most jobs are still within the home-country of the firm, this is not the case for international NGOs. Most multinational firms in the for profit sector work with independent subcontractors in developing countries, with mostly local staff. In international NGOs the dominant model is the subsidiary model, in which local divisions of large international NGOs are established in which international staff fill the top-level positions.

5 The technological lock-in effect is less applicable since NGO aid is not a highly specialized sector, in which past technological decisions create points of no return.

6 These networks are not necessarily stable over time, and one can speak of 'generational networks'. Whereas in the 1970s and early 1980s the solidarity movements and the networks they entertained contributed to a focus on South-American and Southern-Africa, this shifted towards Central American during the mid-and late 1980s. I thank Prof. Dr. P. Hoebink for pointing this out.

7 The most important caveat is thus that international NGOs gave their opinion about the whole of Tanzania, while the local field research only covered the Arusha region. The bias that this generates is likely to be limited, as there is a high likelihood that the opinions of international NGOs on Tanzania are based on their experiences in the Arusha region – after all this is the region in which they are most involved. Yet, the situation of NGOs in Arusha is not fully representative of the rest of Tanzania; the NGO sector in the Arusha region is likely to be more developed. Thus, if there is a bias in the opinion of respondents regarding, for instance, the organizational capacity in Tanzania, it is likely to be a negative one

8 Another difference with respect to the colonial heritage is that Arusha was much more in vogue by settlers, both related to missionary work and colonial efforts. This will be elaborated upon in the section on labour mobility, which will highlight that traditionally there has been a strong presence of foreigners in the Northern part of Tanzania in general and, the Arusha region in particular.

9 This table includes both respondents that were active and that were not active in the respective countries. A breakdown of the table by those that are and those that are not active point in the same direction. Please note that categories, such as '(absence) of (in)formal network' was thus interpreted differently by those that were and those that were not active in the country concerned.

10 Looking at the annual reports of the organizations confirms such a picture. Whereas in the CAR most annual reports consist of a couple of handwritten pages, in Tanzania full-colour and extensive annual reports are available.

11 An inter-agency report by major aid agencies on the CAR warns that 'renting a vehicle for one week can cost as much as 3,500 US dollars in the CAR' (Care International, Norwegian Refugee Council *et al.* 2007). Internet research reveals that this service costs no more than US$500 in Arusha.

12 It is likely that emergency aid, which international NGOs distributed in Indonesia directly after the tsunami, for example, creates less path dependence than structural aid through local partners in Peru, for instance.

5 Do country images affect the concentration of NGOs?

* This chapter is based on a paper presented at the 'International Society for Third Sector Research' conference in Barcelona (2008), which was co-authored by Dik van de Koolwijk and is forthcoming in the conference proceedings.

1 Please note that also in this chapter local NGOs can comprise local subsidiaries of international NGOs, as long as those offices are actually implementing projects in the country/region of interest.

2 These elements were selected on the basis of 20 in-depth interviews with managers of NGOs in the United States, Norway and Germany which revealed that these elements were relevant to geographic choices. More information on those interviews can be found in Chapter 6.

3 The low number of respondents from international NGOs active in the CAR was inevitable because of the limited NGO presence in the CAR.

4 The criteria for interviewing the CAR-based organizations were that the NGOs: (1) were independent from the government and non-profit organizations; (2) were foreign-funded; (3) were involved in development projects in the country; and (4) had an office in the country. The organizations could be local, national or inter-national in scope. Forty-five organizations matched those criteria, all of which were interviewed.

5 A provisional report with results of the survey was discussed in reporting events with the organizations in the CAR. Generally, organizations showed that they recognized the findings (Koolwijk and Koch 2007; Laan 2007). The turnout at those reporting events was 77 per cent.

6 This chapter does not assume that the insiders are automatically right about the country image, and the outsiders are automatically wrong. Insiders might not have adequate comparison material as they are less aware of the situation in other countries, they also might have an interest in portraying a positive image. A difference of view between insiders and outsiders reveals that the public image of a country is not shared by those who work on a daily basis in or with that country.

7 These arguments were: preference of general public; overhead concerns and spending pressure; local corruption; needs population; preference of donors; local climate for NGO operations; potential for results; local security situation; capacity local partners; (no) informal network; possibilities for local funding; general image of country.

8 During the focus-group discussions it was asked whether giving money to a public official at a road block could be labelled as corruption. All participants agreed that this should be seen as such. While there was no discussion on whether this constituted corruption, there was discussion whether this behaviour was acceptable ('these men also need to feed their families and have not received wages in years').

9 Experts were representative of, among others, the European Union, UNDP, UNFPA, World Bank and Ministry of Economics, Planning and International cooperation.

10 For instance, they are not as negative with respect to corruption as the international NGOs, but they recognize that importing goods often poses a problem for

CAR-based NGOs. With respect to NGO legislation, they recognize that the law in itself is appropriate, but that implementation is lacking. With respect to the security situation, they are closer to the opinion of the CAR-based organizations than to those based in the OECD. With respect to the enabling environment they were somewhere between the OECD-based and the CAR-based organizations. They highlighted the constraints that resulted from the meagre human resource base more than the CAR-based organizations did.

11 This effect is sometimes referred to as the 'macchiato effect'. This effect refers to the preferences of expatriates who would be more interested in living and working in countries where already many other westerners are present, as this often means that are good coffee bars where they can get their favourite coffee.

12 Cognitive dissonance is the mental process in which attitudes are adjusted to ensure that they are in line with behaviour. This process is most likely to occur when behaviour cannot be adjusted. The driving factor of this mental process is to ensure that inconsistency between practice and beliefs is reduced Gleitman (1995).

13 *The Economist* claimed that Uganda held the international donors 'to ransom', since international donor had spent so much in Uganda (55 per cent of the GNI of the country) and could not disinvest, for this would indicate that their aid had been ineffective. This resembles a lock-in effect.

14 Albeit slowly, country images can change. The international standing of Tanzania was in 2008 notably more elevated than two decades ago. In 2008 it received the largest Millennium Challenge Account Compact from the US government to date, and was selected by the Chinese government as the sole African country in which the Olympic flag was being toured around.

15 There is no reason to assume that only NGOs are affected by these negative country images – official aid agencies could be equally affected.

6 Back donors' influence on concentration: marketization or slipstream?

*   This chapter is loosely based on an article, co-authored by Judith Westeneng and Ruerd Ruben, which was first published in the *European Journal of Development Research* (2007).

1 The marketization of public services, which will be explained in detail in the analytical and methodological section, is a phenomenon that started to take root in the 1980s and 1990s in the Anglo-Saxon world, and was closely related to the emergence of neo-liberalism and related new public management theories.

2 The organizations in this research are organized in a chain (donor–international NGO–local organization–target group), a framework that is also used in this research. However, not all aid to NGOs is transferred in this rather vertical way: new partnerships emerge between Northern and Southern organizations, which are not based on a funding relation, but on joint programming.

3 An example of the importance of reputation is for instance Plan Nederland (formerly known as Foster Parents Plan Nederland), who saw their donor base decline by more than 50 per cent (from 353,000 to 160,000) in five years, after it became clear they could not keep some of their promises and which even changed its name to reverse this course (Vermaas 2005).

4 One of the implicit assumptions is that the back donor does not correct the value of the success story for the place in which it is achieved; if the back donor would discount the successes in the well-performing countries where many other actors are active, there would be no need for international NGOs to avoid those locations.

5 This is based on the assumption that back donors desire their NGOs to be active in the same countries as where they are active. Whereas exceptions exist, there are indications that this is the case, as Pratt et al. (2006, p.25) demonstrate with accounts of how back donors attempt to influence the country choices of their NGOs.

6 The Netherlands was not selected to be researched for this chapter for methodological reasons. The Dutch co-financing system for NGOs, as described in Chapter 3, is changing from a corporatist system to a liberal system, which would make an analysis on the impact of marketization on concentration difficult.

7 Rondinelli (1982) criticizes the desire of back donors for very specific projects when claiming: '[...] these complex methods of feasibility analysis, appraisal, and selection may introduce a bias toward the choice of projects that are easy to analyse, but are of low priority for development.' Rondinelli sees a desire for specific contracts as a standard feature of every bureaucracy.

8 The term 'closed-shop' refers to the situation that a back donor pre-selects certain preferred international NGOs to submit proposals. This pre-selection is not based on competitive bidding.

9 There are various measures to measure concentration. In earlier work on this topic (Koch 2007), the Lorenz concentration curves and the concomitant Gini coefficients were used to this effect. This measure can adequately assess to extent to which organizations spread their resources equitably over poor countries, or whether their distribution is skewed. Yet, there are also certain shortcomings to this measure. For instance, if an organization chooses to be active in only five countries, its activities to be very concentrated, which will result in a very high Gini coefficient. However, if those five countries happen to be five countries that receive no aid from other NGOs, this NGO is actually making very equality-enhancing choices. Therefore, this chapter has developed a new measure for NGO concentration: the NGO Concentration Index.

10 Country allocations are only one possible indicator reflecting the relative importance that international NGOs attach to certain countries. Other potential indicators are the number of projects or the number of staff working on specific countries. There appears to be a high correlation between these indicators of personnel and allocation, since organizations often peg the number of country desk officers to the turnover in the country concerned (KPMG 2004). It is possible that in poorly performing countries the number of projects is slightly higher than the allocation of funds suggests, as international NGOs attempt to avoid the risks and consequently spread their resources thinner within the country. Still, the total resource allocation provides a good proxy of the relative importance.

11 The Suits index is calculated as follows $= 1 - \sum p_i$ (CA $_i$ + CA $_{i-1}$), with p_i being the share of the number of poor people in country i and CA$_i$ the cumulative aid share of country i and all poorer countries.

12 World Development Indicators. Because of a lack of data, an average is taken from the period 1995–2004. In some cases where the one-dollar-a-day poverty line was not present, the national poverty headline is used.

13 An alternative way of measuring poorly performing countries is by looking at their governance situation. Instead of ranking countries according to their degree of economic development, countries can also be ranked on governance (in this case the factor score of the six Kaufmann indicators on Governance in 2004 was used). The governance-ranked graph (not reported) shows almost the same results as the economic-developed-ranked graph, with the US- and Norway-based organizations again showing a more progressive distribution (-0.21 and -0.19) and Germany a slightly regressive distribution (+0.07).

14 Another reason behind the low poverty focus of German aid could be the inclusion of the political foundations in the sample. They are included because they fulfil the criteria (see note 2). Yet, they see political dialogue as their main intervention strategy, which could have implications for country allocations. When excluding the political foundations from the sample the results remain roughly the same. The marketization index increases somewhat (2.1 instead of 1.9). The Suits index for German Private Aid decreases marginally to +0.14. The correlation

between the individual Suits and Marketization scores remains negative (-0.46), but loses significance.

15 Findings are also in line with research of Scheepers and Grotenhuis (2005)
16 Another example could be that American organizations focus on direct poverty reduction, and not on civil society building, the former presumably being more prevalent in the poorly performing countries.
17 It could also be the case that NGOs and back donors from the same countries operate in the same kind of networks, are subject to the same kind of public pressures and dispose of similar information, and therefore make choices that resemble and co-evolute over time. This can however not explain adequately differences between donor countries in the level of similarity of country choices of NGOs and their back donors.

7 The consequences of concentration: does it affect cooperation?

* This chapter is based on an article forthcoming in *Simulation & Gaming* (2009).
1 Inducements that can be enjoyed by individuals and organizations themselves, without sharing them with others.
2 Olson argues that the behaviour of market groups differs fundamentally from that of non-market groups. A firm in an industry aims to prevent new entrants from coming into the market and to exclude as many as possible of those firms already in the market to leave it. Firms in a given market are competitors. In his opinion, the opposite is true for non-market groups. When a non-market group becomes larger, costs can be shared and the number of opportunities to succeed rises. An increase in the size of the non-market group does not imply increased competition, but may lead to lower costs for those already in the group. The main difference is that in a market environment, supply is fixed while in a non-market environment, supply is not (Olson 1967, p. 37). In the context of Arusha there is a fixed supply, as the aid from international NGOs is finite. NGOs in Arusha thus do, in Olson's term, not meet the criterion to be considered a non-market group. Only when they are jointly operating to reduce the supply constraint can they be considered a non-market group.
3 A classic example of complementarities are education and health. For instance, when one NGO focuses on health and another on education, there are mutual positive spill-over effects, i.e. healthy children are more likely to go to school, and children who attend school can be taught the basic rules of hygiene.
4 The researchers estimate that in this case study Olson would label the organizations in Arusha as an intermediate group. His definition of an intermediate-sized group depends not on the number of actors involved, but on how noticeable each person's action is. At the centre of this and like-minded models is the free-rider problem: whenever one person cannot be excluded from the benefits that others provide, each person is motivated not to contribute to the joint effort, but to free-ride on the efforts of others. In intermediate groups, no single member receives a share of the benefit (e.g. a joint website, a joint training centre) sufficient to give him an incentive to provide the good himself, but which does not have so many members that no one member will notice whether any other member is or is not helping to provide the collective good (Olson 1967, p. 50). In such a group a collective, good may – or equally may not – be obtained, but no collective good can ever be obtained without some group coordination or organization. The game simulation was modelled in such a way that participants faced incentives as if they were in an intermediate group.
5 Scientists who are of the opinion that non-profit agencies are more than just profit-maximizing entities (Young in Rose-Ackerman 1986) argue that this kind of collective action is possible. These scientists argue that NGOs have multiple bottom

lines Anheier (2000) and that other motives, such as concern for quality, can thus play an important role.

6 Between non-market groups it might take place under some severe restrictions (noticability of inputs, small groups, no supply constraint).

7 The underlying assumption is that the Arusha region is not yet so concentrated that it is already past the tipping point of the Wade curve. Since this assumption cannot be verified there is a possibility that this is in fact not the case. When interpreting the results caution is thus needed, as there might potentially thus be a sample selection bias.

8 This is an important element of the game since NGOs need to coordinate and negotiate, but are not allowed to deviate from their original mission. This makes this game quite different from most other games where participants need to play a character, instead of being themselves. It is believed that this enhances the external validity of this simulation game.

9 The joint projects are tailor-made, to ensure that the results between the eight games are comparable. If the players all worked all on the same theme in the same district, the joint projects were related to that theme and that district. In groups in which NGOs were working on the same theme, but in different district, joint projects were related to that particular theme but in different districts. The coordination challenge was thus equally large for the different groups.

10 The debriefings with the game leaders after the test games resulted in significant changes in the design of the game. One element that surfaced during debriefings with the game leaders after the first official game was that small deviations from standard speaking notes and standard duration of the rounds had in some cases clearly affected the behaviour of participants (the sensitivity of players to different wordings has been mapped convincingly by Levitt and List). The three game-leaders agreed that stricter compliance was needed. This led to two changes in the design and execution of the NGO GAME: (1) more elaborate standardized speaking notes for the game leaders; (2) an even stricter compliance with speaking notes and timing by game leaders.

11 The NGO concentration index is calculated on the basis of a geographic and thematic component. As every organization is active in a different set of districts, has head offices in different locations, works on different themes and with different intervention strategies, scores differ for every organization. A higher score indicates that the NGO is active on themes and in districts in which many other NGOs are present. To calculate the geographic concentration component we sum the two subcomponents, that is the NGO target area density indicator and the NGO head office density indicator. We calculate for all districts an NGO target area density indicator by dividing the number of organizations active in a district by the total number of NGOs in the sample. To arrive at the NGO-specific target area density subcomponent, the average of all district-level NGO target area density indicators is taken for all districts in which an organization is active. We calculate the head office component by dividing the number of head offices present in a district by the total number of NGOs in the sample. The geographic component of the concentration index was adjusted to ensure that the maximum reached 1.

To calculate the thematic-concentration component, we sum two subcomponents: the intervention strategy component and the priority theme thematic component. We calculate the intervention-strategy component by dividing the number of NGOs active on one of the intervention strategies (basic service delivery, civil society building, or lobby and advocacy) by the total number of NGOs in the sample. We calculate the priority-theme component by dividing the number of organizations active on a theme by the total number of organizations in a sample.

The thematic component of the concentration index was adjusted to ensure that the maximum reached 1.

8 Implications of the research findings

1 Some argue that this does not go far enough, and that also poor in the rich countries ought to be the focus international NGOs.
2 When dealing for instance with a country's health sector, direct poverty alleviation involves elements such as the construction of hospitals and payment of salaries to health personnel. Civil society building includes elements such as the support to the union of nurses or the establishment of patient councils. Lobby and advocacy activities involve for instance support to a movement that demands the passage of law that gives a right to treatment for marginalized groups in a country. As is becomes evident from the activities cited above, interventions dealing with direct poverty alleviation are much more capital intensive than activities that involve civil society building and lobby and advocacy.
3 Even the definition of what constitutes 'good governance' is hotly contested (Hout 2007).
4 While the need for NGO aid that focuses on 'civil society building' and 'lobby and advocacy' does not depend on other aid actors, the effectiveness of it does (as combined bottom-up and top-down approach can lead to synergies), and effective lobbying can be extremely difficult in dire governance conditions.
5 Dutch organizations have kept for over a decade financial records on which intervention strategies were used. The absolute majority of their aid went to 'direct service delivery'. Dutch NGOs belong to the more politically oriented of the international NGOs, and spend arguably more than other international NGOs on 'civil society building' and 'lobby and advocacy'.
6 This report was discussed at length with local civil society organizations in August 2007 during two national seminars in Bangui, in which 81 per cent of the 65 interviewed organizations were present. The organizational capacity of local organizations was evaluated by taking stock of their material endowments, their level of formalization and the level of human resource development, in line with standard practice in this domain CIDA (2006). Organization Assessment Guide. Ottawa, Canadian International Development Agency.
Interestingly, 68 per cent of the local organizations have a car and more than 90 per cent have a functioning computer and a telephone. Organizations in the capital have in general better facilities than those in the countryside. The level of formalization of organizations is mediocre. Even though 90 per cent is officially registered at the Ministry of Plan and over 90 per cent has a functioning bank account, the Planning, Monitoring, Reporting and Evaluating systems are rather feeble. 58 per cent of the organizations could present an annual report and 43 per cent a financial report. 27 per cent could show a strategic plan and 22 per cent an evaluation report. With respect to human resources opinions differ widely. It is clear that the number of local organizations that has more than 20 paid employees has tripled from five to 15 in ten years. The total number of paid employees in the civil society in the Central African Republic is between 500 and 1,000. The experts indicated that there were quite some problems with the quality of human resources, but these concerns were not shared by local NGOs. All in all, the assumption that local organizations in the Central African Republic need to be 'build up from scratch' is untenable.
Institutional capacity, also dubbed system level capacity, exceeds the level of the individual organizations and deals with the enabling environment of the organizations and cooperation among them. Few practical tools for assessing the institutional capacity of civil society exist. The literature on this topic suggests that

institutional capacity of local civil society can be gauged by their coverage, cooperation among the organizations and cooperation with state agencies DFID (2003), Gordijn (2006). It was therefore chosen to follow these suggestions. The coverage of local organizations is rather equal, but thin. The majority of the local organizations have their main office in Bangui. Bangui and the adjacent regions are best covered by the services of the local organizations, but the distribution over the regions is rather equal. Furthermore, the distribution over the themes is rather equal as well, even though certain themes are more popular, such as HIV/ AIDS, than other themes, such as the environment. Organizations in the CAR do not specialize as they work on a plethora of themes in many regions, despite undersized budgets. The consequence of this is thus that even though coverage is rather equal, it is very thin. Cooperation between the organizations is rather weak, despite certain exceptions. On the operational level there is some cooperation, but not at the strategic or political level. There are some national umbrella organizations, but they are frail. The cooperation with the state is rather good; hardly any problems exist with legislation regarding civil society organizations. Human rights organizations are nonetheless less positive about governmental relations. In sum, despite the rather equal distribution of civil society organizations in the Central African Republic, and their positive experiences with the state, there are certain key institutional weaknesses, such as cooperation between organizations, and their rather thin coverage.

The current level of dependence of potential partners of international NGOs is assessed by determining whether there are many organizations that do not receive any support from international NGOs, the dependence levels of local organizations that do, and the embeddedness of local organizations in the Central African Republic society. Three groups of organizations were found to not receive any support from international NGOs: (1) hundreds of informal functional *groupements* (e.g. groups of youngsters, fishermen, women's groups); (2) a dozen of formal local NGOs that do not receive any international finance; (3) a dozen of formal local NGOs that do receive finance from other international donors, such as the European Commission, but not from international NGOs. This being said, the organizations that do receive international funding are generally very much depending on those donors. For more than 50 per cent of the organizations, their budget was financed for more than 80 per cent by international aid agencies. This does not imply that the organizations do not mobilize other resources from the population: 72 per cent of the organizations have local volunteers and 42 per cent have members. The organizations appear rather well-embedded in the Central African society.

7 A clear example of this came to the fore during the field research in Tanzania. During an informal part of one of the game simulation sessions, two presidents of associations that ran orphanages discussed their concerns. While one of the orphanages was running at full capacity, the other had excess capacity. The latter asked therefore 'Where do you get your orphans?'

8 Why is it, then, that those small informal organizations, whether in the Central African Republic, Guinea, Togo or Yemen, are barely supported by international NGOs? In the 1980s, many international NGOs were focusing on the difficult countries. They worked with local organizations active in undemocratic countries (Philippines, South Africa and Nicaragua) and erected a specialized NGO to work in those environments where local, informal organizations required labour intensive support (ACORD). It is interesting to note that although supporting these small, often rural groups used to be the core-business of the international NGOs, they are increasingly working with urban based professional NGOs (e.g. Steering Group 2002). The growing budgets of international NGOs organizations, in combination with concomitant stricter financial regulations of back donors,

appear to be important drivers towards more established organizations in developing countries (INTRAC 2005; Porter 2000). In certain countries, such as the Netherlands, international NGOs were asked to reduce the number of countries in which they were active. That, in combination with expanding budgets and increasingly strict financial regulations, resulted in an abandonment of those countries where few resources could be spent. Countries such as the Central African Republic (and Yemen, Guinea, Togo and Nigeria) are countries without these professional disbursement machines. Since these organizations were present in more stable and economically faster-growing countries such as Bangladesh, Brazil and South Africa, many international NGOs shifted their focus away from the poorest countries during the 1990s (e.g. Icco, as described and regretted by Rodenburg and Derksen 2007).

9 This is not to suggest that individual NGOs should spread their resources over more countries, as their aid is often already too fragmented, but that the combined effort of NGOs should be more equitably spread.

10 As African states have been engaged in a similar endeavour to promote their tourism industries (Pitt *et al.* 2007).

11 After all, why should only NGOs from one particular donor country focus on the most difficult countries?

12 Besides geographic choices, there are various other major choices that international NGOs face, including decisions regarding themes and intervention strategies. It goes beyond the scope of this research to analysis similarities with these choices in depth, yet an indicative analysis in Annex 9 shows both interesting convergences and divergences.

13 It remains debatable whether these findings on sub-national poverty targeting can be generalized. Arguably, in countries where regional disparities are more pronounced, for example Brazil, there may be potential for better poverty targeting. Nevertheless, they are absent in the countries and regions surveyed here.

14 In line with the present research findings, there is a clear discrepancy in levels of concentration of NGOs (non-financial aspects) between the Central African Republic and Tanzania. Dar es Salaam, the Tanzanian capital, ranks 23rd of all cities worldwide in terms of the ties with international NGOs (Taylor 2004). Bangui falls off the map in this study. The Central African Republic features in the study of Beckfield (2003), but only because he provides an overview of the countries with the fewest ties to international NGOs. The Central African Republic is the second-lowest on his list.

15 There is some overlap between these three types of countries. Since the overlap is not complete, they are presented as separate groups here.

16 It might seem paradoxical to argue on one hand that back donors should provide clearer incentives for NGOs which makes them less autonomous and argue at the other hand that NGOs should become more financially independent from their back donor so NGOs can make more autonomous choices. This paradox can be explained by specifying to which back donors and which international NGOs this advice is given. Back donors that are merely interested in promoting their own interest, instead of stimulating development, are not likely to provide more incentives for NGOs to become more active in the neediest countries. This advice is thus meant for back donors that are truly interested in obtaining development results, and did until now not realize that their NGOs might need some more guidance to make better country choices. The other recommendation, that international NGOs should become more independent from back donors, is mainly aimed for those NGOs that have as a back donor an aid agency that is not really interested in generating development results.

References

Abadie, A. (2005). Semiparametric Difference-in-Differences Estimators. *The Review of Economic Studies Limited* 72(1): 1–19.

Acemoglu, D., S. Johnson and J. A. Robinson (2001). The Colonial Origins of Comparative Development: An Empirical Investigation. *American Economic Review* 91: 1369–1401.

Adam, C. S. and J. W. Gunning (2002). Redesigning the Aid Contract: Donors' Use of Performance Indicators in Uganda. *World Development* 30(12): 2045–56.

Adelman, C. (2003). The Privatization of Foreign Aid: Reassessing National Largesse. *Foreign Affairs* 82(6): 9–14.

Agg, C. (2006). *Trends in Government Support for Nongovernmental Organizations. Is the 'Golden Age' of NGO behind Us?* Civil Society and Social Movements Programme Paper No. 23. Geneva, UNRISD.

Al-Sulaiti, K. I. and M. J. Baker (1998). Country of Origin Effects: A Literature Review. *Marketing Intelligence & Planning* 16(3): 150–99.

Alesina, A. and D. Dollar (2000). Who Gives Foreign Aid to Whom and Why? *Journal of Economic Growth* 5(1): 33–63.

Alesina, A., W. Easterly, A. Devleeschauwer, S. Kurlat and R. Wacziarg (2003). Fractionalization. *Journal of Economic Growth* 8(2): 155–94.

Amin, A. and N. Thrift (1995). Institutional Issues for the European Regions: From Markets and Plan to Socioeconomics and Powers of Association. *Economy and Society* 24(1): 41–66.

Anheier, H. K. (2000). *Managing Non-profit Organisations: Towards a New Approach.* Civil Society Working Paper 1, London School of Economics.

Anheier, H. K. (2004). *Civil Society: Measurement, Evaluation, Policy.* London, Earthscan.

Antonelli, C. (1990). Induced Adoption and Externalities in the Regional Diffusion of Information Technology. *Regional Studies* 34(6): 535–47.

Antonelli, C. (2000). Collective Knowledge Communication and Innovation: The Evidence of Technological Districts. *Regional Studies* 24(1): 31–40.

Ardenne, A. (2004). *Nieuwe partner van formaat op wereldformaat.* [New major partner for major challenges]. Inaugural speech of Partos.

Arellano, M. and O. Bover (1995). Another Look at the Instrumental-Variable Estimation of Error-Components Models. *Journal of Econometrics* 68(1): 29–51.

Armington, P. S. (1969). *A Theory of Demand for Products Distinguished by Place of Production.* IMF staff paper 16:1. Washington DC, International Monetary Fund.

Arndt, C. and C. Oman (2006). *Uses and Abuses of Governance Indicators.* Paris, OECD.

Arthur, W. B. (1994). *Increasing Returns and Path Dependence in the Economy*. Ann Arbor, University of Michigan Press.

AWID (2006). *Where Is the Money for Women's Rights?* An Action-Research Project of the Association for Women's Rights in Development.

Bailey, M. (1999). Fundraising in Brazil: The Major Implications for Civil Society Organisations and International NGOs. *Development in Practice* 9(1–2): 103–16.

Barnabas, A. A. and J. U. Elimimian (1999). Attitudes of Developing Countries towards 'Country of Origin' Products in an Era of Multiple Brands. *Journal of International Consumer Marketing* 11(4): 97–116.

Barr, A. and M. Fafchamps (2005). A Client–Community Assessment of the NGO Sector in Uganda. *Journal of Development Studies* 42(4): 611–39.

Barretaeu, O. and W. Daré (2007). *Role-Playing Games in a Variety of Cultures: Experiences from the ComMod Group*. Proceedings of the 38th Conference of the International Simulation and Gaming Association 9–13 July. Nijmegen.

Bauer, P. T. (1971). *Foreign Aid Forever?* Encounter March.

Bauer, P. T. and B. Yamey (1982). Foreign Aid: What Is at Stake? *Public Interest* Summer.

Baughn, C. C. and A. Yaprak (1993). *Mapping Country of Origin Research: Recent Developments and Emerging Avenues. Product-Country Images: Impact and Role in International Marketing*. N. Papadopoulos and L. Heslop. New York, International Business Press: 89–115.

Baulch, B. (2003). *Aid for the Poorest? The Distribution and Misdistribution of International Development Assistance*. CPRC Working Paper No. 35. Manchester, Chronic Poverty Research Centre.

Bebbington, A. (2004). NGOs and Uneven Development: Geographies of Development Intervention. *Progress in Human Development* 28(6): 725–45.

Bebbington, A. (2005). Donor–NGO Relations and Representatives of Livelihood in Nongovernmental Aid Chains. *World Development* 33(6): 937–50.

Beckfield, J. (2003). Inequality in the World Polity: The Structure of International Organization. *American Sociological Review* 68(3): 401–24.

Bellandi, M. (2003). On Entrepreneurship, the Region, and the Constitution of Economies of Scale and Scope. In: G. Becattini, M. Bellandi, G. D. Ottati and F. Sforzi (eds) *From Industrial Districts to Local Development*. London, Edward Elgar.

Berthélemy, J.-C. (2006). Bilateral Donors' Interest vs. Recipients' Development Motives in Aid Allocation: Do All Donors Behave the Same?. *Review of Development Economics* 10(2): 179–94.

Berthélemy, J. C. and A. Tichit (2004). Bilateral Donors' Aid Allocation Decisions – A Three-dimensional Panel Analysis. *International Review of Economics and Finance* 13: 253–74.

Better Aid (2007). *From Paris 2005 to Accra 2008: Will Aid Become More Accountable and Effective? A Critical Approach to the Aid Effectiveness Agenda*. Better Aid.

Beugelsdijk, S., (2007). The Regional Environment and a Firm's Innovative Performance: A Plea for a Multilevel Interactionist Approach. *Economic Geography* 83 (2): 181–99.

Bhinda, N., J. Leape, M. Martin and S. Griffith-Jones (1999). *Private Capital Flows to Africa Perception and Reality*. The Hague, Fondad.

Biekart, K. (1999). *The Politics of Civil Society Building: European Private Aid Agencies and Democratic Transitions in Central America*. Amsterdam, International Books.

Bielefeld, W. (2000). Metropolitan Nonprofit Sectors: Findings From the NCSS Data. *Nonprofit and Voluntary Sector Quarterly* 29(2): 297–314.

Bielefeld, W. and J. C. Murdoch (2004). The Locations of Nonprofit Organizations and Their For-profit Counterparts: An Exploratory Analysis. *Nonprofit and Voluntary Sector Quarterly* 33(2): 221–46.

Black, M. (1992). *A Cause for Our Times: The First 50 Years of Oxfam*. Oxford, Oxford University Press.

Bornstein, L. (2003). Management Standards and Development Practice in the South African Aid Chain. *Public Administration and Development* 23: 393–404.

Borren, S. (2007). It's a Pity … . *The Broker* 1(4): 2.

Boschma, R. and K. Frenken (2003). Evolutionary Economics and Industry Location. *Review of Regional Research* 23(2):183–200.

Boschma, R. and K. Frenken (2006). Why Is Economic Geography Not an Evolutionary Science? Towards an Evolutionary Economic Geography. *Journal of Economic Geography* 6(3): 273–302.

Boschma, R. and R. Martin (2007). Editorial: Constructing an Evolutionary Economic Geography. *Journal of Economic Geography* 7(2007): 537–48.

Boschma, R. and A. Weterings (2005). The Effect of Regional Differences on the Performance of Software Firms in the Netherlands. *Journal of Economic Geography* 5(5): 567–88.

Bourdieu, P. (1984). *Distinction: A Social Critique of the Judgement of Taste*. London, Routledge.

Bourdieu, P. and T. Eagleton (1992). Doxa and Common Life. *New Left Review* 191 (1): 111–21.

Bradshaw, Y. W. and M. J. Schafer (2000). Urbanization and Development: The Emergence of International Nongovernmental Organizations amid Declining States. *Sociological Perspectives* 43(1): 97–116.

Brakman, S. and H. Garretsen (2003). Rethinking the 'New' Geographical Economics. *Regional Studies* 37(6): 637–48.

Brakman, S., H. Garretsen and C. van Marrewijk (2001). *An Introduction to Geographical Economics: Trade, Location and Growth*. Cambridge, Cambridge University Press.

Brett, E. A. (1998). Autonomy, Diversity and Interdependence in Interorganisational Relationships. *LSE*, Destin, course material.

Brooks, A. C. (2000). Is There a Dark Side to Government Support for Nonprofits? *Public Administration Review* 60(3): 219–29.

Brown, R. (2000). *Group Processes*. London, Blackwell.

Brunner, J. A., A. B. Flaschner and X. Lou (1993). *Images and Events: China before and after Tiananmen Square. Product-Country Images: Impact and Role in International Marketing*. N. Papadopoulos and L. Heslop. New York, International Business Press: 379–400.

Bryson, J. R., M. McGuiness and R. G. Ford (2002). Chasing a 'Loose and Baggy Monster': Almshouses and the Geography of Charity. *Area* 31 (1): 48–58.

Burnside, C. and D. Dollar (1997). *Aid, Policies and Growth*. World Bank Working Paper 1777. Washington DC, World Bank.

Burnside, C. and D. Dollar (2000). Aid, Policies and Growth. *American Economic Review* 90(4): 847–68.

Burnside, C. and D. Dollar (2004). *Aid, Policies, and Growth: Revisiting the Evidence*. World Bank Policy Research Working Paper 3251. Washington DC, World Bank.

Cameron, J. (2000). Development Economics, the New Institutional Economics and NGOs. *Third World Quarterly* 21(4): 627–35.

Canavire, G., P. Nunnenkamp, R. Thiele and L. Triveño (2006). Assessing the Allocation of Aid: Developmental Concerns and the Self-Interest of Donors. *Indian Economic Journal* 54(1): 26–43.

Capacitate (2007). *Issues Paper on: Recent International Debates on The Role of Civil Society in Development Cooperation.* Update of the Danish Strategy for Support to Civil Society. Copenhagen.

Care International, Norwegian Refugee Council and World Vision. (2007). *Inter-agency Mission Report on the Central African Republic.*

Chabal, P. and J. P. Daloz (1999). *Africa Works: Disorder as Political Instrument.* Oxford, James Currey Publishers.

Chambers, R. (2001). *The Best of Both Worlds?. Qual-Quant Qualitative and Quantitative Poverty Appraisal: Complementarities, Tensions and the Way Forward.* Contributions to a Workshop Held at Cornell University 15–16 March 2001. R. Kanbur, Cornell University.

Chambers, R. (2005). *Ideas for Development.* London, Earthscan.

Chandhoke, N. (2002). *The Limits of Global Civil Society. Global Civil Society 2002.* M. Glasius, M. Kaldor and H. Anheier. Oxford, Oxford University Press.

Chang, H. J. (2002). *Kicking Away the Ladder – Development Strategy in Historical Perspective.* London, Anthem Press.

Cheng, S. and R. Stough (2006). Location Decisions of Japanese New Manufacturing Plants in China: A Discrete-choice Analysis. *The Annals of Regional Science* 40(2): 369–87.

Chisik, R. (2002). Reputational Comparative Advantage and Multinational Enterprise. *Economic Inquiry* 40(4): 582–96.

CIDA (2006). *Organization Assessment Guide.* Ottawa, Canadian International Development Agency.

CIDIN (2006). *Evaluation of the Theme-based Co-financing Programme Cross-cutting Study: The Added Value of TMF, Final Report.* Nijmegen, Centre for International Development Studies Nijmegen.

Civicus (2005). *State of Civil Society in Mongolia (2004–2005). CIVICUS Civil Society Index Report for Mongolia.* Ulaanbaatar, CIVICUS.

Civicus (2006). *A Diagnostic Study of Togolese Civil Society. Civil Society Index Report for Togo.* Lomé, CIVICUS.

Clark, G.L., M. P. Feldman and M. S. Gertler (2000). *The Oxford Handbook of Economic Geography.* Oxford, Oxford University Press.

Clarke, G. (1998). Non-governmental Organizations (NGOs) and Politics in the Developing World. *Political Studies* XLVI: 36–52.

Clemens, M. A., S. Radelet and R. Bhavnani (2004). *Counting Chickens When They Hatch: The Short-term Effect of Aid on Growth.* Working Paper 44. Washington DC, Center for Global Development.

Cogneau, D. and J. D. Naudet (2004). *Who Deserves Aid? Equality of Opportunity, International Aid and Poverty Reduction,* CERDI.

Collier, P. (2007). *The Bottom Billion. Why the Poorest Countries Are Failing and What Can Be Done about It.* New York, Oxford University Press.

Collier, P. and D. Dollar (2002). Aid Allocation and Poverty Reduction. *European Economic Review* 46(8): 1470–1500.

Commissie MFP-breed (2002). *Breed uitgemeten: advies van de Commissie Medefinancieringsprogramme-breed inzake toetreding en toewijzing van middelen 2003–2006* [Co-financing unravelled: co-financing programme-broad commission's advise on the admission and allocation of funds 2003–2006]. The Hague, Netherlands Ministry of Foreign Affairs.

Commission of the European Communities (2007). *Communication from the Commission to the Council and the European Parliament. EU Code of Conduct on Division of Labour in Development Policy.* Brussels, Commission of the European Communities.

Comtrade (2007). *United Nations Commodity Trade Statistics Database.* Available at: http://comtrade.un.org/db/.

Concord (2008). *Letter to Mr Craig McQuaide, Head of Unit A3, DG Development,* European Commission, 14 January 2008.

Cooley, A. and J. Ron (2002). The NGO Scramble: Organizational Insecurity and the Political Economy of Transnational Action. *International Security* 27(1): 5–39.

Cordaid (2005). *Cordaid Jaarverslag 2004.* Utrecht, Hoonte Bosch & Keuning.

Cordaid (2006). *Politique République Centrafricaine. Internal mimeo [Policy Central African Republic 2007–2010. Internal Memo].* The Hague, Cordaid.

Cordaid (2007). *Jaarverslag 2006* [Annual report 2006]. The Hague, Cordaid.

Correlates of War 2 Project (2003). *Colonial/Dependency Contiguity Data, 1816–2002.* Version 3.0.

Council of the European Union (2007). *Conclusions of the Council and of the Representatives of the Governements of the Member States Meeting within the Council on EU Code of Conduct on Complementarity and Division of Labour in Development Policy.* Brussels, Council of the European Union.

Creswell, J. W. (2002). *Research Design: Qualitative, Quantitative, and Mixed Method Approaches.* London, SAGE.

Cross, R. M. (2005). Exploring Attitudes: The Case for Q Methodology. *Health and Education Research* 20(2): 206–13.

Devdir. (2007). Directory of Development Organizations: Resource Guide to Development. *Organizations and the Internet.* Vol. 1.A Africa, from http://www.devdir.org/index.html.

DFID (2003). *Promoting Institutional & Organisational Development. A Source Book of Tools and Techniques. A Source Book of Tools and Techniques.* London, Department for International Development.

DFID (2006a). *Civil Society and Development.* London, Department for International Development.

DFID (2006b). *Eliminating World Poverty: Making Governance Work for the Poor.* London, Department for International Development.

Dijkstra, G. (2007). *The Impact of International Debt Relief.* Abingdon, Oxon: Routledge.

Dollar, D. and V. Levin (2006). The Increasing Selectivity of Foreign Aid, 1984–2003. *World Development* 34(12): 2034–46.

Downs, A. (1957). *An Economic Theory of Democracy.* New York, Harper & Row.

Drechsler, D. and F. Zimmerman (2007). *New Actors in Health Financing: Implications for a Donor Darling.* OECD Development Centre Policy Brief 33.

Dreher, A., D. J. Koch, P. Nunnenkamp and R. Thiele (2008). NGO Aid – Well Targeted to the Needy and Deserving? In: *Vox,* 20 May.

Dreher, A., F. Mölders and P. Nunnenkamp (2007). *Are NGOs the Better Donors? A Case Study of Aid Allocation for Sweden.* Working Paper No. 1383. Kiel, Kiel Institute of World Economics.

Dreher, A., P. Nunnenkamp and R. Thiele (2006a). *Does US Aid Buy UN General Assembly Votes? A Disaggregated Analysis.* KOF Working Paper No. 138. Zurich: Swiss Federal Institute of Technology.

Dreher, A., J. E. Sturm and J. Vreeland (2006b). *Does Membership on the UN Security Council Influence IMF Decisions? Evidence from Panel Data.* KOF Working Paper 151. Zurich, ETH.

Easterly, W. (2002). The Cartel of Good Intentions: the Problem of Bureaucracy in Foreign Aid. *Journal of Policy Reform* 1–28.

Easterly, W. (2006). *Planners vs. Searchers in Foreign Aid. Asian Development Bank's Distinguished Speakers Program.* Manila, Philippines.

Ebrahim, A. (2003a). Accountability in Practice: Mechanisms for NGOs. *World Development* 31(5): 813–29.

Ebrahim, A. (2003b). *NGOs and Organizational Change: Discourse, Reporting and Learning.* Cambridge, Cambridge University Press.

ECDPM (2004a). *Partnerschap in een polariserende wereld, eindrapport van de beleidsdialoog 2004 [Partnership in a polarizing world, final report of the policy dialogue 2004].* Maastricht, European Centre for Development Policy Management.

ECDPM (2004b). Renewing Approaches to Institutional Development. *Capacity.org* 20 (January).

The Economist (1999). Reward for a Falling Star. *The Economist* 349(8099): 61.

Edwards, M. (2005). *Have NGOs Made a Difference? From Manchester to Birmingham with an Elephant in the Room. Keynote Speech at the GPRG Sponsored Conference on Reclaiming Development? Assessing the Contribution of Non-Governmental Organizations to Development Alternatives,* Institute for Development Policy and Management, University of Manchester, 27–29 June.

Edwards, M. and D. Hulme (1996). Too Close for Comfort? The Impact of Official Aid on Non Governmental Organizations. *World Development* 24(6): 961–73.

Edwards, M. and D. Hulme (1997). *Too Close for Comfort? The Impact of Official Aid on NGOs. NGOs, State and Donors, Too Close for Comfort?.* M. Edwards and D. Hulme. London, Macmillan Press.

Edwards, M. and D. Hulme (1998). Too Close for Comfort? The Impact of Official Aid on Non Governmental Organizations. *Current Issues in Comparative Education* 1(1): 6–28.

Eifert, B., A. Gelb and V. Ramachandran (2005). Business Environment and Comparative Advantage in Africa: Evidence from the Investment Climate Data. Version 31 August 2005. Original paper presented at the Annual Bank Conference in Development Economics, 27 January 2005. Dakar, Senegal.

Eikenberry, A. M. and J. D. Kluver (2004). The Marketization of the Nonprofit Sector: Civil Society at Risk? *Public Administration Review* 64(2): 132–40.

Esping Andersen, G. (1999). *The Social Foundations of Postindustrial Economies.* Oxford, Oxford University Press.

Evans, B., T. Richmond and J. Shields (2005). Structuring Neoliberal Governance: The Nonprofit Sector, Emerging New Modes of Control and the Marketization of Service Delivery. *Policy and Society* 24(1): 73–97.

Evans, P. (1995). *Embedded Autonomy: States and Industrial Transformation.* Princeton NJ, Princeton University Press.

Fafchamps, M. and T. Owens (2006). *Is International Funding Crowding Out Charitable Contributions in African NGOs?* Global Poverty Research Group Working Paper 55. Oxford, Global Poverty Research Group

Feeny, S. and M. McGillivray (2008). What Determines Bilateral Aid Allocations? Evidence from Time Series Data. *Review of Development Economics* 12(3): 515–29.

Feinstein, A. H. and H. Cannon (2002). Constructs of Simulation Evaluation. *Simulation & Gaming* 33(4): 425–40.

Feinstein, A. H. and H. Cannon (2003). A Hermeneutical Approach to External Validation of Simulation Models. *Simulation & Gaming* 34(2): 186–97.

Feldman, S. (2003). Paradoxes of Institutionalisation: The Depoliticisation of Bangladeshi NGOs. *Development in Practice* 13(1): 5–26.

Ferguson, J. (2006). *Global Shadows: Africa in the Neo-Liberal World Order*. Durham NC, and London, Duke University Press.

Ferguson, N. (2004). *Empire How Britain Made the Modern World*. London, Penguin.

Finke, J. (2006). *The Rough Guide to Tanzania*. London and New York, Rough Guides Ltd.

Fisher, J. (1998). *Non-governments, NGOs and the Political Development of the Third World*. Bloomfield CT, Kumarian Press.

Fisher, W. F. (1997). Doing Good? The Politics and Antipolitics of NGO Practices. *Annual Review of Anthropology* 26(1997): 439–64.

Fowler, A. (1995). *Strengthening the Role of Voluntary Development Organisations: Policy Issues Facing Official Aid Agencies*. Paper presented at conference 'Strengthening Financing for the Voluntary Sector in Development: The Role of Official Development Assistance', New York, 26–28 September 1995.

Fowler, A. (2000). *Civil Society, NDGOs and Social Development: Changing the Rules of the Game*. Geneva 2000 Occasional Paper No. 1, United Nations Research Institute for Social Development.

Fowler, A. (2005). *Aid Architecture*. INTRAC Occasional Papers Series No. 45. Oxford, INTRAC.

Fowler, A. and K. Biekart (1996). *Do Private Agencies Really Make a Difference? Compassion and Calculation: The Business of Private Foreign Aid*. D. Sogge, K. Biekart and J. Saxby. London, Pluto Press: 107–35.

Freedom House. (2006). *Freedom in the World, annual report.* from www.freedomhouse.org.

Frumkin, P. (1998). *Rethinking Public Nonprofit Relations: Toward a Neo-Institutional Theory of Public Management*. PONPO Working Paper No. 248. New Haven CT, Yale University Press.

Fruttero, A. and V. Gauri (2005). The Strategic Choices of NGOs: Location Decisions in Rural Bangladesh. *The Journal of Development Studies* 41(5): 759–87.

Fyfe, N. R. and C. Milligan (2003). Out of the Shadows: Exploring Contemporary Geographies of Voluntarism. *Progress in Human Geography* 27(4): 397–413.

Gatignon, A. (2007). *The Role of NGOs in Financing Development. What Do We Know?* Paris, unpublished Mémoire de fin d'Etudes Sciences Po.

Gauri, V. and J. Galef (2005). NGOs in Bangladesh: Activities, Resources, and Governance. *World Development* 33(12): 2045–65.

German, T. and J. Randel (1999). *Stakeholders: Government–NGO Partnerships for International Development*. London, Earthscan.

Gertler, M. S. (1992). Flexibility Revisited: Districts, Nation-states and the Forces of Production. *Transactions of the British Geographers* 17(3): 259–78.

Giles, M. W. and A. Evans (1986). The Power Approach to Intergroup Hostility. *The Journal of Conflict Resolution* 30(3): 469–86.

Gilles, M., D. H. Perkins, M. Roemer and D. R. Snodgrass (1996). *Economics of Development*. London, W. W. Norton & Company.

Glasius, M., D. Lewis and H. Secikelgin (eds) (2004). *Exploring Civil Society*. Oxford, Routledge.

Gleitman, H. (1995). *Psychology* (4th edn). New York and London, W. W. Norton & Company.

Goodin, R. E., B. Headey, R. Muffels and H. J. Dirven (1999). *The Real Worlds of Welfare Capitalism*. Cambridge, Cambridge University Press.

Gordijn, F. (2006). *The 'What Is' and 'How to' of Capacity Development*. The Hague, PSO.

Grabher, G. and R. Hassink (2003). Fuzzy Concepts, Scanty Evidence, Policy Distance? Debating Ann Markusen' s Assessment of Critical Regional Studies. *Regional Studies* 37 (6): 699–700.

Granovetter, M. (1985). Economic Action and Social Structure: The Problem of Embeddedness. *The American Journal of Sociology* 91(3): 481–510.

Gronbjerg, K. A. and L. Paarlberg (2001). Community Variations in the Size and Scope of the Nonprofit Sector: Theory and Preliminary Findings. *Nonprofit and Voluntary Sector Quarterly* 30(4): 684–706.

Gujarati, D. N. (2002). *Basic Econometrics*. New York, McGraw-Hill.

Han, C. M. and V. Terpstra (1988). Country of Origin Effects for Uni-national and Bi-national Products. *Journal of International Business Studies* 19(2): 235–55.

Hansen, H. and F. Tarp (2000). Aid Effectiveness Disputed. *Journal of International Development* 12(3): 375–98.

Harris, M. (2000). *Instruments of Government? Voluntary Sector Boards in a Changing Public Policy Environment. Change in Practice in Health and Social Care*. C. Davies, L. Finlay and A. Bullman. London, Sage: 277–87.

Harris, S. (2005). *Sri Lanka: Aid Effectiveness: A Scoping of Development Partner Perceptions for DFID-SEA*. London, Department for International Development.

Harrow, J. (2002). *New Public Management and Social Justice. New Public Management, Current Trends and Future Prospects*. K. McLaughlin, S. P. Osborn and E. Ferlie. London, Routledge: 141–59.

Hearn, J. (2007). African NGOs: The New Compradors? *Development and Change* 38 (6): 1095–1110.

Heaton Shrestha, C. (2008). *We Will Not Take a Single Rupee from Any Donor Organisation: Exploring the Changing Conceptions and Practices of Civil Society in Nepal*. Paper presented at the conference: European Development Aid and NGOs: Changing Notions of Civil Society in 'North' and 'South'. London School of Economics, 12–14 March 2008.

Heinrich, V. F. (2005). Studying Civil Society across the World: Exploring the Thorny Issues of Conceptualization and Measurement. *Journal of Civil Society* 1(3): 211–28.

Helmich, H., P. B. Lehning and A. Bernard (eds) (1998). *Civil Society and International Development*. Paris, OECD Development Centre.

Hertz, N. (2004). *The Debt Threat*. New York, HarperCollins Publishers.

Hinchliffe, K. (2004). *Notes on the Impact of the HIPC Initiative on Public Expenditures in Education and Health in African Countries*. Africa Region Human Development Working Paper Series, World Bank.

Hoebink, P. (1988). *Geven is nemen: de Nederlandse ontwikkelingshulp aan Sri Lanka en Tanzania [Giving is taking: Dutch development aid to Sri Lanka and Tanzania]*. Nijmegen, Stichting Derde Wereld Publikaties.

Hofstede, G. J. (2005). *Role-playing with Synthetic Cultures: The Evasive Rules of the Game*. In proceedings of the 9th international workshop of the IFIP Wg 5.7 SIG on Experimental Learning in Industrial Management, Helsinki.

Hood, C. (1995). The New Public Management in the 1980s: Variations on a Theme. *Accounting Organizations and Society* 20(2): 93–109.

Hout, W. (2007). *The Politics of Aid Selectivity. Good Governance Criteria in World Bank, US and Dutch Development Assistance.* Abingdon, Oxon, Routledge.

Hout, W. and D. J. Koch (2006). *Selectiviteit in het Nederlandse ontwikkelingsbeleid 1998–2004.* [Selectivity in Dutch Aid policies 1998–2004]. The Hague, Policy and Operations Evaluations Department (IOB) of the Netherlands Ministry of Foreign Affairs.

Howard, M. M. (2003). *The Weakness of Civil Society in Post-Communist Europe.* Cambridge, Cambridge University Press.

Howell, J. and J. Pearce (2001). *Civil Society and Development: A Critical Exploration.* Boulder CO, Lynne Rienner Publishers.

Hudson, R. (2003). Fuzzy Concepts and Sloppy Thinking: Reflections on Recent Developments in Critical Regional Studies. *Regional Studies* 37(6): 741–46.

Igoe, J. (2003). Scaling Up Civil Society: Donor Money, NGOs and the Pastoralist Land Right Movement in Tanzania. *Development and Change* 34(5): 862–85.

Ilon, L. (1998). Can NGOs Provide Alternative Development in a Market-based System of Global Economics? *Current Issues in Comparative Education* 1(1).

INTRAC (2001). *North–South NGO Partnerships, Legitimacy and Constituencies.* Ontrac 17. Oxford, INTRAC.

INTRAC (2005). *Partners or Contractors? The Relationship Between Official Agencies and NGOs – Kenya and Zimbabwe.* INTRAC Occasional Papers Series No: 16. Oxford, INTRAC.

Jaffe, E. D. and I. D. Nebenzahl (1993). *Global Promotion of Country Image: Do the Olympics Count? Product-Country Images: Impact and Role in International Marketing.* N. Papadopoulos and L. Heslop. New York, International Business Press: 433–52.

Johnson, R. B. and A. J. Onwuegbuzie (2004). Mixed Methods Research: A Research Paradigm Whose Time Has Come. *Educational Researcher* 33(7): 14–26.

Kalb, D. (2005). From Flows to Violence, Politics and Knowledge in the Debates on Globalization and Empire. *Anthropological Theory* 5(2): 176–204.

Kalb, J. (2006). The Institutional Ecology of NGOs: Applying Hansmann to International Development. *Texas International Law Journal* 41: 295–318.

Kanbur, R. (2001). *Qual-Quant Qualitative and Quantitative Poverty Appraisal: Complementarities, Tensions and the Way Forward.* Contributions to a Workshop Held at Cornell University 15–16 March 2001, Cornell University.

Karajkov, R. (2007). *NGOs in the Balkans: Too Much of a Good Thing?* www.worldpress.org.

Kassis, M. (2001). Civil Society and Transition to Democracy in Palestine. *Voluntas: Journal of Voluntary Non-Profit Organisation* 12(1): 35–47.

Kaufmann, D., A. Kraay and M. Mastruzzi (2005). *Governance Matters IV: Governance Indicators for 1996–2004.* World Bank Policy Research Working Paper 3630. Washington DC, World Bank.

Keeble, D., C. Lawson, B. Moore and F. Wilkinson (1999). Collective Learning Processes, Networking and 'Institutional Thickness' in the Cambridge Region. *Regional Studies* 33(4): 319–23.

Khan, M. and K. S. Jomo (2000). *Rents, Rent-seeking and Economic Development: Theory and Evidence in Asia.* New York, Cambridge University Press.

Klees, S. J. (1998). NGOs: Progressive Force or Neo-Liberal Tool? *Current Issues in Comparative Education* 1(1): 49–54.

Klinken, R. V. (2003). Operationalising local governance in Kilimanjaro. *Development in Practice* 13(1): 71–82.

Koch, D. J. (2006). *Blind Spots on the Map of Aid Allocations, the Geographies of Civil Society Aid.* Aid, Principles, Polices and Performance. Conference of the World Institute for Development Economics Research, 14–16 June 2006. Helsinki.

Koch, D. J. (2007a). *Blind Spots on the Map of Aid Allocation. Concentration & Complementarity of International NGO Aid.* Wider Research Paper 2007–45. Helsinki, UNU-WIDER.

Koch, D. J. (2007b). *The NGO Game: Cooperation and Competition between NGOs in Tanzania.* Organizing and Learning through Gaming and Simulation, Proceedings of ISAGA 2007. I. Mayor and H. Mastik. Delft, Eburon: 174–82.

Koch, D. J. (2007c). Uncharted Territories: Geographic Choices of Aid Agencies. *The Broker* 1(3): 9–12.

Koch, D. J. (2008a). De ontwikkelingsorganisatie is een kuddedier [The international NGO is a gregarious animal]. *'Heilige Huisjes: Anders kijken naar internationale samenwerking'.* Amsterdam: Onze Wereld Publishers: 80–90.

Koch, D. J. (2008b). A Paris Declaration for NGOs? The Need for Harmonisation, Co-ordination, Mutual Accountability and Alignment among International NGOs. *Financing Development 2008.* OECD Development Centre. Paris, OECD.

Koch, D.J. (2009, forthcoming) NGOs: cooperation and competition. An experimental gaming approach. *Simulation & Gaming.* DOI: 10.1177/1046878108327956.

Koch, D.J., A. Dreher, P. Nunnenkamp and R. Thiele (2009, forthcoming) Keeping a Low Profile: What Determines the Allocation of Aid by Non-Governmental Organizations? *World Development.*

Koch, D. J. and B. Loman (2008). The Geographic Choices of Dutch NGOs: Myths and Realities. In: P. Hoebink (ed.) *Dutch Yearbook of International Cooperation 2008.* Assen, van Gorcum.

Koch, D. J. and R. Ruben (2008) Spatial Clustering of NGOs: An Evolutionary Economic Geography Approach. Papers in Evolutionary Economic Geography # 08.14. Utrecht University: Urban and Regional Research Centre Utrecht.

Koch, D. J., J. Westeneng and R. Ruben (2007). Does Marketization of Aid Reduce the Country Poverty Targeting of NGOs? *European Journal of Development Research* 19 (4): 635–56.

Koolwijk, D. van de and D. J. Koch (2007). *Où sont les ONG Internationales de développement en République Centreafricaine?* [Where are the international development NGOs in the Central African Republic?]. Presented at the NGO conference, 1–2 August. Bangui, Central African Republic.

Korten, D. C. (1990). *Getting to the 21st Century.* Bloomfield CT, Kumarian Press.

Kotler, P. and D. Gertner (2002). Country as Brand, Product, and Beyond: A Place Marketing and Brand Management Perspective. *Journal of Brand Management* 9 (4–5): 249–61.

KPMG (2004). *Rapportage Doelmatigheidsaudit Medefinancieringsorganisaties* [Effiency audit of co-financing agencies]. Amstelveen, KPMG.

Krugman, P. (1991). *Geography and Trade.* Cambridge MA, MIT Press.

Krugman, P. (1998). *The Role of Geography in Development.* Paper presented at the Annual World Bank Conference on Development Economics, 20–21 April. Washington DC.

Kudva, N. (2005). *Uneasy Relations: NGOs and the State in Karnataka, India.* Paper presented at the Karnataka Conference, Bangalore, 10–12 June, ISEC/Cornell University/The World Bank.

Kuhn, B. (2005). *Entwicklungspolitik zwischen Markt und Staat – Möglichkeiten und Grenzen zivilgesellschaftlicher Organisationen* [Development politics between

Market and State- Possibilities and Boundaries of Civil Society Organizations]. Frankfurt am Main, Campus Verlag.

Kuit, M., I. S. Mayer and M. de Jong (2005). The INFRASTRATEGO Game: An Evaluation of Strategic Behavior and Regulatory Regimes in a Liberalizing Energy Market. *Simulation & Gaming* 36(1): 58–74.

Kuziemko, I. and E. Werker (2006). How Much Is a Seat on the Security Council Worth? Foreign Aid and Bribery at the United Nations. *Journal of Political Economy* 114(5): 905–30.

Laan, J. van der (2007). *Where Do You Get Your Orphans? The Clustering of NGOs in the Arusha Region, Tanzania.* Nijmegen, Radboud University.

Lagendijk, A., (2003). Towards Conceptual Quality in Regional Studies: The Need for Subtle Critique – A Response to Markusen. *Regional Studies* 37 (6):719–27.

Laroche, M., N. Papadopoulos, L. Heslop and M. Mourali (2005). The Influence of Country Image Structure on Consumer Evaluation of Foreign Products. *International Marketing Review* 22(1): 96–115.

Lensink, R. and H. White (2000). Aid Allocation, Poverty Reduction and the Assessing Aid Report. *Journal of International Development* 12(3): 399–412.

Levin, V. and D. Dollar (2004). *Increasing the Selectivity of Foreign Aid.* World Bank Policy Research Working Paper 3299. Washington DC, World Bank.

Levitt, S.D. and J. A. List (2007). What Do Laboratory Experiments Measuring Social Preferences Reveal about the Real World? *Journal of Economic Perspectives* 21(2): 153–74.

Lewis, D. and T. Wallace (2000). *New Roles and Relevance: Development NGOs and the Challenge of Change.* West Hartford CT and Bloomfield CT, Kumarian Press.

Lewis, M. (2005). A War Chest for Fighting HIV/AIDS. *Finance and Development* 42(4).

Lieberman, M. B. and D. B. Montgomery (1988). First-mover Advantages. *Strategic Management Journal* 9: 41–58.

Lipsky, M. and S. Smith (1990). Nonprofit Organizations, Government, and the Welfare State. *Political Science Quarterly* 104(4): 625–48.

Lissner, J., (1977). *The Politics of Altruism: A Study of the Political Behaviour of Voluntary Development Agencies* Geneva, Lutheran World Federation Department of Studies.

Llavador, H. G. and J. E. Roemer (2001). An Equal-opportunity Approach to the Allocation of International Aid. *Journal of Development Economics* 64(1): 147–71.

Low, W. and E. Davenport (2002). NGO Capacity Building and Sustainability in the Pacific. *Asia Pacific Viewpoint* 43(3): 367–79.

Malhotra, K. (2000). NGOs without Aid: Beyond the Global Soup Kitchen. *Third World Quarterly* 21(4): 655–68.

Markusen, A. (2003a). Fuzzy Concepts, Scanty Evidence, Policy Distance: The Case for Rigour and Policy Relevance in Critical Regional Studies. *Regional Studies* 37 (6): 701–17.

Markusen, A. (2003b). On Conceptualization, Evidence and Impact: A Response to Hudson, Lagendijk and Peck. *Regional Studies* 37(6): 747–51.

Markusen, A. (1996). Sticky Places in Slippery Space: A Typology of Industrial Districts. *Economic Geography* 72(3): 293–313.

Marshall, M. G. and K. Jaggers (2004). *Political Regime Characteristics and Transitions – Polity IV Project.* College Park MD, University of Maryland.

Martens, B., U. Mummert, P. Murrell and P. Seabright (2002). *The Institutional Economics of Foreign Aid.* Cambridge, Cambridge University Press.

Martin, R. (1999). The New 'Geographical Turn' in Economics: Some Critical Reflections. *Cambridge Journal of Economics* 23: 65–91.

Martin, R. and P. Sunley (2006). Path Dependence and Regional Economic Evolution. *Journal of Economic Geography* 6(4): 395–437.

Marysse, S., A. Ansoms and A. Cassimon (2007). The Aid 'Darlings' and 'Orphans' of the Great Lakes Region in Africa. *The European Journal of Development Research* 19(3): 433–58.

Maskell, P. and A. Malmberg (1995). *Localized Learning and Industrial Competitiveness*. BRIE Working Paper 80. Berkeley, University of California.

Masud, N. and B. Yontcheva (2005). 'Does Foreign Aid Reduce Poverty? Empirical Evidence from Nongovernmental and Bilateral Aid. IMF Working Paper No. 100'. Washington DC, International Monetary Fund.

May, A. and J. Magongo (2005). *NGOs in Development and Poverty Reduction, and Their Relationships with Donors and the State in Tanzania: Views from Civil Society.* Dar es Salaam and Dublin, REPOA and Dublin City University Press: 1–64.

Mavrotas, G. and M. McGillivray (2009, forthcoming) *Development Aid: A Fresh Look.* Basingstoke: Palgrave McMillan.

McCleary, R. and R. Barro (2006). *U.S.-Based Private Voluntary Organizations: Religious and Secular PVOs Engaged in International Relief & Development.* NBER Working Paper No. 12238. Working Paper Series. N. B. o. E. Research.

McGillivray, M. (2003). *Descriptive and Prescriptive Analyses of Aid Allocation.* Discussion Paper No. 2003/21. WIDER.

Meijer, S., G. Zúñiga-Arias and G. Sterrenburg (2005). *Experiences with the Mango Chain Game.* Paper presented at: The IFIP WG 5.7 Special Interest Group on Experimental Interactive Learning in Industrial Management, Espoo, 2–5 July.

Mercer, C. (2003). Performing Partnership: Civil Society and the Illusions of Good Governance in Tanzania. *Political Geography* 22: 741–63.

Meredith, M. (2005). *The State of Africa. A History of Fifty Years of Independence.* London, Free Press.

Meyer, C. A. (1995). Opportunism and NGOs: Entrepreneurship and Green North–South Transfers. *World Development* 23(8): 1277–89.

Michael, S. (2004). *Undermining Development: The Absence of Power among Local NGOs in Africa.* Bloomington, Indiana University Press.

Migdal, J. S. (2001). *State in Society: Studying How States and Societies Transform and Constitute Each Other.* Cambridge, Cambridge University Press.

Milligan, C. (2007). Geographies of Voluntarism: Mapping the Terrain. *Geography Compass* 1/2: 183–99.

Mitlin, A., S. Hickey and A. Bebbington (2007). Reclaiming Development? NGOs and the Challenge of Alternatives. *World Development* 35(10): 1699–1720.

Monteiro, M. (2007). NGOs Are as Complex as Their Environment. *The Broker* 1(4): 2.

Morena, A. (2006). Funding and the Future of the Global Justice Movement. *Development* 49(2): 29–33.

Morosino, P. (2004). Industrial Clusters, Knowledge Integration and Performance. *World Development* 32(2): 305–26.

Mosse, D. (2005). *Cultivating Development. An Ethnography of Aid Policy and Practice.* London, Pluto Press.

Myrdal, G. (1957). *The Economic Theory and Under-Developed Regions.* London, Duckworth.

Nagashima, A. (1970). A Comparison of Japanese and U.S. Attitudes toward Foreign Products. *Journal of Marketing* 34(1): 68–74.

Nancy, G. and B. Yontcheva (2006). *Does NGO Aid Go to the Poor? Empirical Evidence from Europe.* IMF Working Paper. Washington DC, IMF Institute.

Netherlands Ministry of Foreign Affairs (1966). *Nota hulpverlening aan minder ontwikkelde landen* [White paper on development assistance to lesser developed countries]. The Hague, Netherlands Ministry of Foreign Affairs.

Netherlands Ministry of Foreign Affairs (1976). *Bilaterale ontwikkelingssamenwerking – Om de kwaliteit van de Nederlandse hulp* [Bilateral development cooperation – for the quality of Dutch aid]. The Hague, Netherlands Ministry of Foreign Affairs.

Netherlands Ministry of Foreign Affairs (1995). *Budget for the year 1996.* The Hague, Netherlands Ministry of Foreign Affairs.

Netherlands Ministry of Foreign Affairs (2000). *Toespraak Minister voor Ontwikkelingssamenwerking: Naar nieuwe taakverdeling: Overheid en particuliere organisaties niet inwisselbaar* [Speech by the Minister for Development Cooperation: Towards a new division of tasks: Government and private aid organisations: not interchangeable]. The Hague, Netherlands Ministry of Foreign Affairs.

Netherlands Ministry of Foreign Affairs (2001). *Civil Society and Poverty Reduction.* The Hague, Netherlands Ministry of Foreign Affairs.

Netherlands Ministry of Foreign Affairs (2006). *Beleidsreactie IOB-evaluatie inzake Sectorale Benadering. 26 april 2006. Brief aan de Tweede Kamer 30548, nr. 1.* [Policy reaction, IOB evaluation of the Sectoral Approach. 26 April 2006, Letter to the Parliament 30548, no. 1]. The Hague, Netherlands Ministry of Foreign Affairs,

Netherlands Ministry of Foreign Affairs (2007). *Our Common Concern; Policy Note Dutch Development Cooperation 2007–2011.* The Hague, Netherlands Ministry of Foreign Affairs.

Neumayer, E. (2003). *The Pattern of Aid Giving: The Impact of Good Governance on Development Assistance.* London, Routledge.

Novib (1998). Instructions for the GRAP 2. Internal mimeo. The Hague, Novib.

Novib (2003). *Guidelines for Focus Instrument.* Internal mimeo. The Hague, Novib.

Nunnenkamp, P. (2008). The Myth of NGO Superiority. *Development & Cooperation* 49(5).

Nunnenkamp, P., J. Weingarth and J. Weisser. (2008). *Is NGO Aid Not So Different after All? Comparing the Allocation of Swiss Aid by Private and Official Donors.* Kiel Working Papers No. 1405.

Observatoires des Médias (2008). *Le monde dans les yeux d'un rédac chef.* Blog of 24 March.

OECD (2007). *International Development Statistics Online.* Available at: http://www. oecd. org/dac/stats/idsonline.

Olson, M. (1967). *The Logic of Collective Action.* Cambridge MA, Harvard University Press.

Oosten, H. V. and A. Badjeck (2006). *Etude sur la société civile Centrafricaine* [Research on civil society in the Central African Republic]. The Hague, Cordaid.

Opheusden, E. (2007). Boekhouders aan de macht [Accountants in power]. *Vice Versa* 41(2): 10–17.

Oxfam Novib (2007). *East Africa Regional Cluster – Strategic Plan 2007 – 2010.* The Hague, Novib.

Oxfam Novib (n.d.). *Mission.* The Hague, Oxfam Novib. Available at: http://www. oxfamnovib.nl.

Oyugi, W. O. (2004). The Role of NGOs in Fostering Development and Good Governance at the Local Level. *Africa Development* XXIX(4): 19–55.

Page, S. (2005). What's New about New Public Management? *Public Administration Review* 65(6): 713–27.

Paine, A. D. M. (1985). 'Ergodic' Reasoning in Geomorphology: Time for a Review of the Term? *Progress in Physical Geography* 9(1): 1–15.

Papadopoulos, N. and L. Heslop (2002). Country Equity and County Branding: Problems and Prospects. *Journal of Brand Management* 9(4–5): 294–314.

Paswan, A. K., S. Kulkarni and G. Ganesh (2002). Nation Branding; Loyalty towards the Country, the State and the Service Brands. *Journal of Brand Management* 10 (3): 233–51.

Peck, J., (2003). Fuzzy Old World: A Response to Markusen. *Regional Studies* 37(6): 729–40.

Pelkmans, M. (2005). On Transition and Revolution in Kyrgyzstan. *Focaal* 46: 147–57.

Peng, S. and Y. Zou (2007). The Moderating Effect of Multicultural Competence in Brand-of-Origin Effect. *International Management Review* 3(3): 57–65.

Peterson, R. A. and A. J. P. Jolibert (1995). A Meta-analysis of Country of Origin Effects. *Journal of International Business* 26(4): 883–900.

Petras, J. (1997). Imperialism and NGOs in Latin America. *Monthly Review* 49(7): 10–27.

Pitt, L. F., R. Opoku, M. Hultmann, R. Abratt and S. Spyropoulou (2007). What I Say about Myself: Communication of Brand Personality by African Countries. *Tourism Management* 28: 835–44.

Plan International (2007). *The Effectiveness of Plan's Child-centred Community Development. Plan Program Review (2003 to 2006)*. Woking, Surrey, Plan International.

Ploumen, L. (2007). Hope to Meet You Sometime in Bangui!. *The Broker* 1(4).

Polgreen, L. (2007) *World Briefing | Africa: Central African Republic: Aid Worker Shot Dead*. New York Times of 12 June 2007.

Population Council & Planned Parenthood Association of Ghana (2000). *An Assessment of the Community Based Distribution Programs in Ghana*. Accra, Population Council & Planned Parenthood Association of Ghana.

Porter, G. (2003). NGOs and Poverty Reduction in A Globalizing World: Perspectives from Ghana. *Progress in Development Studies* 3(2): 131–45.

Porter, M. (2000). Location, Competition, and Economic Development: Local Clusters in a Global Economy. *Economic Development Quarterly* 14(1): 15–34.

Pratt, B., J. Adams and H. Warren (2006). *Official Agency Funding of NGOs in Seven Countries: Mechanisms, Trends and Implications*. INTRAC Occasional Papers Series No. 46. Oxford, INTRAC.

Ravallion, M. (2001). *Can Qualitative Methods Help Quantitative Poverty Measurement? Qual-Quant Qualitative and Quantitative Poverty Appraisal: Complementarities, Tensions and the Way Forward*. Contributions to a Workshop Held at Cornell University 15–16 March, 2001R. Ithaca NY, Cornell University Press.

Rawls, J. (1973). *Theory of Justice*. London, Oxford University Press.

Renzio, P. de. and J. Hanlon (2007). *Contested Sovereignty in Mozambique: The Dilemmas of Aid Dependence*. Global Economic Governance Working Paper 2007/25.

Rhodes, R. A. W. (1999). Traditions and Public Sector Reform: Comparing Britain and Denmark. *Scandinavian Political Studies* 22(4): 341–70.

Riddell, R. C., A. Bebbington and L. Peck (1995). *Development by Proxy: An Evaluation of the Development Impact of Government Support to Swedish NGOs*. Stockholm, SIDA.

Riddell, R. C. and M. Robinson (1995). *Non-Governmental Organizations and Rural Poverty Alleviation*. Oxford and London, Clarendon Press and ODI.

Ritzen, J. (2005). *A Chance for the World Bank*. London, Anthem Press.

Roberts, W. T. (2005). The Uneven Globalization of Civil Society Organizations and the Consequences for Cross-National Disparities in Human Development. *International Journal of Sociology and Social Policy* 25: 118–34.

Robinson, M. (1997). Privatizing the Voluntary Sector: NGOs as Public Service Contractors? In: D. Hulme and M. Edwards (eds) *NGOs, States and Donors: Too Close for Comfort?* London: Pergamon Press.

Rodenburg, J. and H. Derksen (2007). The Times, They Are a-Changin. *The Broker* 1(4).

Rogerson, A. (2004). *The International Aid System 2005–2010: Forces For and Against Change*. London, Overseas Development Institute.

Rondinelli, D. A. (1982). The Dilemma of Development Administration: Complexity and Uncertainty in Control-Oriented Bureaucracies. *World Politics* 35(1): 43–72.

Roodman, D., (2006). *How to Do xtabond2: An Introduction to 'Difference' and 'System' GMM in Stata*. Working Paper 103. Washington DC, Center for Global Development.

Rose-Ackerman, S. (1986). *The Economics of Non-profit Institutions: Studies in Structure and Policy*. New York, Oxford University Press.

Ruben, R. (2007). *Development through Cooperation*. Inaugural speech delivered on accepting the office of professor Development Studies in the Radboud University, Nijmegen, on Wednesday, 23 May 2007.

Sadoun, B. (2006). Donor Policies and the Financial Autonomy of Development NGOs. *Development* 49(2): 45–51.

Sakabe, Y. and M. Eloundou-Enyegue (2006). The Emergence of African NGOs: Functional or Opportunistic Response? Africa Notes. Ithaca NY, Institute for African Development, Cornell University, 2–7.

Salomon, L., S. W. Sokolowski and R. List (2003). *Global Civil Society: An Overview*. Baltimore MD, Johns Hopkins University.

Saxenian, A. (1994). *Regional Advantage: Culture and Competition in Silicon Valley and Route 128*. Cambridge MA, Harvard University Press.

Scheepers, P. and M. Te Grotenhuis (2005). Who Cares for the Poor in Europe? Micro and Macro Determinants for Alleviating Poverty in 15 European Countries. *European Sociological Review* 21(5): 453–65.

Schmid, H. (2003). Rethinking the Policy of Contracting out Social Services to Nongovernment Organizations. *Public Management Review* 5(3): 307–23.

Schmitz, H. (2000). Does Co-operation Matter? Evidence from Industrial Clusters in South Asia and Latin America. *Oxford Development Studies* 28(3): 323–36.

Schooler, R. D. (1971). Bias Phenomena Attendant to the Marketing of Foreign Products in the U.S. *Journal of International Business Studies* 6 (Spring): 71–80.

Schulpen, L. (1997). *The Same Difference – a Comparison of Dutch Aid Channels to India*. Saarbrücken, Breitenbach.

Schulpen, L. and P. Hoebink (2001). *Ontwikkelingssamenwerking via particuliere ontwikkelingsorganisaties – de MFO's in perspectief* [Development cooperation through private organisations – the cofinancing organisations in perspective]. Hulp in ontwikkeling. S. Schulpen. Assen, Koninklijke Van Gorcum.

Sforzi, F. (2002). The Industrial District and the 'New' Italian Economic Geography. *European Planning Studies* 10(4): 439–47.

Sharma, M. and M. Zeller (1999). *Placement and Outreach of Group-based Credit Organizations: The Cases of ASA, BRAC, and PROSHIKA in Bangladesh*. Food

Consumption and Nutrition Division. Discussion article no. 59. Washington DC, FNCD.

Shellman, S. M. and K. Turan (2003). The Cyprus Crisis: A Multilateral Bargaining Simulation. *Simulation Gaming* 34: 281–91.

Shivji, I. G. (2004). Reflections on NGOs in Tanzania: What We Are, What We Are Not, and What We Ought To Be. *Development in Practice* 14(5): 689–95.

Sloover, S., de. (2007). Hulporganisaties spelen kluitjesvoetbal in de Derde Wereld ['NGOs demonstrate herding behaviour in developing world']. *De Volkskrant* (21 August): 5.

Smillie, I. (1997). NGOs and Development Assistance: A Change in Mind-set? *Third World Quarterly* 18(3): 563–78.

Smillie, I. (2000). NGOs: Crisis and Opportunity in the New World Order. In: J. Freedman (ed.) *Transforming Development*. Toronto: University of Toronto Press.

Smith, J. and D. Wiest (2005). The Uneven Geography of Global Civil Society: National and International Influences on Transnational Association. *Social Forces* 84(2): 622–51.

Sogge, D., K. Biekart and J. Saxby (eds) (1996). *Compassion and Calculation: the Business of Private Foreign Aid*. London: Pluto Press.

Starkey, B. A. and E. L. Blake (2001). Simulation in International Relations Education. *Simulation Gaming* 32: 537–51.

Steering Committee for the Evaluation of the TMF-programme (2006). *Synthesis Report*.

Steering Committee for the Impact Study on the Co-financing Programme (1991). *Betekenis van het medefinancieringsprogramma: een verkenning* [Significance of the co-financing programme: an exploration]. The Hague, Libertas.

Steering Group (2002). *Final Report of the Evaluation of the Cofinancing Programme*. Amsterdam, MFP-breed.

Sumner, A. and M. Tribe (2004) *The Nature of Epistemology and Methodology in Development Studies: What Do We Mean by 'Rigour'?* Paper prepared for: 'The Nature of Development Studies', DSA Annual Conference, 'Bridging Research and Policy', Church House, London, 6 November.

Takala, T. E. (2005). *Education Sector Programmes in Developing Countries*. Tampere, Finland, Tampere University Press.

Tan, C. T. and J. U. Farley (1987). The Impact of Cultural Patterns on Cognition and Intention in Singapore. *Journal of Consumer Research* 13 (March): 540–44.

Tanzania Association of Non-Governmental Organization (2001). *NGO Directory 2001: Answers the Question of Who Is Doing What and Where*. Dar es Salaam, Tanzania Association of Non-Governmental Organization.

Tashakkori, A. and C. Teddlie (eds) (2003). *Handbook of Mixed Methods in Social & Behavioral Research*. London, Sage.

Taylor, P. J. (2004). The New Geography of Global Civil Society: NGOs in the World City Network. *Globalizations* 1(2): 265–77.

Tendler, J. (1982). *Turning Private Voluntary Organizations into Development Agencies: Questions for Evaluation*. AID Program Evaluation Discussion Paper No. 12.

Teune, B. and T. Dietz (2003). Hoe de wereld van Novib een stukje kleiner werd [How Novib's world became slightly smaller]. *Geografie* 12(3): 20–23.

Thirlwall, A. P. (1987). *Nicholas Kaldor, Grand Masters in Economics*. Brighton, Harverster Press.

Townsend, J., G. Porter and E. Mawdsley (2002). The Role of the Transnational Community of Non-government Organizations: Governance or Poverty Reduction? *Journal of International Development* 14(6): 829–39.

Transparency International (2008). *Corruption Perception Index – Online Database.* Available at: www.transparency.org.

Trefon, T. (ed.) (2004). *Reinventing Order in the Congo: How People Respond to State Failure in Kinshasa.* London and New York, Zed Books.

Tsunami Evaluation Coalition (2006). *Joint Evaluation of the International Response to the Indian Ocean Tsunami, Synthesis Report.* London, Tsunami Evaluation Coalition.

Tvedt, T. (1998). *Angels of Mercy or Development Diplomats. NGOs and Foreign Aid.* Trenton NJ, Africa World Press.

Tvedt, T. (2002). Development NGOs: Actors in a Global Civil Society or in a New International Social System. *Voluntas: International Journal of Voluntary and Non-Profit Organizations* 13(4): 363–75.

Umbrella NGO Training Project (n.d.). *NGO directory Tanzania.* Arusha and Dar es Salaam, The East and Southern Africa Management Institute & National Income Generation Program.

United Nations Development Programme (2003). *Human Development Report 2003.* New York, Oxford University Press.

United Nations Development Programme (2006a). *Human Development Report 2006.* New York, Oxford University Press.

United Nations Development Programme (2006b). *Plan Cadre des Nations Unies pour l'aide au développement – République Centrafricaine 2007–2011* [Project framework of the United Nations for development aid – Central African Republic 2007–2011]. New York, United Nations Development Program.

United Nations Development Programme (2006c). *Une stratégie de croissance pro-pauvre et au service du développement humain – Contraintes et défis pour la République Centrafricaine* [A pro-poor growth strategy for human development – constraints and challenges for the Central African Republic]. New York, United Nations Development Program.

United Nations Millennium Project (2005). *Investing in Development: A Practical Plan to Achieve the MDGs.* London, Earthscan.

USAID (1999). *Lessons in Implementation: The NGO Story. Building Civil Society in Central and Eastern Europe and the New Independent States.* Washington DC, United States Agency for International Development.

Veen, R. van de (2004). *What Went Wrong with Africa?* Amsterdam: KIT Publishers.

Venables, A. J. (2001). *Trade, Location, and Development: an Overview of Theory. Paper Prepared for the World Bank Project Patterns of Integration in the Global Economy.* Washington DC, World Bank.

Verlegh, P. W. J. and J. B. E. M. Steenkamp (1999). A Review and Meta-analysis of Country of Origin Research. *Journal of Economic Psychology* 20(5): 521–46.

Vermaas, P. (2005). Wat zijn zij nu weer van Plan? [What are they planning to do now?]. *Onze Wereld,* October.

Vincent, F. (2007). NGOs, Social Movements, External Funding and Dependency. *Development and Change* 49(2): 22–28.

Visscher, R. (2008). NGO's maken zich schuldig aan kuddegedrag [NGOs display herding behaviour]. *Transfer Magazine* 15(9): 24–25.

Visser, E. J. (1999). A Comparison of Clustered and Dispersed Firms in the Small-scale Clothing Industry of Lima. *World Development* 27(9): 1553–70.

Wade, R. H. (1988). *Village Republics, Conditions for Collective Action in Southern India.* Cambridge, Cambridge University Press.

Wallace, T. (2003). Trends in UK NGOs: A Research Note. *Development in Practice* 13(5): 564–9.

Wallace, T. (2000). *Introductory Essay. Development Management and the Aid Chain: The Case of NGOs. Development and Management.* D. Eade, T. Hewitt and H. Johnson. Oxford, Oxfam Publishing: 18–39.

Wallace, T., L. Bornstein and J. Chapman (2006). *The Aid Chain: Coercion and Commitment in Development NGOs.* Rugby, Warks, Intermediate Technology Publications Ltd.

Wang, S. (2006). Money and Autonomy: Patterns of Civil Society Finance and Their Implications. *Studies in Comparative International Development* 40(4): 3–29.

Weisbrod, B. (1988). *The NonProfit Economy.* Cambridge MA, Harvard University Press.

Wenting, R., O. Atzema and K. Frenken (2008). Urban Amenities or Agglomeration Economies? Locational Behaviour and Entrepreneurial Success of Dutch Fashion Designers. Papers in Evolutionary Economic Geography #08.03. Utrecht, Urban and Regional Research Centre Utrecht University.

Werkgroep Evaluatie Nederlandse Ontwikkelingshulp (1969). *Evaluatie van de Nederlandse Ontwikkelingshulp* [Evaluation of Dutch development aid].

Williams, A. (1990). A Growing Role for NGOs in Development. *Finance and Development* 27(4): 31–33.

Wolch, J. R. (1999). Decentring America's Non-profit Sector: Reflections on Salamon's Crises Analysis. *Voluntas* 10(1): 22–36.

Wolch, J. R. and R. K. Geiger (1983). The Urban Distribution of Voluntary Resources: An Exploratory Analysis. *Environment and Planning* 15(8): 1067–82.

World Bank (1998). *Assessing Aid, What Works, What Doesn't and Why?* New York, Oxford University Press.

World Bank (2006). *World Development Indicators.* CD-ROM. Washington DC.

World Bank (2007). *CAR – Enhanced Heavily Indebted Poor Countries (HIPC) Initiative – Preliminary document; Report no. 38675.* Washington DC, World Bank.

Zeller, M., S. Manohar, U. A. Akther and R. Shahidur (2001). *Group-based Financial Institutions for the Rural Poor in Bangladesh.* Research Report 120. Washington DC, International Food Policy Research Institute.

Zetter, R. (1996). Refugee Survival and NGO Project Assistance: Mozambican Refugees in Malawi. *Community Development Journal* 31(3): 214–29.

Zhang, Y. (1997). Country of Origin Effect: The Moderating Function of Individual Difference in Information Processing. *International Marketing Review* 14(4): 266–87.

Zoete, C. de (2006). *Dutch Support to Civil Society in Tanzania: An Inventory.* Dar es Salaam, Royal Netherlands Embassy.

Index

For Product Safety Concerns and Information please contact our EU
representative GPSR@taylorandfrancis.com
Taylor & Francis Verlag GmbH, Kaufingerstraße 24, 80331 München, Germany

www.ingramcontent.com/pod-product-compliance
Ingram Content Group UK Ltd.
Pitfield, Milton Keynes, MK11 3LW, UK
UKHW021119180425
457613UK00005B/154